B&T
4/28/82
?.95

W9-CDC-932

The Making of the 20th Century

This series of specially commissioned titles focuses attention on significant and often controversial events and themes of world history in the present century. Each book provides sufficient narrative and explanation for the newcomer to the subject while offering, for more advanced study, detailed source-references and bibliographies, together with interpretation and reassessment in the light of recent scholarship.

In the choice of subjects there is a balance between breadth in some spheres and detail in others; between the essentially political and matters economic or social. The series cannot be a comprehensive account of everything that has happened in the twentieth century, but it provides a guide to recent research and explains something of the times of extraordinary change and complexity in which we live. It is directed in the main to students of contemporary history and international relations, but includes titles which are of direct relevance to courses in economics, sociology, politics and geography.

The Making of the 20th Century

Series Editor: GEOFFREY WARNER

Titles in the Series include

Already published

South and South-east Asia, 1945–1979: Problems and Policies

B. N. Pandey

St. Martin's Press   New York

Wingate College Library

© B. N. Pandey 1980

All rights reserved. For information write:
St. Martin's Press, Inc., 175 Fifth Avenue, New York, N.Y. 10010
Printed in Great Britain
First published in the United States of America in 1980

ISBN 0–312–74710–1

Library of Congress Cataloging in Publication Data

Pandey, Bishwa Nath, 1929–
    South and South-East Asia, 1945–1979.

    (The Making of the 20th Century)
    Bibliography: p.
    Includes index.
    1.   South Asia—Politics and government.
2.   Asia, Southeastern—Politics and government.
I.   Title.
DS341.P36   1980   959'.053   79–26753
ISBN 0–312–74710–1

085931.

Contents

For
my daughter Tara

Preface

This work is a modest exercise in comparative contemporary history. It takes the whole of South and South-east Asia as a unit to study certain common problems which the fourteen countries of this region have faced since their independence, and the policies they have adopted to resolve them. It focuses mainly on political problems and policies, and poses and suggests answers to some basic questions. How differently were these countries conditioned by the differences in their colonial legacies? For what reasons did all the countries adopt democratic institutions at the beginning of the period? How and why did democracy come to be discarded by most of them? What indigenous surrogates for Western democracy were evolved and with what results? Under what constraints has democracy functioned in Sri Lanka, India, Malaysia and Singapore? What are the factors which have threatened national integration and how has each country managed to deal with them? Why did the communist insurgencies fail, and why has constitutional communism not succeeded so far in capturing the central power in any country outside Indo-China?

This study also surveys the bilateral conflicts and wars over disputed lands, and investigates the nature of minority problems. It assesses the roles these countries have played, individually and collectively, in bringing to an end the era of cold war and confrontation, and in sustaining the present era of *détente* and co-operation. It ends with an enquiry into economic and social problems. Here it traces the progress made by individual countries in handling the harrowing problems of poverty and illiteracy, and suggests a tentative answer to the often-asked question: can the gap between the haves and have-nots of the world ever be closed?

So far, no general work of this kind has been done. Scholars have abstained, perhaps wisely, from including South and South-east Asia within the scope of a single enquiry. The first and so far the only work of any distinction to deal with contemporary South and South-east Asia is *Politics in Southern Asia*, ed. Saul Rose (London, 1963). It includes some excellent articles, but is limited in its scope in so far as it focuses only on political problems and excludes some countries from its treatment. Besides, it was published as long ago as 1963, since which date much has happened in that part of the world.

There was thus no 'model' in the field from which I could find guidance. However, I have been fortunate in having as my friend and colleague Dr Malcolm Yapp, who has in recent years promoted the cause of comparative history. Throughout the time that this book was in the making, I derived inspiration and support from him. Though the views expressed in this book are entirely mine, Malcolm has read the chapters and saved me from making many technical errors. I take this opportunity of expressing my very deep sense of gratitude to him. I am also deeply obliged to my wife, Valerie, who, as usual, made it possible for me to write this book in peace and seclusion without ever losing the warmth and togetherness of the family. I am grateful to my publishers, particularly to Derick Mirfin, his successor, Sarah Mahaffy, and the general editor of this series, who have treated me with infinite patience and the utmost kindness. I would also like to thank Janet Marks for typing the text. Without her co-operation I would not have met the deadline.

June 1979   B. N. PANDEY
London

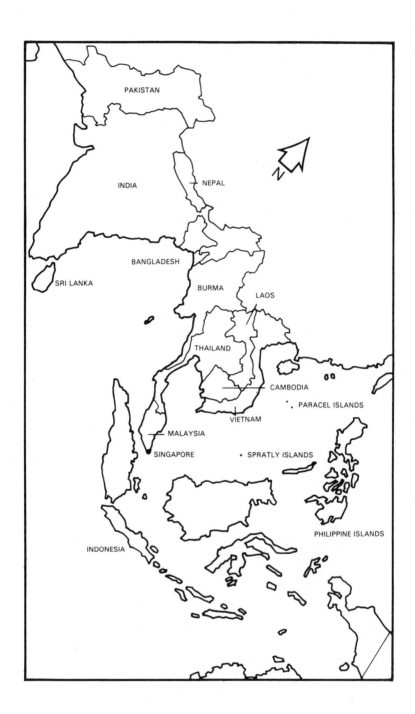

1 Decolonisation and the Emergence of South and South-east Asia

South and South-east Asia – stretching from Pakistan in the west to the Philippines in the east, consisting of fourteen states (taking into account the emergence of Bangladesh in 1971 and the unification of North and South Vietnam in 1975), with a total population in the 1970s of about 1100 millions (nearly one-third of the world's total population of 4000 millions) – were substantially under Western dominance for roughly 250 years; some areas had fallen under the imperial power of Portugal and Spain as early as the beginning of the sixteenth century. Thus from the beginning of industrial civilisation to the coming of the nuclear age the Western colonial powers ruled over South and South-east Asia, except for the interregnum between 1941 and 1945 when they were temporarily ousted by Japan. The Second World War brought decolonisation in its wake: the first state to gain independence was the Philippines in 1946, and the last was Malaya in 1957. Except for a few small areas of Portuguese territory (Goa, Daman and Diu in India and the island of Timor in the Indonesian archipelago) and the Dutch possession (Western New Guinea), Western domination ended in a remarkably short period of time, and the states of South and South-east Asia entered into the era of independence, still fettered however by the legacies of their colonial past.

Immediately before decolonisation began, four different colonial systems functioned in this area: the American, Dutch, French and British. All four had introduced into their respective dependencies, in greater or smaller measure, the ideas and institutions of the industrial age – reason, individual liberty and an impersonal system of law – and thereby caused a conflict between the modern and traditional systems, the latter resting on religion, personal authority and customary obligations. But the conflict was not resolved. The champions of the modern age could not fight for the cause in their imperial holdings, because a colonial regime was not rooted in public support and therefore lacked the self-confidence to institute major changes.[1] Besides, in order to preserve its rule it had to become cautious and conservative, and even to seek allies in the traditional order to counterbalance the upsurge of modern forces.

This policy of cautious conservatism, demonstrated by all colonial powers, was in part responsible for putting new life into the traditional institutions and ideas, and setting in motion religious (or cultural) nationalism against secular nationalism, caste against class, regionalism against federalism, separatism against union, status against merit, authority against reason, and so on. However, these diverse forces only represented competition for power among the various élites, and these conflicts would not have grown so fierce but for the sharing of enormous powers which the state, for the first time in Asia, had come to acquire during the colonial period. States, governments and empires had existed in Asia before, but only as the preserve of the chosen few – the hereditary rulers. Colonialism brought in its wake the Western principles of liberty and democracy which made it possible for almost every élite group to aspire to political power.

A sense of Western superiority, precariously based on the supremacy of the 'white' race, was the other feature common to all the colonial powers. This caused among the subject Asians an emotive reaction against a Western rule which seemed to them utterly alien, exclusive and hypocritical. Partly as a result of this the national movements in South and South-east Asia acquired some special features: utter rejection of Western superiority, anti-racism, pan-Asianism, and a bias towards the Soviet system, which seemed openly hostile to colonialism and racism and successful in fully assimilating its Asian colonies; some of these features (rejection of the West, and Asianism), however, did not survive for long during the post-independence period. Japan had boosted the morale of Asian nationalists in 1905 when it defeated Russia. It did so again during 1941–2 by ousting the Americans, Dutch, French and British colonial powers from South-east Asia, in less than a year. Japan's victory demolished many myths that had come to be associated with colonialism. For example, it irreparably damaged one of the justifications the colonial powers had so often sought for their existence in Asia – that they defended their dependencies from foreign aggression. But the racial legacy of the colonial period was not fully buried and forgotten in the whirlwind of Japanese ascendency. It continued to influence East–West relationships in the post-independence era.

Beneath these similarities there were differences in the styles of the colonial regimes caused partly by differences in the systems of the metropolitan countries, and partly by the variations in the historical traditions and environments that obtained among the dependencies. The British and American colonial systems were the most liberal: they introduced the rule of law, constitutionalism and Western education in their colonies; they admitted that a dependency was entitled to self-government once it had proved its fitness; and they associated the subject people with the running of the regime. In consequence the Philippines, Ceylon and India stood well ahead of other dependencies in terms of political development. Though a British colony, Malaya lagged behind because the Malayan States did not come under British rule until 1896, and even after 1896, when the Malayan federation emerged, a majority of the States remained under the indirect rule of the British, maintaining thereby their autonomy and their traditional order. Throughout the colonial period legalism and constitutionalism remained the twin features of the British Raj, and even during the fiercest phases of the national movements the British never abandoned their law courts and legislative councils. These features of the Anglo-American colonial system affected the composition of the new middle class and consequently, in some measure, the very style of the national movement. For example, the English-educated Indian middle class (in itself the outcome of various political, economic and legal changes introduced by the British in India) was virtually dominated and led into the national movement by lawyers who by training and profession were attached to constitutionalism and liberal democracy and, consequently, allergic to revolution, terrorism or bloodshed. Such men felt much more at home fighting for independence in the legislative council than on the battlefield. Evolution, not revolution, was throughout the leitmotiv of the national movement in India, Ceylon, Malaysia and the Philippines. The peaceful transfer of power that took place in these dependencies, and the way they all began to march confidently and firmly towards a democratic way of life in the post-independence era, may in some measure be related to the style of Anglo-American colonial rule. But even within this group of dependencies there were some regional variations: in the character and composition of the middle class, in the style of the national movement, and in the political and economic developments during the post-independence era – caused by differences in the historical traditions and environments of the individual countries. For example, the Filipino élite or *ilustrados* was different from its Indian counterpart in composition and size. As a legacy from Spanish rule, the Filipino élite consisted mostly of landlords and numbered not more than 600 individuals. During American rule wealth, power and leadership remained concentrated in their hands, and this had its bearing on the exclusively élitist nature of the Filipino national movement and on the country's half-hearted march towards economic and political democracy during the post-independence period.

As compared to the British and American colonial systems, those of the Dutch and French were less conducive to the growth of modern education, a professional middle class and constitutionalism in their respective dependencies. Dutch rule in Indonesia was both excessively paternalistic and exclusive. The Dutch method has been well described as, 'Let me help you, let me show you how to do it, let me do it for you.' Modern education had a late start and was restricted only to a small fraction of the population. For example, in 1924 not more than 2600 Indonesians were attending schools giving Western secondary education. The Dutch positively discouraged the learning and use of the Dutch language by the Indonesians. The Indonesians were encouraged to use a bazaar Malay, which grew into a national language and became an important integrating factor in the national movement. The Dutch made a beginning with representative government in 1918, but the People's Council, based as it was on a very narrow franchise and invested with virtually no legislative powers, turned out to be a feeble adventure in constitutionalism and was ignored and abandoned by the Indonesian élite. The Indonesian élite was thus denied the opportunities of growing in size as a class distinct from the rural populace and gaining any training in the running of a democractic political structure. Their involvement in the modernising process was minimal, and so their cultural and political bonds with the Netherlands remained relatively weak.

Despite their earlier mission to civilise and assimilate Vietnam into the metropolitan system – a policy which was later abandoned in favour of association between the ruler and the ruled – the French were too afraid of the political consequences of education to embark upon a thorough-going expansion of schools and colleges.[2] In Cochin-China (or South Vietnam), which the French directly administered, a modest beginning was made to secure collaborators, but by 1913 there were only 12,103 pupils in government primary schools. The Colonial Council, which the French established in Cochin-China, was an apology for a representative system. Severely restricted in size, franchise and powers, the Council failed to feed the constitutional stream into Vietnamese life. As a result the constitutionalists in Cochin-China were weakened and the political initiative passed to more extreme leaders who were the forerunners of the communists. In the protectorates of Annam and Tongking the advisory councils remained non-elective. Thus northern Vietnam, denied from the very beginning a constitutional channel for its nationalist urges, harboured underground nationalist societies. The other two French protectorates, Cambodia and Laos, remained virtually insulated from what little modern influence the French had brought, rather inadvertently, to Cochin-China.

However, the French and Dutch, as compared with the British, manifested little racial aggression and discrimination against their colonial subjects. The French, having been (like the Portuguese and Russians) the missionaries of assimilative colonialism, were naturally disposed towards accepting an Indo-Chinese as a fellow human being provided the latter was cultured by French standards. The Dutch, concerned as they were only with the economics of their empire, had no strong racial feelings and often married Indonesian or Eurasian women. Unlike the Anglo-Indians, who suffered in some ways more than Indians from British discrimination, the Eurasians in Indonesia were accepted as Netherlanders and often held the highest posts.[3] There was thus no biological barrier between the French and the Indo-Chinese, between the Dutch and the Indonesian. As a result the Indo-Chinese and Indonesian élites, compared to their Indian counterparts, were racially less sensitive towards their Western rulers.

If the 'racialism' of the Portuguese, Dutch and French was respectively religious, economic and cultural, it was political considerations more than anything else which determined British insularity in their imperial possessions. It was writ large on the British imperial mind that familiarity with the subject people might breed in them contempt or fellowship for the rulers and in either case was incompatible with the preservation of the empire, which rested in such a vast country as India more on the image of the moral and physical prowess of the British people than on the reality. Like a teacher's aloofness from his pupils or a politician's remoteness from his constituents, British isolation from the subject people was initially designed to promote respectability. The British showed fear, jealousy, even contempt, towards those colonial élites who emulated and tried to excel them. But having laid the foundations of the rule of law, a widespread modern educational system and constitutionalism, the British could not long remain insulated from the indigenous aspiring élites. When the time came they gave in, reluctantly but with a certain amount of grace.

To a few Churchillites the end of the British empire in India seemed premature. But it was inevitable when it happened in 1947. By then colonialism had lost all justification for perpetuating itself in Asia. Any attempt to preserve it further, apart from the exceptional case of Malaya, was bound to fail dismally as happened with the Dutch and French.

The fall of the empires was inevitable after 1945;[4] firstly, because of the Second World War, which coincided with the intrusion of Japanese military power into South-east Asia. Japan occupied all European posessions in the east up to the borders of India and northern New Guinea, and shattered both the mystique and the institutions of Western colonialism. The Japanese encouraged and strengthened the nationalist forces where they already existed in Indonesia, Vietnam, the Philippines and Burma, and created national consciousness in less advanced dependencies such as Malaya. In projecting further its image as a liberator Japan supported the Indian leader, S. C. Bose, in forming the Indian National Army and the Free Indian Government with headquarters in Singapore. Secondly, the war brought a change in the European attitude towards empire and weakened, in the case of Britain, the will to rule. Attlee's Labour government, which came to power in 1945, was determined to liquidate its Indian empire. The war also brought in its wake the Atlantic Charter, the United Nations and the Trusteeship Council, all designed to protect the dignity and freedom of nations. Colonialism suddenly became immoral. The emergence of Russia and the United States as the two super powers of the world, and the ensuing competition between them to gain support and allies among the nations of Asia and Africa, accelerated the process of decolonisation. America laid pressure on its European allies to decolonise in order to enable the Western bloc to win friends in the Eastern world. Among other things, the Cold War helped Indonesia to win its freedom from the Dutch in 1949.

We may now briefly turn to the process of decolonisation in the individual countries.

NEPAL AND THAILAND

Nepal and Thailand are the only two countries in this region never to have come under Western colonial rule. But it was sheer chance that they managed to retain their sovereignty.

The Himalayan kingdom of Nepal (about 520 miles long and 100 miles wide) escaped British penetration and remained one of the 'closed countries' of the world till the middle of the present century. This was so mainly because the kingdom did not present, directly or indirectly, any threat to the adjoining British Raj in India, except once in 1814, when the Gurkha army penetrated into British Indian territory, the British retaliated and the Treaty of Segawli (1816) was signed between the British and the Raja of Nepal. Also, from 1768, when the kingdom of Nepal began to assume its present shape, to 1950, when Tibet fell under communist China's rule, there was no danger of Nepal being swallowed by any other power. Such a danger might have accentuated British concern about Nepal and the kingdom would most certainly have fallen into the vortex of the international power game. When this happened for the first time in the post-colonial period, that is when China occupied Tibet and came close to the Nepalese-Indian border, the government of India tightened its control over Nepal. Also Nepal as an independent kingdom served the British imperial interest well in India. The Gurkha army, which the British recruited from Nepal, could be set against the Hindu, Sikh and Muslim soldiers if ever these elements, which constituted the Indian army, united against their British masters. Nepal was thus left alone because it never became a bone of contention between two imperial powers.

Thailand's case was the opposite. In the 1890s Thailand came between the expanding empires of Britain and France. Expanding eastward from its Indian base Britain had by then occupied Burma and established a foothold in Malaya. The French empire had moved westward from Vietnam, occupied Cambodia and Laos, and now it stood on the eastern frontiers of Thailand. To complete the boundaries of its Laotian protectorate France demanded all Thai territories east of the Mekong River, and determined to enforce its demand by penetrating deep into Thai territory. It was in British imperial interests to avoid having frontiers with the French colonial regimes, which could be done only by preserving Thailand as a buffer state between British and French possessions. Thus it was mainly because of British pressure that the independence of Thailand was guaranteed by the Anglo-French Agreement of 1896. Thailand had to concede territories to France in Laos and later to Britain in Malaya. But it retained its sovereignty.

Thailand and Nepal entered the modern world in 1932 and 1951 respectively. In both cases the breakaway from the traditional political structure was caused by the indigenous élites aspiring for power. The Thai revolution of 1932 was caused by a group of professionals, most of whom had received their education in Paris. This group of middle-level military and civil officials, finding their way to the chamber of power blocked by the continuing omnipotence of absolute monarchy, organised a *coup d'état* which ended the control of the royal family over the government. The monarchy was not abolished, but was made constitutional, and the constitution of 1932, while promising full democracy in due course, established in the initial period a quasi-parliamentary constitution. Half the members of parliament were to be appointed by the government. From 10 December, when the King (Rama VII) proclaimed the new constitution, until 1973, Thailand was virtually ruled by a military dictatorship, and its internal politics were in large measure a matter of factional infighting between competing élites. The political structure – with the Prime Minister, the Cabinet and the National Assembly – had the appearance of liberal democracy but the power, none the less, remained concentrated in the executive, and the National Assembly never succeeded in developing its potential authority.

However, Thailand's experiment with democracy lasted for only three years, from 1973 to 1976. For the military, a democratic government was a weak government which Thailand could not afford, especially after Indo-China fell into the communist lap in 1975. Consequently, in October 1976, the military took over the government. With a view to restoring a restricted form of democracy to Thailand, the military junta drafted a new constitution, the thirteenth since 1932.

For various reasons modernisation has been slowest in Nepal. Apart from being a mountain kingdom with the most primitive means of transport and communication, and having a traditional educational system and an utterly feudal society, Nepal was ruled autocratically by an oligarchy of Ranas for 104 years, beginning in 1846 when Jung Bahadur Rana usurped power from the Shah dynasty. The monarch was kept in captivity and all powers were exercised by the Rana Prime Minister in the name of the king. A modern middle class grew at a snail's pace. The very few well-to-do Nepalese who could acquire modern education in the Indian universities were absorbed into the bureaucratic structure of their country. Any contest with the Rana regime was overlaid by, among other things, the respect in which the Ranas and the country (the only Hindu independent nation in the world) were held by the Hindu nationalists in India. However, the number of Nepali students in India went on increasing through the 1930s and 1940s. Their indoctrination with democratic principles and the decreasing number of opportunities for them to share power, made the students restive. They formed the Nepal National Congress, which met on British Indian territory in 1946, a year before India's independence, and resolved to overthrow the Rana regime, revive the monarchy to form a constitutional framework, and establish democratic rule in Nepal. But the Nepali Congress could make no headway against the autocratic Rana regime without support from a foreign power. India, on achieving independence, was engrossed in its own internal problems, but soon after the emergence of communist China in 1949 and its conquest of Tibet in 1950 Nehru's concern about Nepal was aroused. Nepal should be made strong as a buffer state between India and China, and the only way this could be done, Nehru thought, was to set up a democratic government with wide mass support. A democratic Nepal would have natural bonds with India and therefore would stand firm against any Chinese penetration. India thus lent a hand, unofficially, in organising the Palace revolution which took place in Katmandu in November 1950. On that day the captive King Tribhuvan managed to escape into the Indian Embassy building in Katmandu. He was now on Indian soil. The Rana Prime Minister was persuaded to allow the King to leave for India. All disaffected forces rallied round the King and sporadic revolts erupted in a number of places. India exercised pressure on the Rana regime, agreement was reached on 12 February 1951 between all parties concerned (the Ranas, the King and the Nepali Congress), and a coalition government was formed. Thus ended the Rana regime, but this was not the beginning of democratic rule in Nepal.

The King experimented with democratic institutions, but perhaps the change was too sudden and the proper social, economic and political base to support such experimentation had not yet developed. On 18 February 1955 King Tribhuvan issued a proclamation from his sick bed in France dissolving the Nepalese parliament (the Royal council of State) and vesting all power in the Crown Prince. He died the following month and King Mahendra Shah ascended the throne as an absolute monarch.

Since then Nepal has experimented in vain, even with its own version of democracy – the village-based democracy of the National Panchayat. The trappings of a modern political system remain – the Prime Minister, the Cabinet, the National Panchayat – but the king (now Birendra Shah) rules with supreme powers.

THE PHILIPPINES (1946)

The archipelago has some unique features. It comprises 7107 islands and islets, of which only 2713 have names. But most importantly, it is the only nation in South and South-east Asia to have been in a tribal state of development when it became subject to Western colonialism. The people's religion was substantially animism; Islam had reached only the southern islands (Sulu and Mindano). The archipelago had neither a central governmental structure ruling over a large territory nor a traditional élite centred round a royal court. It had evaded the cultural impact of both China and India. Coming thus under Western dominance at an early stage of cultural and political development, the Philippines underwent a greater degree of conversion to Western ways than any other country in this region of Asia.[5] Under three hundred years of Spanish rule (from 1571 to 1898) the people embraced Christianity; today over 90 per cent of the population is Christian (80 per cent Roman Catholic and 8 per cent Protestant). Under Spanish rule the Filipino middle class also grew, consisting mostly of landed gentry and dominated by the *mestizos* of mixed blood. The Spanish regime provided a sound educational system (in 1898 there were nearly 200,000 children in school) in which the Filipino élite could grow.

After annexing the archipelago in 1898 as a result of the Spanish-American war, the United States improved upon this seemingly sound base for modernisation. In a generation the school population expanded by 500 per cent. Under American colonial rule English became the common language of the well educated throughout the country. However, by supporting a free economy in a capitalist framework, America further strengthened the position of the Filipino ruling class (the *ilustrados*) with their large rural estates (in 1966–7, 42 per cent of the gross national income was appropriated by 10 per cent of the population). In a predominantly agricultural country the ownership of land remained concentrated in a few hands, and nearly 50 per cent of the cultivators existed as landless labourers. Here lay a potentially dangerous situation for a nation which was being shepherded by the Americans towards a democratic way of life. It was to these *ilustrados* that the United States first transferred power in 1935, when the Philippine Commonwealth became the first self-governing state in South and South-east Asia, headed by a Filipino President. The conduct of foreign relations and national defence were to remain in American hands for ten years, after which time the Philippines were to attain full independence.

The war broke out and the Japanese occupied the archipelago after defeating the Americans and the Filipinos in their heroic battle of Bataan. In their rule over the nation from 1942 to 1945 the Japanese, however, did not change the social structure and the composition of the political élite. In 1945 the Americans came back, and on 4 July 1946 the country acquired its independence, and Manuel A. Roxas became the first President of the Republic of the Philippines. The Philippines marched on the democratic path with a presidential system supported by a bicameral legislature (the Senate and the House of Representatives). However, a potential danger to democracy lay, among other things, in the preponderant constitutional power held by the Philippine President, which allowed him to encroach upon the powers of the legislature. With almost all the classical conditions suitable for the proper functioning of democracy, the country carried on with its Western legacy for twenty-five years and then in 1972 it was placed under martial law. Since then President Ferdinand Marcos and his beautiful wife, Imelda, have been running the country, as a Marcos opponent – now safely in exile – put it, under 'conjugal dictatorship'.[6]

INDIA AND PAKISTAN (1947), BANGLADESH (1971)

Of all the Afro-Asian national movements against Western dominance, the Indian was the most modernised and its leadership

possessed the most quality and integrity. Indian nationalism involved a great deal of mass participation and was in principle a
secular and democratic movement. However (from the beginning of
the twentieth century) the Indian national movement was con-
fronted by Muslim separatism. This was a unique Indian phenomenon caused by the peculiarities of the Indian situation. The Muslims
in India were a strong (over 20 per cent of the total population),
unintegrated and a power-conscious political minority. They derived their political consciousness partly from the fact that they
constituted the ruling class in India immediately before the British
take-over. A second peculiarity lay in the geographical spread of this
minority. The Muslims were in the majority in the north-western
(the Punjab, the North-West-Frontier Province, Sind, Baluchistan)
and the north-eastern (which now constitutes Bangladesh) regions
of India. Muslim separatism thus had a potential territorial base.

The national movement was represented by the Indian National
Congress and the Muslim interest by the All-India Muslim League.
The latter struggled till 1939 to obtain for the Muslims, from any
constitutional scheme devised for the Indian Union, one third to one
half of the power, at all levels and in each area. The Muslim demand
had the support of the British, one of whose motives in offering such
support was to weaken the Congress movement for independence.
To Congress,however, the Muslim demand seemed unreasonable
and undemocratic – the concoction of a handful of self-seeking
Muslim leaders. Instead of being browbeaten, the Muslim League
leader, M. A. Jinnah, raised his demands higher and in 1940 asked for
a separate Muslim state. At that time nobody, not even Jinnah,
believed that Pakistan would ever come into existence. But the idea
of Pakistan, advanced in the first instance possibly to strengthen the
League's bargaining position, began to grip the Muslim imagina-
tion. In the period from 1940 to 1947 many factors combined to turn
the idea into a reality. The communal holocaust, fanned by the
League's 'Islam in danger' crusade, and combined with the various
acts and omissions on the part of all the parties concerned (the
British, Congress and the League) as well as some individuals, led
the country to partition. In August 1947 British power was withdrawn from the Indian sub-continent, and India and Pakistan (consisting of two wings separated by 1000 miles of Indian territory)
began their independent lives in a democratic style. Pakistan, however, had no foundation to support a democratic structure. The
Muslim League, now the ruling party of Pakistan, had been run
dictatorially by one man, Jinnah. Consequently it had been unable to
develop any democratic traditions or a wide range of leadership.
Jinnah himself was too secretive and introverted to have any liking
for popular democracy. Suspicious of all his colleagues and hardly

believing in the integrity of any of them, he kept all the power in his own hands. Soon after his death in 1948 the scramble for power began among the Pakistani politicians, and with it also began the tension between the two wings of the country – west and east Pakistan. The half-hearted experimentation with democracy finally came to an end in 1958 with the military *coup*. The tension between the two wings escalated into war in 1971 and east Pakistan finally broke away and became the independent state of Bangladesh.

India's wholehearted adoption of the Westminster style of democracy was facilitated mainly by Congress and its wide range of leadership. Since its inception in 1885 Congress had remained committed to a democratic and secular system, and in 1947 its leadership was large, respectable and mature enough to provide a lead in that direction. Perhaps no Afro-Asian leader was as much of a devout democrat as Nehru. It was because of him that the liberal democratic order flourished in India for over a quarter of a century, surprisingly without mutilation or modification. Nehru has been blamed by some of his countrymen for perpetuating in India a system which other countries in South and South-east Asia had wisely abandoned because of its inadequacy to cope with their wide range of new problems. Whether it was the inadequacy of the system or of the leadership, or a combination of both, which led to the undemocratisation of South and South-east Asia will be investigated later. Suffice it here to mention that India, hitherto the world's largest democratic country, suspended the system, in June 1975, but only for twenty months. It was revived in March 1977 under the leadership of the Janata Party.

CEYLON (SRI LANKA) 1948

For 450 years, from 1505 to 1948, Ceylon was ruled successively by the Portuguese, the Dutch and the British. But it was only during the second decade of the twentieth century that the national movement emerged. Nowhere in Asia was the national movement so élitist, so constitutional and peaceful, as in Ceylon. As a result Ceylon slid gently through a series of constitutional reforms into independence. The Ceylon National Congress, the vehicle of the national movement, emerged in 1918 and, throughout its existence, consisted mostly of the English-educated, upper-class Ceylonese professionals. The national movement in Ceylon did not thus involve the masses in the same manner or scale as did the Congress movement in India. Nor was it seriously handicapped by the communal (or minority) problem. Indeed the Hindu Tamils made up a formidable minority, but they were advised by Indian nationalists, particularly by Nehru, to join hands with the Sinhalese Buddhist majority and present a united front against the British till independence was won. Thus the gulf between leaders and followers, the conflict between majority and minority interests, remained concealed, mainly due to the character and style of the national movement.

Through a series of constitutional reforms, introduced in 1883, 1920 and 1931, Ceylon had come to acquire an elective legislature with an unofficial majority. The Ceylonese had also been given the opportunity to participate in the running of the colonial government through various executive committees. At almost every stage of constitutional development the nationalists wanted more than they were given by the British, but they never practised non-cooperation or rebellion. The Ceylon National Congress went into a decline in 1945, when the Ceylonese leader D. S. Senanayake refused to have any truck with it because of the presence of communists in its ranks. In the same year Britain set up a commission (the Soulbury Commission) to devise a constitution for an independent Ceylon. In 1947 Senanayake organised the United National Party (UNP). The Independence Bill had a smooth run in the House of Commons as well as in Ceylon's House of Representatives. On 4 February 1948 Ceylon became independent as a dominion of the British Commonwealth.

The uniqueness of Ceylon's political development since independence lies in the running of the Westminster-style democracy on a two-party system. D. S. Senanayake's party ruled the country until 1956, when it was defeated at the polls by S. W. R. D. Bandaranaike's Sri Lanka Party (SLFP). In 1959 Bandaranaike was assassinated by a Buddhist monk. His widow, Mrs Sirimavo Bandaranaike, took over the leadership of the party and defeated the UNP in the second general election of 1960. She became the world's first woman Prime Minister. The UNP won the general election in 1965 and remained in power until the next election of 1970, when it was replaced by the SLFP. Mrs Bandaranaike became Prime Minister for the second time. In December 1971, on her initiative, Ceylon adopted a new constitution whereby it became a free, sovereign and independent republic. The Soulbury Dominion Constitution of Ceylon came to an end. At the same time Ceylon was renamed Sri Lanka.

Mrs Bandaranaike, however, lost popular support during the Emergency, the longest in the country's history, which she had declared in 1971. As a result, her party suffered a crushing defeat in Sri Lanka's fifth election, held in July 1977. The UNP once again came to power with J. R. Jayewardene as the Prime Minister. Jayewardene, however, was committed to rejecting the country's Westminster form of government, on the grounds that the fickleness

Wingate College Library

of parliamentary factions had made for weak government, and he substituted a French-style presidential form of government. The constitution was accordingly amended, and in February 1978 Jayewardene became the country's first executive president.

BURMA (1948)

Conquered by the British between 1826 and 1885 and administered as a province of British India until 1935, Burma was in fact never considered, by either Burmese or Indians, as an integral part of India. Not a single Indian nationalist of any consequence raised his voice against the separation of Burma from India in 1935. The Indian National Congress did maintain a provincial branch in Burma until 1935, but it was insignificant. It was run by Indians and was virtually confined to the city of Rangoon.

Until the outbreak of the Second World War, Burma did not have a mass-based national movement run by a modern political party, such as Congress in India. Political agitation began as late as 1917. Students and Buddhist monks played leading roles in the first tide of the national movement. The political party of some significance was the General Council of Burmese Associations (GCBA), but soon after its foundation in 1921 it split into factions mainly over the question of accepting the constitutional reforms introduced by the British, or remaining aloof and fighting for a new political system. Some Burmese nationalists, like Ba Maw and U Saw, participated in the implementation of the 1935 Act, which provided for a cabinet government wherein nearly all internal subjects were transferred to ministers responsible to the parliament. This experiment in near self-government was halted by the Second World War.

The militant and revolutionary phase of the Burmese nationalist movement began with the 'Thirty Heroes' – a group of young Burmese who were smuggled out of Burma prior to the war and trained by the Japanese in military warfare so that they would form the core of the Japanese drive against the British in Burma. Led by Aung San they formed the Burmese Independence Army and followed the invading Japanese from Thailand to Burma. Japan was instrumental in the creation of a political army in Burma, as elsewhere in South-east Asia. Aung San's 'Independence Army' turned into a 'National Army' in 1943 when Japan granted nominal independence to Burma. At this time a modern political party came into existence, the Anti-Fascist People's Freedom League (AFPFL). The party opened its ranks to all Burmese irrespective of race, religion and political beliefs. The leadership of the party included those who were co-operating with the Japanese.

After the British reoccupation of Burma in the spring of 1945 the AFPFL with its 'National Army' came to play the leading role in Burmese politics. The AFPFL demanded immediate independence for Burma, which the British then seemed unwilling to concede. But the tide turned with Prime Minister Attlee's announcement on 20 December 1946 of Britain's firm intention to transfer power to Burma. Negotiations began and elections were held in April 1947. In July 1947, in the midst of mapping the political future of Burma, Aung San and six of his colleagues were assassinated. Thakin (or U) Nu became the new leader of the AFPFL and head of the Executive Council. The constitution of Burma was completed and the final agreement signed on 17 October 1947. On 4 January 1948 Burma became a fully sovereign and independent state, but unlike India, Pakistan and Ceylon it opted to remain outside the British Commonwealth.

Burma entered the post-independence era with U Nu as its first Prime Minister, the AFPFL as its ruling political party, and all the democratic freedoms of a Westminster type of liberal democracy: a Cabinet system of government, a bicameral parliament, and an independent judiciary. But with independence also began the struggle for power and more power between the élites in the AFPFL and between the ruling party on the one hand and the communists and minority groups (like the Christian Karens) on the other. Insurrections and revolts drew the country into a state of semi war. The ruling party (AFPFL) split up in 1958. Democracy led a precarious existence for another four years and finally collapsed on 2 March 1962 when the military took over the government. The 1947 constitution was abolished and military rule began under General Ne Win and the Revolutionary Council. Since 1962 Burma has been striving towards a socialist society in a Burmese way under the supreme command of General Ne Win.

INDONESIA (1949)

'We have ruled here for 300 years with the whip and the club and we shall still be doing it in another 300 years.'[7] This statement, made in 1936, by the Dutch Governor-General of Indonesia (B. C. de Jonge), epitomises Dutch thinking on its empire. Even in the 1930s it was inconceivable to the Netherlands that the empire would ever come to an end. The Second World War did not shake the Dutch belief. On reoccupying Indonesia (or parts of it) in 1945, Holland held it even more tenaciously than before. Many factors combined to put pressure on the Dutch finally to relinquish their empire in Indonesia in December 1949.

The most important factor was Indonesian nationalism, which suddenly became vigorous, militant and revolutionary during the Japanese occupation of the archipelago from March 1942 to August 1945. The Japanese interregnum in Indonesia was catalytic. It was instrumental in destroying the political authority and prestige of the traditional élites – the indigenous nobility of the Javanese *priyayi* class – who alone had been associated by the Dutch in the colonial administration of the country up to 1942.[8] The Japanese were also instrumental in reviving and bringing into the forefront modern élite groups represented by secular Muslims like Sukarno, Hatta and S. Sjahrir. Also under Japanese auspices a number of quasi-military youth organisations were founded. The emergence of different élite groups – all militant and all contending between themselves for power – was the significant political development during the Japanese rule. Political parties too were revived during this period, each representing different élite interests, but no one succeeded then or in subsequent years in overshadowing the others. Absence of a strong nationalist political party may in some measure account for the instability in the post–independence period. The Dutch colonial system was indeed responsible for choking the growth of a nationalist party in Indonesia. Both Sukarno's Indonesian Nationalist Party (PNI), founded in 1927, and the Indies Communist Party (PKI), founded in 1920, were suppressed and banished by the Dutch soon after their inception. The Japanese created a party of Indonesian Islamic Federation, the Masjumi, in 1943. The PNI was also revived during the Japanese rule and the PKI during the revolution, from 1945 to 1949. It was, however, the Masjumi and the PNI which carried the government, sometimes in coalition but always with the bitterest of rivalry subsisting between them, through the first phase of independence – the liberal period from 1949 to 1958.

The Japanese occupation thus gave life, pace and a revolutionary character to the Indonesian national movement. On 17 August 1945, two days after the Japanese surrender, Sukarno and Hatta proclaimed the Republic of Indonesia. Soon the Dutch landed under British cover, and the armed struggle, which was to last for nearly five years, began between the Republic and the Dutch. Soon after its own independence in 1947 India lent full support to the Indonesian war of independence. During 1948 American public opinion changed in favour of the Republic. The United States put pressure on The Hague by threatening to suspend aid under the Marshall Plan. The Netherlands was finally persuaded to change its policy and transfer full sovereignty to Indonesia. The Federal Republic of the United States of Indonesia was established on 27 December 1949, but the Dutch retained their hold on West New Guinea (West Irian).

Since 1949 Indonesia has passed through three political phases of independence: the liberal period 1949 to 1958, the period of guided democracy from 1958 to 1967 and the period of military rule under General Suharto since March 1967. It was during the first phase that Indonesia experimented with the principles and forms of liberal democracy – the power of President Sukarno and the army was effectively limited, parliament enjoyed some authority and the political parties wielded real power. Several factors, not least his own ambition, induced Sukarno to arrogate to himself the supreme powers of the state. In 1958 Indonesia abandoned the constitutional democracy and opted for an 'Indonesian form of democracy' suited to the genius of the people and to the style and ambition of their charismatic leader – Sukarno.

VIETNAM, CAMBODIA, LAOS (1954)

The three French possessions in South-East Asia (collectively called Indo-China) have been victims of incessant strife and warfare and have figured prominently in international politics for almost thirty years, from 1946 to 1975. The story began with North Vietnam turning to communism; it ended in December 1975 with the whole of Vietnam, Cambodia and Laos becoming communist states. A number of questions have been posed over the last twenty years. Why did North Vietnam become communist? Was it inevitable, or could it have been prevented? In what measure did the American intervention facilitate the fall of Cambodia and Laos to communism? As for the future, will these communist countries of Asia form a united front against the 'free world' or will each go its own way? Some observations will be made on these questions later. Here we will just outline the sequence of events which led these countries to full independence in 1954.

Vietnam consisted of three territorial zones: northern (Tongking), central (Annam) and southern (Cochin-China). France annexed Cochin-China in 1867 and established its protectorate over Annam and Tongking in 1883. Thus the French ruled directly over the southern part, penetrating down to district and village level. Over the rest of Vietnam they ruled indirectly through the Vietnamese emperor based at Hué. For all practical purposes the French were masters of Annam and Tongking, but their system did not penetrate down to district and village level. A modicum of traditional order persisted in these parts of Vietnam. Perhaps this may explain in some measure why Annam and Tongking, when compared to Cochin-China, maintained a high degree of cultural, religious and social homogeneity. Twentieth-century Cochin-China, divided as it was between mutually antagonistic and exclusive forces – social, religious and ethnic – lacked a common will and common loyalties.[9] The Cambodian and Laotian monarchies became French protectorates by 1864 and 1895 respectively. Thus French rule over Indo-China was just over seventy years old when the Second World War broke out and the Japanese entered the area. Overrun and occupied by Germany, France, under the Vichy regime, was not at war with Japan in 1941. Thus when the Japanese landed in Indo-China, in 1941, they recognised French sovereignty over these countries and left local administration and security functions in French colonial hands. This arrangement lasted till March 1945, when the Japanese military command took over the colonial administration, imprisoned the French administrators, and induced the monarchs of Annam, Cambodia and Laos to declare the independence of their respective kingdoms from French imperialism.

As decided at the Potsdam Conference (July–August 1945) by the combined Chiefs of Staff, the whole of Indo-China was to be divided into north and south at the 16th parallel, and after the Japanese surrender the British forces were to take charge of the south and the Chinese of the north. Consequently South Vietnam and Cambodia fell under the charge of Lord Louis Mountbatten, the Supreme Allied Commander of South-east Asia, and Annam, Tongking and Laos went to the care of the Chinese task-force. Lord Mountbatten regretted this arbitrary division implying the emergence of two different types of political development in the north and south of Indo-China during the postwar period.[10] The British and Chinese forces allowed the French to reoccupy the whole of Indo-China by September 1946. If the British had prevented the French from re-entering Indo-China, some scholars have argued, the postwar history of Indo-China might have taken a different turn. The consequences of French re-entry might be interpreted in various different ways. Suffice it here to observe that the national movement in North Vietnam had already become communist and revolutionary before the French forces arrived on the scene.

In fact the Vietnamese national movement had been revolutionary and militant from the very beginning. This was so partly because of the French colonial system, which offered very little scope for nationalist aspirations to grow on constitutional lines. Founded in 1927 the Vietnam Quoc Dan Dang (VNQDD – Vietnamese Nationalist Party) was the first major non-Marxist party, but it was destroyed by the French in 1930 after it had attempted to foment a general revolution. It was, however, Ho Chi Minh and the Indo-Chinese Communist Party (ICP) which he founded in 1930 which carried the banner of revolutionary nationalism. The ICP was suppressed by the French in 1931 but unlike VNQDD it did not die. During the war the ICP leaders decided to give first priority to national unity and independence. With this in view they launched in May 1941 an all-inclusive, co-ordinating political party – the Vietnam Independence League – better known as the Viet Minh. Following the Japanese surrender, the Viet Minh forced the Vietnamese Emperor Bao Dai to abdicate in favour of the provisional government of the Democratic Republic of Vietnam (DRV) which was established in Hanoi under the presidency of Ho Chi Minh. The DRV gathered strength during the Chinese occupation of North Vietnam.

The French, having consolidated their position in South Vietnam, made their own entry into North Vietnam possible by recognising the DRV as a free state with its own government, parliament, army and treasury, and belonging to the Indo-Chinese Federation and to the French Union. France also offered to hold a referendum to determine whether Tongking, Annam and Cochin-China should be united. In March 1946 the DRV allowed the French troops to enter North Vietnam to relieve the Chinese occupation. Negotiations began between the French government and the DRV but no agreement was reached on the future of the free state of Vietnam. In November 1946 fighting broke out between the French and DRV forces and lasted until May 1954, when the Vietnamese forces under Vo Nguyen Giap inflicted a crushing defeat on the French at Dien Bien Phu. This humiliating defeat of the flower of the French Expeditionary Corps at the hands of 'Vietnamese peasants' shattered the confidence of the Western world in its conventional forces and of France in its Indo-Chinese empire. In July 1954 at the Geneva Conference France finally agreed to grant independence collectively to North and South Vietnam, Cambodia and Laos. It was agreed at the Geneva Conference to hold a free election in Vietnam, in 1956, for the unification of the two zones. The elections were never held and the inter-state war between Ho Chi Minh's North Vietnam and Ngo Dinh Diem's Republic of South Vietnam continued. With American support South Vietnam fought North Vietnamese aggression and infiltration until 1975 when it finally capitulated. On 30 April 1975 communist forces took over Saigon and renamed it Ho Chi Minh City. After thirty years of war Vietnam emerged united under communist rule. On 24 June 1976 the united Vietnam held its first National Assembly session in Hanoi.

National movements in Cambodia and Laos were born only during the war under Japanese occupation, and in both countries the movements were fomented and run by the royal families. The national movement in Cambodia was represented by King Norodom Sihanouk himself. It began in 1945 after the Japanese surrender, when the question arose as to whether the country was prepared immediately to opt for full independence. The King did not believe that it was. But there were parties and groups consisting of young university-educated men, including some members of the royal family, who wanted full independence and the establishment of a liberal democracy based on universal suffrage. Then there were the communists, who began to gain support from the Viet Minh of North and South Vietnam, who too were willing to use militant and revolutionary tactics against the French. By 1953 the communists in Cambodia had come to present themselves as the real freedom fighters, which galvanised the colourful King into negotiation with the French government for full independence. When the French ignored his overtures, the King dramatised his position by departing for voluntary exile in Bangkok, vowing not to return to his palace until Cambodia was free. This embarrassed the French and they eventually agreed to concede full independence. The King returned to his country in triumph. Cambodia's independence was formally conceded at the Geneva Conference, and China and North Vietnam acknowledged the legitimacy of King Sihanouk's government. DRV further agreed to withdraw Viet Minh forces from Cambodia.

From 1954 to 1970, under the leadership of Sihanouk, Cambodia experimented with democracy under most difficult conditions. Its internal unity was threatened by contending élites and its autonomy by outside interference from the Americans and the Vietnamese communists engendered by the continuing war in Vietnam. In order to foster national unity the King stepped down from the throne, in March 1955, appointed his father as his successor, and entered into politics as a 'humble citizen'. In trying to preserve the sovereignty of his state against American interference he veered more towards China. This angered the Nixon administration, and in 1970, while Prince Sihanouk was abroad in the Soviet Union, his government was overthrown by a military coup organised by General Lon Nol. Sihanouk lived in exile in Peking for five years. He returned in the wake of the Cambodian communist's (Khmer Rouge) victory over the American-backed regime of Marshal Lon Nol in April 1975. Prince Sihanouk remained the titular head of the state till April 1976, when he resigned and retired from politics and was replaced by Khieu Samphan, the Khmer Rouge war hero.

Laos like Cambodia was a protectorate, but of the five *pays* of French Indo-China, it was the least touched by the French system and retained in French eyes its image of Rousseau's 'noble savage', till its independence in 1954. A modern middle class or a national consciousness hardly existed. Under French supervision the ad–

ministration of the country was carried on by a ruling class of about 2,000 persons consisting of the King, descendants of the royal and quasi-royal families and some commercial leaders of the towns. Political developments in Laos were initiated by and thrived on factional rivalries for power among the traditional élites, especially after the promulgation on 11 May 1947 of a constitution which curtailed the powers of the King by turning him into a constitutional monarch, thereby providing an opportunity for the élites to enter the power-game.

An élitist movement against French rule was born in March 1945, when the Japanese asked the Laotian King to declare the independence of his country. The King vacillated but his Prime Minister, Prince Phetsarath, opted for independence. The national movement began in the form of a conflict between the King and the Princes. It grew strong during the Chinese occupation of Laos from August 1945 to August 1946. By the time the French colonial regime was reinstated (August 1946) a significant development had already taken place. Prince Souphanouvong (half-brother of Prince Phetsarath) had given a communist dimension to the national movement. He had leagued with the Viet Minh and with their support gained control of most of central Laos.

The communist movement grew even stronger during the French reoccupation from 1946 to 1954. In 1949 Souphanouvong gave it form by founding the militant Pathet Lao (Lao National Movement). By 1954 the Pathet Lao had come to occupy the two provinces of Sam Neua and Phong Saly – both bordering on North Vietnam. For the North Vietnamese communists it was a great strategic gain, for they could now use the eastern region of Laos as a trail for infiltration into South Vietnam. The Pathet Lao had thus brought North Vietnam into Laotian politics and thereby made American intervention inevitable.

America's resolve to intervene was determined by France's decision in 1953 to withdraw from Laos by transferring power to its royal government. This French act was formalised at the Geneva Conference of 1954. In American eyes the French withdrawal from Indo-China created a vacuum. Unless this vacuum was filled by American forces, so American thinking ran, the whole of South-east Asia might be overrun by the communists. America wanted to turn Laos into a strong buffer state between communist China and North Vietnam in the north and Thailand and Cambodia in the south. In 1955, with the visit of Secretary of State Dulles to the Laotian capital Vientiane, American military and financial aid began pouring into the country. From its independence in 1954 to its total capitulation to communism in 1975 Laotian politics were divided between three parties. The first consisted of those élites who were pro-Western and relied on American–Thai support; the second, comprising the communist Pathet Lao and its political organ – Neo Lao Hak Xat (NLHX) – relied on North Vietnamese and Chinese support; and the third headed by Prince Souvannaphouma wanted to steer a middle course between 'right' and 'left'. It was this third party which under the prime ministership of Souvannaphouma strove to preserve national unity by pursuing a neutral policy through a coalition government which included the communists. This party suffered most at the hands of the Americans, who then believed neither in the concept of neutrality nor in the principle of coexistence, and considered that all communists – whether Russian, Chinese, Vietnamese or Laotian – were alike. As in Vietnam and Cambodia so in Laos the Americans failed to resist the communist forces. The inevitable happened in December 1975 when the communist Lao Revolutionary Party took hold of the entire country. The king abdicated, the republic was proclaimed and three million Laotians were shepherded on to the path of 'true democracy'.

MALAYA (1957) SINGAPORE (1965)

The root cause of Malaya's late independence may lie in the composition of its population. In 1940 the total population of the nine Malayan States and the three Straits Settlements (Malacca, Penang and Singapore) was estimated to be 5·5 million persons, consisting of 2·3 million Malays (Muslims of Malaya), 2·4 million Chinese, and 0·75 million Indians. The indigenous Malays were thus in a minority, overshadowed by Chinese and Indians, many of whom had originally entered the country as labourers during the British colonial regime to work in the mines and on the plantations. From this calculation is excluded the dominant Muslim Malay population of the north-western coastal area of the island of Borneo (consisting of the States of Sarawak and North Borneo), which if added to the Malaysian population would have tipped the balance in favour of the Malays. But until 1963 these Borneo States, separated from the Malay peninsula by 400 miles, were British Crown Colonies and as such played no part in the politics of the peninsula.

Evenly balanced between the Malays, Chinese and Indians, Malayan society lacked cohesion and common will. The complex administrative divisions which the British had imposed upon Malaya further diversified the situation. The first British possessions (Penang, Malacca and Singapore), acquired between 1786 and 1819, were in 1867 turned into crown colonies and as such were much more exposed to British penetration, and modernisation. But the bulk of the Malayan peninsula (consisting of nine states), which came under British suzerainty between 1896 and 1909, was ruled indirectly through the sultans and rajas. Even among these nine states there existed a division: four were grouped in a federation and five remained unfederated, which in practice meant that the British indirect rule was more of a reality over the unfederated states. The traditional order persisted in these states thus choking the growth of modern élites.

During the Japanese occupation of the peninsula (1942–45) a feeble national movement developed; even so it spoke with different voices. The Japanese favoured the Malays and induced them to think in terms of the eventual independence of their country. The Indians were encouraged to fight for India's independence. The Chinese were ill-treated, and alone formed the resistance movement against the Japanese. Many of the underground Chinese fighters were communists. The Japanese occupation thus resulted in stirring Malay political consciousness, in articulating communal antipathy between Chinese and Malays and in improving the Communist Party's organisation.

On their re-entry into Malaya the British experimented with a few administrative changes, finally opting, in February 1948, for constituting the country into a federation. The federal government (consisting of all nine states, Penang and Malacca) was to be run by the British, but the rulers of states were given the same measure of autonomy that they enjoyed before the war. The federal arrangement thus seemed a backward step to the communists, a revival of the partnership between British imperialism and Malayan feudalism. In June 1948 the Malayan Communist Party went into an armed rebellion, which was to last until 1960.

The non-communist politicians took to constitutional politics in meeting the pre-conditions of self-rule (national unity, and the restoration of law and order) imposed by the British at the time of concluding the Federal Agreement. As national unity could not be based on cultural fusion the politicians went for co-operation between the communities. Three parties – the United Malays National Organisation (UMNO) of Tunku Abdul Rahman, the Malayan Chinese Association (MCA) and the Malayan Indian Congress (MIC) – formed the Alliance, and won an overwhelming victory at the first national election held in July 1955. The victory of the Alliance symbolised the national unity of the kind that was feasible in Malayan conditions. The British entered into negotiations with the Alliance leaders for the granting of full independence to Malaya. On 31 August 1957 power was transferred to the Alliance and independent Malaya marched forward with a democratic structure and with

Tunku Abdul Rahman as its first Prime Minister. Singapore and Borneo remained Crown Colonies.

From 1946 the national movement in Singapore was led by the People's Action Party (PAP), and its leader Lee Kuan Yew had secured, by 1959, a virtually autonomous status (though not complete freedom) for the island. But in 1961 the militants in his party broke away and under the leadership of Lin Chin Siong formed their own organisation, the Barisan Sosialis. This split not only weakened the PAP but also aroused Malayan apprehension of Singapore becoming Malaya's 'Cuba'. This could be prevented by securing the merger of Singapore in a Malaysian Federation while Lee Kuan Yew, a keen proponent of such a merger, was still in power. With this objective in view, Tanku Abdul Rahman proposed in May 1961 that a plan be devised whereby Malaya, Singapore and the three Borneo states could be brought closer in a Federation. Merger with the predominantly Chinese Singapore necessitated that the predominantly non-Chinese populations of the Borneo States joined the Federation in order to preserve Malay numerical predominance.

In 1963 with British support the plan for the greater Malaysian federation was implemented. Singapore and the two states of Borneo (Sarawak and Sabah – British North Borneo) joined the Federation; Brunei chose to remain outside. Inclusion of the Borneo states in the Federation aroused the apprehensions of Indonesia, which saw in it the rise of neo-colonialism and the upsetting of the *status quo* of the whole region of South-east Asia. As most of Borneo (Kalimantan) belonged to Indonesia the merger of the north-western coastal area into Malaysia made the two countries next-door neighbours. The thought made President Sukarno uneasy and the 'confrontation' between Indonesia and Malaysia began in 1963 and lasted until Sukarno's fall from power in 1965. The Philippines too became involved in the dispute by claiming residual sovereignty over North Borneo. But this claim was later dropped and the tension between Malaysia on the one hand and Indonesia and the Philippines on the other subsided in the mid-1960s.

The expanded Federation, however, shrank in 1965 with the expulsion from it of Singapore. The volatile and ambitious Lee Kuan Yew soon entered into a trial of strength with Tunku, and finding no room in Malaysian politics for his style of leadership, he took Singapore out of the Federation, to the great relief of the Malaysian Prime Minister.

Malaysia has, like Sri Lanka, preserved till now the framework of liberal democracy. But since the emergence, in 1975, of the communist regimes in Laos, Cambodia and Vietnam, the Malaysian communists have intensified their guerrilla warfare. As a result, since the beginning of 1976, the Malaysian government has been obliged to restrict some democratic freedoms.

We have examined the process of decolonisation in individual states. Also, we have traced, in broader outlines, the political development in each country from independence to the present time. Beneath this panoramic view of the political changes in South and South-east Asia since 1945 lie the enthusiasm and the struggle of individual nations to cope with their problems. The problems fall into four broad categories: political, foreign relations, economic and social.

We turn now to the identification and analysis of these problems.

2 The Crisis of Democracy

At the dawn of independence, all the countries of South and South-east Asia, except North Vietnam, opted for a democratic form of government. Some adopted the system substantially, some superficially. In the course of time most of them abandoned or suspended the system. In India, where democracy found firmer roots during the first seventeen years of independence and brought about the world's largest free country, the system was eventually suspended for about twenty months, from June 1975 until March 1977. Only Malaysia, Sri Lanka and, in a restricted sense, Singapore, continued to practise the system.

Why, we may ask, did the countries of South and South-east Asia adopt democracy in the first place? How and why did they come to discard it? How and in what form has the system functioned in the states of Malaysia, Singapore and Sri Lanka? These questions will be examined in this chapter. In Chapter 3 we will look at the functioning of the authoritarian system which was adopted by a number of states as an alternative to the democratic system.

Perhaps it would be appropriate to begin this enquiry by first defining parliamentary democracy, communist totalitarianism, and non-communist authoritarianism. Parliamentary democracy refers to a political system based on the Western model which provides regular constitutional opportunities for changing the government, and it implies, as a minimum, 'free elections, the legal recognition of more than one political party, a free press and an independent judiciary'.[1] A communist totalitarian state is characterised by a one-party dictatorship. In such a state the communist party has the monopoly of power and means of mass communication, elections are restricted and unfree, the judiciary lacks independence, and coercion rather than persuasion is applied in transforming a given society into a 'perfect' one. An authoritarian state is neither democratic nor totalitarian. It occupies an intermediate position between the two and may contain some aspects of both systems. It has no fixed features and abounds in varieties. At present most of the states of South and South-east Asia fall into this third category.

Never during the colonial period did the Asian nationalists ever question the suitability of a democratic system of government for their countries. The idea of democracy had filtered imperceptibly into their political thinking and came to dominate their aspirations for the future. For some, democracy had become a synonym for independence itself. Nehru, for example, could not 'conceive of independence without democracy in India'.[2] He believed that the two hung together.

Behind this acceptance of democracy, however, lay certain reasons. For example, the concept of majority rule which democracy held was particularly useful to the constitutionally minded Indian nationalists. When labelled by their colonial masters as a handful of unrepresentative, self-seeking individuals, the Indian nationalists began acquiring the semblance or substance of mass support for their movement. Common people were enrolled as party members and shepherded to annual conferences. On the basis of this the nationalists attacked the colonial government more for being a minority than an alien rule. The weapon of majority rule was also used by the nationalists in fighting their separate battle against the communal and regional politics of the minorities. Democracy thus came to be regarded as the panacea for all the ills of colonialism. This formal acceptance of democracy, however, took place mainly in the British and American colonies – India, Ceylon, Burma, Malaya, Singapore, the Philippines – where democratic institutions had been introduced, and democratic principles had come to determine the rules of the game.

Nations with very little experience in constitutional politics had to make their choice at the time of their independence. In this they were highly influenced by the postwar mood of the West. The Second World War had been fought and won to protect and preserve the democracies of the world. Fascism, the old enemy of democracy, lay defeated and disgraced. The United States had turned its back on isolation, and openly bestowed its favours on the newly born independent nations if they presented a democratic appearance and were prepared to resist the communist challenge. Democracy, thus, was in fashion. The new nations of Asia accepted the system almost as a matter of course. It would have seemed unfashionable and uncivilised not to have done so.

The nationalists of Indonesia, South Vietnam, Cambodia and Laos were influenced by such considerations, even though they had a very poor understanding of the system, for the Dutch and the French had severely restricted the infiltration of democratic institutions in their imperial holdings. The Indonesian leaders, for example, put their own mystical interpretation on democracy: democracy is the unity of God with his servant and, according to Sukarno, democracy

meant jointly formulating truth.[3] In Indonesian thinking on democracy the idea of representation was almost entirely absent and there
was no stress on majority rule and minority rights.[4] Thus, from the
very beginning of their country's independence the Indonesian
leaders, having on the one hand formally accepted the Western form
of democracy, were on the other searching for an Indonesian version
which could be more comprehensible to them and more suitable to
the genius of their people. Indonesia's was the clear case of an
accidental acceptance of democracy. The system was formally
adopted in 1949, having already been in operation since 1945,
because the United Nations' Commission for Indonesia would have
frowned upon the country if its leaders had opted for an alternative
model, and because it was unthinkable for the national leaders not to
follow the example set by India and Burma.

Thailand and Nepal, however, form a category of their own. In
both countries the aspiring élites based their bid for power on
democratic principles. Democracy alone could legitimise their claim
to share power with their hereditary rulers. Thus in these countries
democracy served as an instrument for destroying the traditional
reserve of power.

For various reasons, therefore, the nations of Southern Asia
accepted a democratic form of government. The Philippines, South
Vietnam and Indonesia became democratic republics with a presidential form of government. The remaining countries accepted the
parliamentary form of democracy with a Prime Minister as head of
government, and a monarch (as in Malaysia, Cambodia, Laos,
Nepal, Thailand), a President (as in India, Bangladesh, Burma,
Singapore) or a Governor-General (as in Ceylon and Pakistan) as
head of state. Only the Democratic Republic of North Vietnam
began its independent existence as a communist state with powers
vested, under the Constitution of 1959, in a unicameral legislature
(the National Assembly with a four-year term of office), its Standing
Committee, the President of the Republic and, to a lesser extent, the
Council of Ministers. This system would not have seemed so
radically different from a democratic structure but for the supreme
power the communist party (Vietnam Lao Dong Dang or Workers'
Party) exercised over the government, the military, the people and
even over such extra-territorial organisations as the National Front
for the Liberation of South Vietnam (NFLSV) which was founded
somewhere in South Vietnam in 1960.[5] As the Party Congress was to
meet every four years the real power was exercised by its Central
Executive Committee and the Politburo; the latter was a small body
which included the top leaders of the government, the military and
the party. Ho Chi Minh, being the Chairman of the Party and

President of the Republic, wielded supreme power. The fact that other political parties – the Democratic Party and the Socialist Party – were allowed to exist and their leaders sometimes included in the National Assembly and the Council of Ministers might have suggested that the Workers' Party in North Vietnam did not exercise an absolute monopoly over mass communication. But this was not so. These other parties functioned under the auspices of the Workers' Party. Their separate existence was justified on the grounds that they contained the national bourgeoisie and gradually transformed it along socialist lines.[6] They did not, therefore, constitute a true opposition.

From the middle of the 1950s, however, the liberal face of Southern Asia began to change. In 1955 the constitutional monarchy of South Vietnam was changed to a republic which quietly passed under the dictatorial rule of its first president, Ngo Dinh Diem. In the same year King Mahendra of Nepal dissolved and disbanded the parliamentary institutions. Indonesia abandoned its democratic system in 1957, as did Thailand for the second time in the same year, Pakistan in 1958, and Burma in 1962. Cambodia's skeletal democracy collapsed in 1970. In 1972 the Philippines came under martial law. In January 1975 Sheikh Mujibur Rahman effected the Fourth Amendment to the constitution of Bangladesh whereby parliamentary democracy was abolished, political opposition outlawed and the press nationalised. In June of the same year Mrs Gandhi placed India in a state of emergency. In December 1975 Laos fell to the communists.

Turning now to the second question as to why these democracies collapsed in South and South-east Asia, it may be mentioned at the outset that the conventional explanations offered from time to time by scholars and journalists have not sufficiently taken into account the fact that liberal democracy, on the very first stage of its journey in Asia, was called upon to perform certain functions which it had never discharged before in the entire history of its birth and growth in the Western world. The Asian votaries of the system expected that it would destroy the roots of tradition, preserve the precariously balanced unity of the state, establish social and economic equality and, above all, that it would perform these functions in the minimum possible time. Democracy was thus put to a severe test which it had never stood before. And as it turned out, it could not stand the test on its own. In some countries it collapsed. In others it just managed to survive, mainly because it was supported by such additional devices as the emergency.

We may now ascertain some specific factors which led to the collapse of democracy in Southern Asia. They are mainly three: the undemocratic competition for power and lack of national consensus among the political élites; the political role of the military; the communist challenge and American intervention. The first factor is the most important and complex, and is mainly responsible for the fall of democracy in the Philippines, India and Nepal. The second emerges out of the first and explains the collapse of the system in Indonesia, Pakistan, Thailand, Burma and Bangladesh. The third is mainly applicable to South Vietnam, Laos, and Cambodia.

In any society political élites have always been, and still are, in a minority. Before the advent of universal suffrage they could remain isolated from, and virtually uninfluenced by the masses, for the government changed hands among them without the invocation of popular mass consent. After all, democracy of the classic liberal kind functioned in Europe for centuries without universal suffrage, and amidst mass poverty and illiteracy. With the coming of universal suffrage (in Europe in the late 1920s and in South and South-east Asia at the dawn of independence) the masses were drawn into politics, and even though the political élites were still in a minority they could no longer remain unaffected by the life-style of the common people. Poverty, illiteracy, and the tradition-mindedness of the masses came to have a bearing on the political style of both the governing and aspiring élites. This created problems. Take, for example, India and the Philippines. Both countries adopted universal franchise, though the Philippines enfranchised only its literate citizens, which in effect made little difference because the literacy rate there was among the highest in Asia. But as compared to those in the West, the Indian and Filipino societies had a much wider gulf between the political élites and the masses, far too high a level of poverty and illiteracy, and tradition had a much more powerful grip on the peoples' lives and attitudes. These social features are usually interlinked. But this connection is not true, say, in India, where an educated and well-to-do citizen may still be deeply rooted in tradition. True, all human beings are loyal, in some measure or other, to some traditions. (Tradition here is used in its popular sense of being an active process; entailing some degree of respect and duty, hence standards, values and customs which are two generations old may pass as tradition.) But it is the age of traditions and the degree of irrationality involved in adhering to them which make the difference. In the case of a Hindu who respectfully believes in caste obligations, the tradition is age-old. However, if he is an ordinary poor peasant his beliefs, on their own, may not hold any imminent danger for a secular democracy. It is only when his beliefs are exploited by a politician for political gains that the danger arises. Thus, when universal suffrage brought the political élites face to face with the mute millions the former had the option of nourishing, exploiting or redeeming the conservatism of the latter. The success of democracy greatly depended on whether politicians treated the ignorance, beliefs, and poverty of their constituents as political assets or national liabilities. In this complex relation between the élites and masses strange things may happen. A committed democrat may lose popular support by trying to redeem the conservatism of his constituents. On the other hand, a power-seeking authoritarian may achieve his ends by nourishing, or following, as it were, the dictates of his followers.

INDIA

Looking first at the political élites of India one finds that it was only after the death of Nehru in 1964 that the struggle for power between the opposition and the ruling élites became intensely personalised, more unprincipled and unashamedly degenerate. There were in Nehru's era too right-wing and left-wing politicians, both inside the ruling Congress Party and outside in the opposition, who were susceptible to feeding and exploiting the traditionalism, ignorance and poverty of the masses. There were the Hindu communalists of the Rashtriya Swayamsevak Sangh (RSS), Hindu Mahasabha, Jan Sangh, Ram Rajya Parishad (RRP), the Ganatantra Parishad, and the communists of the Communist Party of India, whose ideologies and methods posed threats to the very life of the incipient democracy. These threats were real for they were based on conviction. In fact, during Nehru's era the politics of the opposition showed more of an ideological bias and less individual greed for power. But Nehru kept it within bounds by the sheer force of his charismatic leadership. He had the rare advantage of being recognised even by his most critical opponents as the indispensable leader of the nation. Above all, he was firmly committed to and determined to fight for the life of secular democracy, for the planting of which on Indian soil he was more responsible than any of his colleagues. 'I am greatly conscious of the delay that the democratic processes involve,' he avowed, 'but still I am convinced that for my country this system of parliamentary democracy is the best.'[7]

None the less it was a difficult task even for Nehru to lay, in only seventeen years, any deep foundations for democracy. His own overshadowing personality, together with the prestige and omnipotence which the ruling Congress Party had acquired through being, for over half a century, the vehicle of India's freedom movement, stunted the growth of a strong and confident opposition in India. It was hard for the opposition to gain a foothold, partly because of the stigma attached to anybody who opposed Nehru and his national Congress, but mainly because of Congress's all-inclusive character, which enabled it occasionally to take over the opposition's programmes. The worst sufferers on this count were the socialist parties, which if united would have provided a viable alternative to Congress rule. But Congress undermined their strength by adopting, in 1955, a programme for a socialist pattern of society. Besides undermining the prospect of an alternative party rule, Congress, by playing the dual roles of a party and government, was in one capacity virtually strengthening the very traditional forces which it was committed to annihilating in its other capacity. The Congress government was concerned with modernising society and the economy but the Congress Party had to adapt itself to the local environment, and in effect anchor its organisation among the dominant castes, in order to win elections.[8] Here we see a paradoxical situation arising out of the conflict between democratic ideas and democratic methods. A progressive government, committed to the task of modernising society, becomes traditionalised in the process of seeking support from the electorate.[9] Nehru's government was thus obliged to make many compromises, some on basic issues. For example, the much needed land reforms, which if introduced would have modernised cultivation and increased the total agricultural output, could not be carried through. Congress could not afford to alienate the rich peasants and landlords – the classes who were opposed to such reforms – for not only were they the party's active supporters, they were also strongly linked with the ruling junta at state level. Consequently Nehru's plans, particularly the one which purported to introduce co-operative farming, were often defeated by his own colleagues – the party barons and chief ministers of the states.

Nehru's mottos – 'revolution by consent', 'change with continuity' – though truly echoing the spirit of nineteenth-century liberalism, were quite ineffective in producing those structural changes which the 'twentieth-century democratic model' required for its smooth running in India. Nehruism, envisaging for India a modernised, secular, democratic structure resting on the pillars of parliamentary government, central planning, large-scale industrialisation and the socialist pattern of society, was indeed a worthy attempt to combine the best of the two systems – the liberal Western and the communist Russian – and it was perhaps also based on that Indian mode of thought which sees basic underlying agreement between opposing views and which was best expressed by the Indian philosopher, Radhakrishnan – 'Why look at things in terms of this or that? Why not try to have both this *and* that?'[10] But in the Indian context Nehruism was destined to bring more continuity than change, more compromises than radical reforms. For its fulfilment Nehruism needed time, patience and consensus among political élites. But the post-independence era, surcharged with high expectations, a sense of urgency and a race for political power, was least conducive to the growth of Nehruism, particularly without a Nehru.

In view of the unique problems facing democracy on the first lap of its journey through Asia, it was no mean achievement by Nehru to have run the system, almost smoothly, for the last seventeen years of his life as India's first Prime Minister. Under his guidance the world's most populous democracy passed elegantly through the first three general elections (1952, 1957, 1962) with the electorate rising from over 173 million in 1952 to 210 million in 1962. It was mainly due to Nehru's charisma that Congress was returned to power in each election, at the centre as well as in the states, except in Kerala, where the communists, having been voted into power, ruled the state democratically for a short time, from 1954 to 1959. The hegemony of the Congress government over the whole of India was to disappear after Nehru's death, but while it lasted it gave the impression to the whole world that democracy had acquired a firm basis in India. Perhaps it had.

While Nehru ruled, Congress was in the mainstream of Indian politics, and the opposition was restricted to its backwaters. Frustrations were rampant, particularly among the new recruits to the opposition parties. This was partly because of Nehru's socialism, which had undermined the prestige which went with certain professions, and the sense of security and incentive among businessmen and industrialists, leaving few avenues open for ambitious young people to acquire wealth, power and prestige. Consequently, bureaucracy and politics, in that order, had become enormously attractive professions. India's young people aspired to be government servants; the rejects went into politics, hoping to lord it over the government servants. In India there was always a stigma attached to the acquisition and demonstration of wealth. Consequently, the style of a rich Indian differed from that of a Filipino or an American. He had to be apologetic for being rich. But no such stigma was attached to the acquisition of political power and distribution of patronage. When Nehru was gone the scramble for the prize began.

With the end of the Nehru era the political culture of the country suddenly changed. The national consensus which Nehru had evolved and imposed upon the political élites began to disintegrate. The élites were no longer in agreement about the ends and purposes of the government. Secondly, the paramountcy of Congress was

shattered. It had always been a large national organisation, consisting of diverse elements, and accommodating a host of different
interests. It had never been a cohesive organisation with a distinct
personality of its own. Its unity had been maintained by the sheer
charisma of Gandhi and Nehru. Now after Nehru the struggle for
governmental power began, first within Congress itself, and then
between Congress and the opposition. Between 1964 and 1966
Congress was increasingly weakened by the two wars of succession
fought within the party itself, first in choosing the successor to
Nehru in 1964, and second in choosing the successor to Lal Bahadur
Shastri, who died in 1966 while in office.

When in 1966 Mrs Gandhi emerged as India's third Prime Minister
she was utterly lacking in charisma but at the same time filled with
determination to rule the country in her own right and not as the
daughter of the great Nehru or the puppet of the Congress barons
who had put her on the throne. Much of her time, courage and skill
was spent in proving herself, in acquiring legitimacy for her leadership. The more she was challenged and pushed the more assertive
and ruthless she became.

India's fourth general election of 1967 was of most consequence in
giving a market-place style to the country's politics. The age-old
hegemony of Congress was broken. Though returned to power at
the centre with a small majority, Congress lost six of the states where
non-Congress governments were formed. It was a boom year for
the opposition parties, some for the first time obtaining the plums of
power, but as none of them secured an absolute majority in any of
the states, the non-Congress governments came to be precariously
balanced on coalitions of parties. This in turn brought about among
the politicians the most unstabilising practice of 'crossing the floor'.
A promise of ministership was enough to induce an M.L.A.
(Member of a State Legislative Assembly) to discard his party
loyalty and cross the floor in order either to support a ruling caucus
or to bring it down. Thus began the era of power-mongering among
India's political élites. The political game was more often played
through 'unholy alliances' – a secular party aligning itself with a
communal, a national with a regional, a right-wing with a left-wing
– and through the exploitation of people's parochialism, conservatism, ignorance and prejudices. Personal ambition more than political ideology came to determine the behaviour of politicians, to cause
splits in the existing political parties, and to give birth to new
national and regional parties. Personal ambition and jealousy among
their leaders also made it impossible for the opposition parties to
unite against what all or most of them considered to be their
common enemy – Mrs Gandhi's Raj. Mrs Gandhi's survival was first

threatened by the very Congress barons who had put her in power. Here again ideological differences played little part, though Mrs Gandhi used all the socialist idioms and slogans in her campaigns to isolate and discredit her opponents in Congress. The fight was personal. The party bosses, finding that Mrs Gandhi was becoming increasingly independent of them and at times treated them with indifference and subjected them to slights, began plotting, rather naïvely, her removal from office.[11]

In her fight against the party bosses Mrs Gandhi used a new technique – 'directly appealing to the people'. By gaining the semblance or reality of mass support through carefully organised mass rallies and demonstrations in her support, Mrs Gandhi succeeded in defying the dictates of her party: and, consequently, in splitting Congress. The Congress split of 1969 was significant in that a faction of Congress comprising the so-called old guard now joined the opposition ranks, leaving Mrs Gandhi's ruling Congress with a slender majority in parliament. But more significant to Indian politics was her technique. Its potential to undermine the parliamentary system of government was sufficiently revealed when the opposition itself began using the same technique against Mrs Gandhi herself.

The liberal democratic system depends upon the willingness of those with grievances to seek a remedy through the processes of representative government, and above all through orderly discussion.[12] It assumes that until the law is changed the law is obeyed. These necessary conditions for its survival were utterly denied to Indian democracy between 1970 and 1975. The political life of the country in those years was characterised by strikes of all descriptions, student revolts, *gheraos* (encirclement of an individual or an institution by strikers), and violence practised by extreme right and extreme left. The politicans of the opposition, having been bitterly disappointed at the parliamentary election of 1971 and again at the state elections of 1972 (in both of which Mrs Gandhi had swept the polls and increased her party's majority in parliament, as well as regaining most of the states she had lost to the opposition since the 1967 election), were now bent on using any means whatsoever to bring down what they called the corrupt regime of Mrs Gandhi. In their thinking Mrs Gandhi had never succeeded in establishing her legitimacy to the high office of Prime Minister. If she had been returned to power in the past, it was, so the reasoning went, mainly because the simple people of India always bowed to the person or party in power, and also because Mrs Gandhi misused her power and held out false promises to win their support. In the eyes of educated Indians, however, the opposition itself did not constitute a viable alternative to Mrs Gandhi's Raj. Its political behaviour had not been above board. Some Indians began to wonder whether it would not be a good thing for India to change to a strong authoritarian system rather than to persist in experimenting with democracy, which was becoming enormously wasteful and hopelessly ineffective.

It was against this background that the crisis came in 1974, when the opposition parties for the first time put up a united front, and, with student support, launched a mass movement against the democratically constituted government of Gujarat. The Congress government fell. Encouraged by this success, all the opposition parties, except the Communist Party, rallied round the seventy-three-year old J. P. Narayan, who launched a mass movement against the 'corrupt' Congress government of Bihar. But this time Mrs Gandhi would not give in. She condemned Narayan's method as undemocratic, one which favoured deciding matters in the streets and not at the polling booths. Narayan's movement was modelled on Mahatma Gandhi's *satyagrahas* of the past. It called for total non-cooperation with Mrs Gandhi's Raj. In one of his speeches Narayan appealed to the army and police to disobey orders.[13]

Narayan was not an ordinary opponent of Mrs Gandhi. He was possibly the only leader whose integrity had never been questioned. He had never aspired to government power, and on many occasions in the past, during Nehru's Prime Ministership, he had refused offers to join the government. Had he sought power, so Indians believed, he would most certainly have become Nehru's successor. Narayan carried enough weight and credentials among the people and was the only leader who could outdo Mrs Gandhi in rallying mass support. Mrs Gandhi was thus outwitted when in March 1975 Narayan led a massive people's march in New Delhi. In the continuing confrontation between Narayan and Mrs Gandhi the balance turned decidedly in favour of the former when in June the Allahabad High Court found Mrs Gandhi guilty of corrupt electoral practices, and disqualified her from contesting an election to parliament or a state assembly for the next six years. A further blow to Mrs Gandhi was administered by the Gujarat election. Her party was defeated by the United Opposition Front. Then followed, on 21 June, the Supreme Court ruling rejecting her petition for an 'unconditional' stay of the High Court order but allowing her to continue in her office, without any right to vote in parliament or to draw any salary until the proper hearing of her appeal in the Supreme Court, which was fixed for 14 July. Encouraged further by the ruling of the Supreme Court the opposition mounted its attack on Mrs Gandhi and planned to begin a nationwide movement demanding that she quit her office at once.

Mrs Gandhi, however, did not step down. If she had done so she might have gained sympathy from all over the world, but possibly,

in her own calculation, lost her office for ever. She was not conditioned to stoop in order to conquer. Besides, she distrusted her
colleagues in the Cabinet, and feared that once she was out of office
they would contrive to keep her there. Further, she was not certain
which way the judgement of the Supreme Court might turn. She
therefore decided to stay 'for the sake of the people'. And on 26 June
1975 she declared a state of emergency in India in order 'to protect
democracy', as she claimed, from 'a deep and widespread
conspiracy'.[14]

The decline of the democratic order in India was thus mainly
brought about by the political élites, in power and in opposition. No
such factors as communist subversion, armed rebellion, foreign
invasion or intervention had any significant role to play in this
drama. It should also be noted that, though the scramble for power
became increasingly undemocratic and personalised, it was not
stained by any large-scale bloodshed. Ideologies played little part in
this warfare. All professed to be fighting their individual battles in
the name of the mute millions and for the welfare of the country. But
there existed among them hardly any consensus on what constituted
the welfare of the people and nation.

THE PHILIPPINES

Turning now to the Philippines we must first consider President
Marcos's own explanation of what went wrong with 'the showcase
of American democracy in Asia', and why he had to bring the
country under martial law on 21 September 1972. Marcos puts the
main blame on the political and media élites.[15] Both 'the reactionary
Right and the radical Left' had joined forces in leading the country
into a state of anarchy. Within this unholy alliance each party was
scheming to outdo the other in the final run for power. The
reactionaries, for example, hoped to organise a *coup d'état* with
military support, before the communists came round to doing so.
The main target for both groups was President Marcos himself. His
assassination would bring complete chaos from which both the
right-wing and the communists intended to benefit to the exclusion
of the other. In their political warfare, as Marcos goes on to say, the
politicians were supported by the newspaper barons, who fabricated
false and scandalous news in order to run down the government.
Other factors are also held responsible for weakening the government: the Philippine Congress for consistently using its legislative
powers to block the President's executive decisions; the secessionist
movement of the Muslims in Mindanao and Sulu. But it was the
foreign-supported rebellion of the Mao communists and their 'link

up' with the leaders of the Liberal Party (then in opposition) which
Marcos held were principally responsible for forcing his 'duly
constituted government' into resorting to martial law.

One may not feel inclined to accept Marcos's explanation at its
face-value. As in India, personal ambitions, suspicions and intrigues
had come to determine political behaviour in the Philippines. Marcos, the Philippines' sixth President, 'is a man obsessed with history
and his place in it'.[16] Ambitious throughout his political career he
stressed in his inaugural speech after his first election in 1965 that the
people's mandate was not for change, but for greatness: 'This is your
dream and mine. By your choice you have committed yourselves to
it. Come then, let us march together towards the dream of
greatness.'[17] He was the only President in the country's history to be
re-elected to the office, in 1969. The dream of greatness, however,
appeared to be cut short when, in January 1972, the Constitutional
Convention laid down that he was not to continue in power beyond
the end of his second term.[18] But perhaps it would be simply
conjecture to infer from this that personal ambition more than
anything else induced the President to defeat the Convention's
mandate by rushing the country, in the same year, into a state of
martial law.

None the less, the fact remains that the political élites of the
Philippines had ceased to observe the rules of the game and had made
a mockery of democracy. Though far ahead of India in terms of *per
capita* income and education, the Philippines exhibited a very wide
gap between the have-nots and the haves, the latter constituting not
more than 10 per cent of the population but monopolising all wealth
and power. Unlike those of India the Filipino economic and political
élites largely overlapped, and it was common for economic power
to beget political power.[19] The worship of private enterprise, unhealthy competition, and the open demonstration of wealth and
power characterised the Philippine élites. The Filipinos 'took all the
evils of the American system – and improved on them', and as a
result the country came to be populated by 'cut-price Americans'.[20]
Personal advancement rather than loyalty to the party determined
the behaviour of the politicians. There were hardly any ideological
differences between the two major parties, and as the joke went the
Nacionalists and the Liberals were as separate and distinct from one
another as Coca-Cola and Pepsi-Cola. The politicians changed their
parties as easily as their shirts. Marcos himself abandoned his Liberal
Party to win his first presidential election as a Nacionalist.

It was not only the composition and motivation of the Filipino
élites, but also their insensitivity towards the poor masses and the
excessive violence they used in furthering their individual or

factional ends, which brought democracy to the point of collapse. Philippine elections were notorious for their corruption, violence and extravagance, and political warlords controlled them through private armies. This was sufficient to discredit the system in the eyes of the students and the communists, who became increasingly rebellious from the start of Marcos's second term of office in 1970. Bombing of government offices, banks, airline offices, department stores, became a daily occurrence. Crimes of every nature thrived: kidnappings, robberies, street shoot-outs between crime lords. Manila came to be regarded as the most insecure metropolis in the world. In September 1971 Marcos suspended the privilege of the writ of habeas corpus. This had been done only once before, in 1950, by President Quirino in order to enable the government to suppress the Huk communist resurgence. The suspension restored law and order, in some measure. But when the suspension order was lifted in January 1972, there was a sudden recurrence of violence and terrorism, caused by subversives of all kinds: the leftists, rightists, Muslim secessionists and crime lords. A series of events, including the Digoya discovery of 4 July which, according to Marcos, proved that the Communist New People's Army was receiving firearms from a foreign power, led him to declare martial law.

As in India, we find that the immediate cause for the suspension of democratic rights and institutions was the élite's bid to win political power unconstitutionally. Behind this lay a host of other factors, of which the most significant for the Philippines was the great distance that separated the poor millions from the rich few.

NEPAL

In Nepal, the problem which Prime Minister B. P. Koirala faced in 1960 was basically the same as that which Marcos was to face in 1972 and Indira Gandhi in 1975. In fact all three used the same language in blaming the opposition for putting democracy in jeopardy. In 1960 just before the King suspended democracy in Nepal and put his Prime Minister in prison, Koirala, while commenting on the role of political élites, particularly of the opposition (which consisted of feudal lords and politicians of different denominations), said that though the opposition was not anti-national it most certainly played an anti-democratic role, in utilising the rights which democracy conferred 'to produce such conditions as would destroy the very existence of democracy'.[21] Here in Nepal, however, the role of the 'saviour' was played by King Mahendra. It is doubtful whether the King regretted doing what he did on 15 December 1960: dismissing the government, dissolving Nepal's first elected parliament and, a little later, banning all political parties. The King had never intended to become titular head of state, and the constitution which he gave the nation on 14 February 1959 gave him enough leverage to assert his personal rule if the parliamentary system of government failed to function. According to the constitution, the King was to be the judge of whether the elected government was working in the interests of the nation. Even so, it would have been almost impossible for the King to suspend the system *ad libitum* and establish his personal rule if the political élites had behaved differently during those crucial months from June 1959 (when the democratic system was inaugurated) to December 1960 (when it was put into cold storage). After all, monarchy was resurrected in 1951 by the political élites themselves, aided by the government of India, and the King would not have found it easy to clamp down upon his rescuers if the latter had been firm and united on some vital principles of government, and furthermore observed the rules of the game among themselves. But this was not to be.

During each of its two spells of existence – 1951 to 1955 and May 1959 to December 1960 – the democratic government in Nepal was torn asunder by the personal ambition and jealousy of the political leaders. During the first phase, in 1952, the leading national party of the country – the Nepali Congress – split into four factions, mainly on account of the rivalry between two brothers, M. P. and B. P. Koirala. Expelled from the Nepali Congress, M. P. Koirala formed his own party – a small group of dissident Nepali Congressmen – and with the support of King Tribhuvan functioned as Prime Minister throughout this phase except for a brief period from November 1951 to August 1952. However, parties and politicians, inside and outside the government, wildly pursued their political warfare throughout, in consequence weakening and discrediting the politics of the parties and at the same time strengthening the hand of the King against democracy. The King played the role of a biased umpire. In 1954, by amending the interim constitution of 1951 for the third time, he arrogated supreme power to himself, and bent on exercising this power in full he was waiting eagerly for the right moment to arrive when he could call off the political game.

The opportunity arrived when the coalition government of M. P. Koirala was pushed to the brink by in-fighting among its ministers. Serious charges against each other, for example, were exchanged between the Prime Minister and the Home Minister. The Advisory Assembly of 106 members (an apology for a parliament), though a forum of the parties in power, turned against the government itself and rejected a few official bills. In this state of affairs, when the politicians seemed to be grossly involved in preventing each other from holding the reins of power, the King thankfully assumed the role of saviour. The dying King Tribhuvan invested Crown Prince Mahendra with all his royal authority, and the Prince lost no time in dissolving the national government and promulgating the direct rule of the crown. As for the plea of mercy on the ground that democracy in Nepal was merely an infant, the Prince retorted – 'But infants do not indulge in bribery and corruption.' So, in March 1955, the four-year-old infant democracy was put away in a reformatory.

How and why was democratic rule restored in Nepal, even though for only a short while, from May 1959 to December 1960? This question may as well be asked of some other non-communist countries in Southern Asia, where democracy was suspended and then restored. The answer to this question lies in two features common to the civilian authoritarian regimes. One is the sense of consciousness among such authoritarians that they should not appear, in the eyes of the free world, as the annihilators of democratic order. This consciousness has been more alive among the civilian authoritarians (Mrs Gandhi, Mrs Bandaranaike, Z. A. Bhutto, Lee Kuan Yew, Sukarno, F. Marcos) than among the military dictators (Ayub and Yahya Khan of Pakistan, Ziaur Rahman of Bangladesh, Ne Win of Burma, Suharto of Indonesia). The other feature is the continuing existence of opposition under civilian regimes. The general practice of keeping the opposition alive, even though in chains, has been observed with very few exceptions. There have been cases of torture and harassment, and of wide-scale imprisonment in India, Sri Lanka, Nepal, Burma and the Philippines, but never any organised massacre of the opposition. The agonies of the non-communist authoritarians thus lie in this paradoxical situation where they have to maintain a democratic façade for their dictatorial rule. In pursuing this ritual some have occasionally been trapped and overtaken by the democratic forces.

These two factors were mainly responsible for the brief revival of democracy in Nepal. Conscious that he would incur Nehru's condemnation should he appear to have utterly rejected the democratic form, King Mahendra, throughout his personal rule (1955 to 1959), left the country's discredited parties and politicians at liberty. It was not a heavy risk to take, for he believed that the back of the party system was already broken and there was no fear that real power would ever pass away from him to an ill-assorted group of politicians who seemed to have no following or credit among the people. But as soon as the politicians realised that they were being gradually pushed away from the corridors of power, they began to close ranks and to put united pressure on the King in order to bring his personal rule to an end. The leading Nepali Congress joined hands with the two other parties and formed the Democratic Front. For a while the King played the 'divide and rule' game but without much success. He gave in to the politicians, hoping that they would fail to hold the ground for any length of time. In 1959 he awarded a constitution (which vested the crown with supreme powers), and conceded a general election, the first to be held in the history of the country. Ten political parties contested the election for 109 seats in the lower house. The Nepali Congress won 74 of them. On 27 May 1959 the elected Nepali Congress Ministry was formed with B. P. Koirala as Prime Minister.

With the revival of democracy, to the King's delight internecine political warfare began. Almost instantly the parties in opposition were united (the communists joining hands with the rightists of the Gurkha Parishad) and the National Democratic Front was formed. The Congress government was branded as anti-national and re-actionary. Some modest reforms which the government proposed to introduce in order to abolish the age-old feudal proprietorship of land provoked the landlords into taking law and order into their own hands. Religious leaders were encouraged to play on the ancient prejudices and fears of the poor peasants. A civil war seemed imminent. M. P. Koirala, the brother of the Prime Minister, joined the opposition and appealed to the King to save the country from what he called the dictatorial rule of the Congress government. On 15 December 1960 the King responded and the allegedly dictatorial government of the Congress was replaced by the monarch's personal rule.

★

Whereas the irresponsible and undemocratic behaviour of the political élites, both ruling and aspiring, led to the collapse of democratic order and the rise of civilian authoritarian rule in the Philippines, Nepal, and for a while in India, the circumstance of the military acting as a political force led to the emergence of a military dictatorship in Thailand, Indonesia, Pakistan, Burma and Bangladesh.

The story of the emergence of the military Raj differs from country to country. But most of the countries had two features in common. First, all except Burma were handicapped by an underdeveloped party system. Secondly, all except Pakistan began their independent lives with highly politicised armed forces. These two features were mainly responsible for the collapse of the democratic experiment in these countries. In all of them at some stage the civilian government came to be precariously balanced on political factions and cliques rather than based on the support of a strong national party. In times of crisis such governments tended to stagger and disintegrate. The military, as the only integrated national force, was in some instances (Burma and Pakistan) called upon to take over; elsewhere (Thailand, Indonesia, Bangladesh) it had to intervene on its own initiative.

THAILAND

In tracing briefly the impact of these two features on the politics of the countries concerned, we turn first to Thailand. Unlike other countries in this group, Thailand entered the modern age, in 1932, already saddled with a military dictatorship. Since then military rule has been the general practice, interrupted by only three spells of democratic experiment: 1944–7, 1955–7, 1973–6. It was almost inevitable that the military should play a leading role in the country's affairs, for it was the only institution which was centralised, run by professionals, dedicated to nationalism, and above all politically oriented.[22] But, having captured political power, the military could no longer remain immune from its corrupting and divisive influences. In competing for supreme power high-ranking military officers often caused divisions in the armed forces. The results were *coups* and counter-*coups* perpetrated by military officers against each other. A sense of insecurity haunted both the ruling and the aspiring generals, and at least one of them, Field-Marshal Phibun Songkhram (a promoter of the *coup* in 1932 and Prime Minister from 1938 to 1944 and again from 1947 to 1957) tried to gain security from popular support for his personal rule by introducing democratic institutions, from 1955 to 1957. In 1957, however, Phibun was overthrown by his rival, General Sarit Thanarat, and the second experiment with democracy was abruptly ended.

Civilian democratic governments in Thailand were, thus, short-lived, and therefore unable to cultivate a viable party system. Parties sprouted on the eve of every general election. In the general election of 1973, forty-two parties competed, of which eight won enough seats to put them into double figures. Thirty-nine parties participated in the 1976 election. Except perhaps for the Democratic Party, all were newly formed, and most of them had no substance, representing neither a political philosophy nor any social grouping but only the following of a particular leader. The resulting coalition governments (as in 1973 and 1976) had thus no defined political base. Such civilian governments were weak and under the constant surveillance of the military, which distrusted them. Any crisis, whether arising out of an alleged communist threat or student riot, was used by the military as an excuse for bringing the civilian interlude to an

end. On 6 October 1976, after overthrowing the coalition government of Seni Pramoj, Admiral Sangad Chaloryu declared: 'The
government cannot govern the country properly and in order not to
let Thailand become a prey to communists and to uphold the
monarchy and royal family, this council has seized power.'[23] It must,
however, be admitted that the communist threat to Thailand seemed
more real in 1976 than it was in 1957. Of the countries bordering
Thailand two, Laos and Cambodia, had turned into communist
states by 1975. The military, ever distrustful of politicians' ability to
handle grave situations, had a better excuse this time for sending
packing the civilian government.

INDONESIA

Indonesia, like other states in South-east Asia, inherited at its
independence a political army. A large part of what constituted
Indonesia's armed forces had been drilled by the Japanese between
1943 and 1945, and had begun their military careers fighting for the
country's independence, between 1945 and 1949. At the dawn of
independence the Indonesian military thus possessed the potential as
well as the willingness to act as a political force. Much therefore
depended on how strong a civilian government the politicians and
political parties could offer in order to counteract the possibility of a
military intervention. Under the able leadership of Sukarno and
Hatta and with four political parties of national status (PNI, Masjumi, the Socialist Party, and the communist PKI) Indonesia made a
promising start with a constitutional democracy. However, none of
Indonesia's political parties ever acquired the requisite strength to
form a viable government on its own. As a result the constitutional
phase, from December 1949 to March 1957, contained no less than
seven coalition governments none of which lasted as long as two
years. Each coalition government was torn by sharp conflicts between its components and between factions inside each component.
Also, during this phase some parties – the socialist PSI and the
Masjumi – were discredited (and later, in 1960, banned) for sponsor-
ing the regional revolution in Sumatra, in alliance with the local
army, and founding, in 1958, the rival Revolutionary Government
of the Republic of Indonesia (PRRI).

President Sukarno himself played an important part in discrediting the party system, humiliating the civilian governments, and
encouraging the military to intervene frequently in the political
affairs of the country. He did this mainly to keep himself in supreme
power. Finally, on 5 July 1959, he abolished constitutional democracy and brought into being his 'guided democracy'. On that day,

President Sukarno re-enacted by decree the constitution of 1945, which vested the President with supreme powers. In this he was supported by the military, with the result that members of the armed forces came to occupy for the first time a quarter of all posts in the new Indonesian cabinet.[24] Little did the President realise then that henceforth the greatest threat to his power was to be posed by the military.

Before 1955 the Indonesian military had on many occasions disobeyed the orders of the civilian government and resisted political interference in its internal affairs. From 1955 onwards it began to play an increasingly active role in politics. It was in that year that a group of rebel army officers began plotting against the civilian government, and succeeded, in 1958, in establishing a counter-government in Sumatra. The senior officers, however, remained loyal to the government in Djakarta and the regional rebellion was easily suppressed. The episode, however, betrayed the fact that the Indonesian military was not united and its officers could be played off against each other.

This must have been a comforting thought for Sukarno. Now that he was saddled with the overbearing presence of the military in the government, his only hope of curbing its increasing strength lay in pursuing a 'divide and rule' policy. From 1959 until his downfall in 1965, President Sukarno followed the strategy of dividing the military, making it more submissive, while contriving to bring the Communist Party (PKI) gradually to power.[25] The PKI was, during this period, the only party with some political force which could be set against the military. Fortunately for Sukarno these two had an inherent abhorrence for each other.

Whether Sukarno overshot the mark is the question which must be asked of what occurred on 1 October 1965. On that day six generals were arrested by soldiers and brutally killed in public. This was done, as an army officer proclaimed, to forestall an army *coup* against the President. So far no real evidence has come to light to prove conclusively that any such plan on the part of the dead generals existed. On the other hand, circumstantial evidence strongly suggests that the killing of the generals was sponsored by the PKI, possibly with the President's blessing. One of the generals who was not on the conspirators' list of victims was General Suharto. He acted cautiously but decisively, in extending his command over the unaffected units, and overpowering the conspirators in less than forty-eight hours. President Sukarno was now virtually a prisoner of General Suharto. From October 1965 the country was governed by General Suharto, though Sukarno was allowed to retain the presidency until March 1968, when it was officially resumed by Suharto.

But the most appalling offshoot of what happened in October was the massacre of the communists. This was one of the bloodiest massacres in modern history – by the end of 1965 at least half a million were slaughtered by soldiers and civilians. The PKI had lost its life force long before it was officially dissolved by General Suharto in March 1966.

BANGLADESH

Bangladesh is the only country in Southern Asia to have acquired its sovereign status through a war. It thus began its independent existence with a political army, consisting of the guerrilla freedom-fighters – the Mukti Bahini. But the country was also endowed with a powerful and much-loved civilian leader – Sheikh Mujibur Rahman. Why should he have been eliminated on 15 August 1975 by a gang of army officers? Bangladeshi experts have offered some explanations.[26] It is said that Mujib alienated the popular armed forces by showing, from the very beginning, his distrust of them. He lost no opportunity to denigrate the forces in general, and some army officers in particular. The one instance generally cited is that of Major Sheriful Huq (known as Major Dalim) who was prematurely retired at twenty-eight by Mujib. It was this Major Dalim who, on 15 August 1975, broke the news to a startled nation that Sheikh Mujib and his 'autocratic regime' had been terminated. At the same time, it is alleged, Sheikh Mujib was very partial towards the Rakhi Bahini – highly trained and well-armed storm-troopers personally loyal to him – a fact which was very much resented by the personnel of the regular armed forces. In spite of this mounting tension between him and the military, in 1974 Mujib employed the army and navy in the fight against smuggling and corruption. This offered the military the opportunity to see for the first time how grossly the affairs of the country were mismanaged by politicians.

Added to this were two other factors which together brought about the downfall of Mujib. In 1972 Mujib's disestablishment of Islam as the state religion caused strong resentment among the orthodox sections of the community and some army officers. Finally, in 1975, Mujib's assumption of absolute presidential power, abandonment of the parliamentary system, and imposition of one-party rule, left no channel for any future political transition. The only way now open for his opponents to remove him was by assassination.

These explanations carry some weight, but it would be wrong to infer from them that a general discontent against Mujib had come to prevail among the masses or even in the rank and file of the armed forces. The *coup* of 15 August was the work of a handful of misguided young army officers, infatuated by personal grievances against Mujib. The senior military officers were as much taken by surprise as the people at large. It was a meaningless event, hardly a *coup*. The junior officers who performed the slaughter achieved nothing for themselves. They had to flee the country. Senior military officers stepped into the power vacuum that was created, and the net outcome of the whole episode was the replacement of Mujib's personal rule by the military dictatorship of Major General Ziaur Rahman, who through two further *coups*, in November 1975 succeeded in assuming supreme power as President.

BURMA

Burma began its independent life with a political army. Most of the army officers were involved in the independence movement, and after independence they were assigned in almost random fashion to careers in the army.[27] Apart from this, the military and political leaders in Burma shared a common social background and there existed between them the closeness of associates. However, unlike Indonesia the military in Burma was firmly united and the officers displayed no overt inclination, at least in the first decade of independence, to share political power with the civilian leaders. The country had a leader of integrity in U Nu, who ruled democratically as Prime Minister from 1948 to 1958, except for a brief period of nine months when he voluntarily stepped out of office in order to reorganise and rejuvenate his ruling party, the AFPFL. But the factor which increasingly weakened the government of U Nu was the recurring armed insurgency of the communists, and of the minority communities – Karens, Mons, Arakanese, Shans, Kachins, Chins – who, having experienced British protection from the dominant Burmans in the days of the Raj, now after independence demanded separate autonomous states for themselves. To suppress these revolts the government had to employ the army. The army, while operating in the districts, tended to revive and consolidate the authority of the civilian officers against the local politicians of the AFPFL. As a result, a certain measure of tension grew between the army and the ruling political party. It was against this background that the split in the AFPFL occurred in 1958. U Nu's public rejection of Marxism as a guiding philosophy antagonised the socialist wing of the party. The socialists with their leaders, Ba Swe and Kyaw Nyein, quitted the party to form their own 'stable' AFPFL, leaving U Nu with the rump of the so-called 'clean' AFPFL. With no clear majority in parliament, U Nu's government staggered on for a few months, and on 28 October 1958 the Prime Minister announced that he was handing over power to General Ne Win and the army.

Thus began the caretaker military administration of General Ne Win. The third general election was fixed for February 1960. The army supported the stable AFPFL, but ironically was to some extent responsible for the defeat of the stable AFPFL at the polls.[28] First, army rule had become unpopular and the people expressed their resentment by voting against the army's civilian ally – the stable AFPFL. Secondly, the military administration had destroyed the effectiveness of party organisations in the country. But the stable AFPFL was to suffer more on this account than the clean AFPFL, for the former, having no charismatic leader like U Nu, could compete with the latter only if it possessed an elaborate party organisation, which it lacked.

At the election the clean AFPFL won a landslide victory. General Ne Win promptly handed back the premiership to U Nu. With the restoration of constitutional democracy the old problems were revived – the secessionist movements of the minorities, militant strikes by students, and so on. Through 'reconciliations and compromises' U Nu might have succeeded in overcoming these problems, but now his government was under the constant surveillance of the military, which had not overcome its frustration at the defeat of its ally, the stable AFPFL. Besides, there was an influential group in the armed forces which had never accepted the desirability of a return to parliamentary government.[29] It was this group which eventually prevailed upon General Ne Win to intervene. On the night of 2 March 1962, General Ne Win and the army overthrew the constitutional government by arresting the members of the government, dismissing parliament, and abolishing the constitution of 1947.

PAKISTAN

Like India, Pakistan inherited a non-political military. Like India again, it faced many political problems in the first decade of independence. But, unlike India, it was not endowed with a strong party and a charismatic leadership committed to democracy. Jinnah was a strong leader but an autocrat by force of circumstances and by temperament. He ruled the Muslim League at will. While he spent the last year of his life nominally as Governor-General of Pakistan, he in fact ruled the country as a constitutional dictator. Thus democracy could not have gained any ground even if the father of Pakistan had lived longer than he did. After Jinnah's death in 1948, Prime Minister Liaquat Ali Khan held the fort till October 1951 when he was assassinated. Pakistan was left with no leader of continental status, no party of any strength, no constitution, and no general election so far on record. A Pakistan Constituent Assembly had been in existence since 14 August 1947, but it had not come round to drafting even the preamble of a constitution. Thus no substance was put into the framework of democracy which the Act of 1935, under which Pakistan continued to be governed, initially set up for the Dominion.

The spectacle which the partyless civilian politicians presented, in the period from 1951 to 1958, was perhaps the poorest in Southern Asia. A war raged between the Constituent Assembly and the government, the former gradually turning into a battleground of factional and regional disputes.[30] The central and provincial governments were at loggerheads. Tension grew between the west and east wings of Pakistan, and occasionally broke out in violence. In 1953 the situation went beyond civilian control when sectarian riots broke out in the Punjab between the Ahrars and the Ahmadiyas. Martial law was declared and the army was called in to restore order for the first time. In the following year, 1954, the army was brought closer to the government when the continuing conflict between the Constituent Assembly and the Governor-General was terminated by the dismissal of the former by the latter. A state of emergency was declared and Pakistan's Commander-in-Chief, General Ayub Khan, was included in the new cabinet.

It was now only a matter of time before the army took over the administration of the country. The sparks of hope for political stability ignited by the formation of the second Constituent Assembly in 1955, and the adoption of a new constitution on 23 March 1956, died out when the struggle for power between East Pakistan's Suhrawardy and West Pakistan's Feroz Khan Noon resulted in the collapse of the civilian government. President Iskander Mirza, now under pressure from General Ayub Khan, declared martial law on 7 October 1958. The constitution was abrogated, legislatures were dissolved, political parties were banned, and General Ayub Khan was appointed Chief Martial Law Administrator. Three weeks later, on 27 October, General Ayub Khan dismissed the President and assumed full control of the government.

VIETNAM, LAOS AND CAMBODIA

Regarding the third factor – the communist challenge and American intervention – it should be observed at the outset that liberal democracy had only shallow roots in South Vietnam, Laos and Cambodia. The system would have collapsed in far less strenuous situations than those which these countries had to endure. In the twentieth century, no people have suffered so much, for so long, and for so little, as have the Vietnamese, Laotians and Cambodians, during the twenty-five years from 1950 to 1975.

In American thinking the communist threat to the non-communist countries of Southern Asia began with the establishment of communist rule in China (1949), and the recognition, by China and the Soviet Union in 1950, of Ho Chi Minh's communist government in North Vietnam. Fear that the communist powers would openly attack the non-communist neighbouring countries, or would organise infiltration into them, or otherwise aid the communist guerrillas already operating there, was based on communist pronouncements frequently made in Peking and Moscow, on resolutions passed at communist conferences such as the Calcutta Conference of South-east Asian Youth in February 1948, as well as on the more tangible evidence of actual communist uprisings in Malaysia, Burma, India and the Philippines. The threat thus seemed real and consequently most disturbing to the Eisenhower administration, particularly to the Secretary of State, John Foster Dulles, who religiously believed that the postwar world was irrevocably split into two unified and hostile blocs, and that in such a world the threat of communism was indivisible and the obligation to oppose that threat unlimited.[31] The American obligation to contain communism became more pressing after the French withdrawal from Indo-China in 1954. In the same year an effective American intervention in South Vietnam began with President Eisenhower's letter to Prime Minister Ngo Dinh Diem, in which the former pledged American support in developing South Vietnam into a viable state, capable of resisting attempted subversion or aggression through military means.[32] The pouring into South Vietnam of American money and military skill, and later in 1965 the deployment of American ground forces, failed to achieve America's main objective of halting communism north of the 17th parallel in Vietnam. Instead American intervention further increased the determination of the communist forces (Viet Minh and Viet Cong) to liberate South Vietnam. In the process the North Vietnamese forces came to use tracts of land in Laos and communist sanctuaries in Cambodia, thereby bringing these two countries into the orbit of the Vietnamese war.

The first victim of this war was democracy itself. America's concern for democracy, so unequivocally proclaimed during the Second World War, was in the postwar period swallowed by its fear of communism. Deprived of any high principles, American foreign policy was thus less likely to have any creative or renovative impact on any situation to which it was applied. Instead it brought out the worst in individuals over whom it extended its patronage. Having come under American protection, Ngo Dinh Diem, once a nationalist and democrat, now turned into a dictator. After he had sent packing Emperor Bao Dai and had assumed the presidency of the Republic of Vietnam himself in 1955, he continued to destroy the saplings of democracy and grab more and more power for himself. As a result, South Vietnam came to be autocratically ruled by Diem and his brother Ngo Dinh Nhu. Diem's authoritarianism did not anger the Americans. They were disappointed in him because he had failed to deliver the goods and had also antagonised the Vietnamese army. With hindsight it can be said that Diem was blamed for not achieving the impossible. With all their supremacy in nuclear and conventional warfare, the American forces and American-trained South Vietnamese, Laotian and Cambodian armed forces were no match for the guerrilla war waged by the communists. The irresistibility of the communist strength lay in the fact that the guerrillas moved among the people as fish swam in the sea. It was late in the day, in 1961, that a counter-insurgency plan was prepared by the Kennedy administration, but it had only the half-hearted support of the American generals, and, like any scheme imposed from above, it failed to gain the sympathy, co-operation and assistance of the Vietnamese people. Diem had also lost his value to the Americans. And as soon as he was abandoned by his patrons the Vietnamese generals pounced upon him. The *coup* of 1 November 1963 brought to an end the civilian dictatorship. Diem and his brother were murdered. The military rule, which began on that day, was also doomed to fail in saving South Vietnam for the 'free world'.

American attention was drawn towards Laos because it was strategically situated between China and North Vietnam on the one hand and the neutral and western allied nations of South-east Asia on the other. If the communists gained possession of the Mekong valley in Laos, they could intensify their pressure against South Vietnam and Thailand. In the Dulles plan for communist containment Laos thus became a 'bulwark against communism' and a 'bastion of freedom'. By the end of 1960, America had poured into Laos 300 million dollars, 85 per cent of which went into training and outfitting the Laotian army in the American style.[33] As a result the Laotian troops came to learn, not counter-guerrilla warfare, but conventional manoeuvres. And the flood of American bounty brought in its wake corruption, and the demoralisation of army officers. Above all, it widened the gap between the capital, Vientiane, and the countryside. This misbegotten American investment implied that the Laotian government remained closely allied to the United States. Hence conflict arose between the Americans and Prince Souvannaphouma, head of the Laotian government for most of the years between 1954 and 1977. Prince Souvanna wanted his country to steer a middle course. He believed that the survival of his country as an independent democratic state was possible only if his government pursued a neutral policy, which in Laotian conditions sometimes implied forming a coalition government with the leaders of the communist Pathet Lao. This was Prince Souvanna's way of keeping Laos non-communist. In this he drew inspiration from the example set by India's Nehru. But for the Americans neutrality was an immoral policy, and a coalition with communists a downright surrender. Souvanna was suspected of being a communist. How else could he negotiate and form a coalition government with the Pathet Lao, as he did in November 1957? The Eisenhower administration (State, Defence and the CIA) decided that Souvanna must go. Souvanna was refused rice and oil which he badly needed to relieve the needs created by the Thai blockade. Souvanna then turned to the Russians, who immediately came to his rescue. But this was too much for America to bear. In December 1958, Souvanna was thrown out of office. The *coup* was entirely planned by American agents and advisers operating in Laos. Two *coups* took place in 1960; the first brought Souvanna back to power, the second, once again led by Phoumi Nosavan and backed by the Americans, drove him out. Souvanna fled to Cambodia and soon afterwards came to terms with Souphanouvong – the Pathet Lao leader. Thus the Eisenhower administration, by rejecting the neutralist alternative, had driven the neutralists into closer alliance with the communists and, furthermore, provoked open Soviet aid to the Pathet Lao.

The Kennedy administration was faced with a civil war in Laos between the right-wing government and the Pathet Lao, the latter having come to control nearly half the country. In order to retrieve the situation President Kennedy accepted in principle the neutralisation of Laos, and with Nehru's intervention succeeded in getting the Russians to agree to negotiate. The Geneva settlement of 1961, asking all foreign forces to withdraw from Laos, was never fully implemented. It did, however, succeed in restoring Souvanna in 1962, at the head of a coalition government. Partly because of persistent American hostility towards Souvanna, and partly because of continuing disputes among the three components of the coalition government, the coalition did not last. The third and last coalition government, with Souvanna as Prime Minister, was formed on 5 April 1975; the negotiations for this had begun early in 1973, but were not finalised sooner because of American opposition. By 1973 the Pathet Lao had come to control 80 per cent of the country. In the coalition government it occupied 50 per cent of the ministerial posts.

It was now beyond Prince Souvanna ever to resume full control of the government. After the fall of South Vietnam and Cambodia in April 1975, the Pathet Lao assumed effective control of Laos. In December 1975 the communists seized total power and the era dominated by Prince Souvannaphouma and his half-brother, Prince Souphanouvong, came to an end.

More tragic than that of Laos is the story of Cambodia, which gradually lost its democratic appearance and neutrality, and slid into the communist fold. The country suffered most perhaps because it was forced into the Vietnamese whirlwind by a more aggressive American administration than that of Eisenhower, Johnson and Kennedy. Nixon and Henry Kissinger have jointly been held responsible by their critics for the total tragedy enacted here in the name of global American 'credibility'.

Before the Nixon administration appeared on the stage in 1969, Prince Sihanouk had ruled Cambodia for over fifteen years, experimented with a multi-party democratic system, and in the process devised his own version of 'a one-party democratic government', which he thought was 'something very rare in South-east Asia, and did much to preserve national unity'.[34] The principal object of the innovations which Sihanouk introduced in 1955 was to prevent a naked struggle for power raging between parties and politicians – a phenomenon which all the countries in Asia faced in the early stages of their experiments with Western-style liberal democracy. The mushroom-like growth of political parties and the wranglings that went on between them had been one of the main causes of the disappearance or weakening of the democratic order in a number of countries. Even in India – the citadel of democracy in Asia – this posed a serious threat to the stability of the democratic order. Sihanouk tried to overcome this danger by forming a party of all parties – the Sangkum Reastr Niyum (People's Socialist Community) – which he hoped would eventually absorb and replace parties. It was his party, and though he did not officially ban other parties, by 1957 the Sangkum had managed to force many, including the Democratic Party, out of circulation; in the post-1957 period only one party – the left-wing Pracheachon – managed to hold its ground against the Sangkum. To further ensure that the Sangkum and the parliament did not come to monopolise all power, soon after the 1955 election in which his party won 83 per cent of the seats in the National Assembly, he created the National Congress – a biannual forum of delegates chosen by provincial bodies and by peasants – which, he thought, would encourage greater popular participation in politics.

The National Congress was to determine Cambodia's policies,

which the National Assembly was to enact and the government to implement. Not trusting even the National Congress itself, which might in due course become highly politicised and accordingly disintegrate into factional wranglings, Sihanouk kept open the option of referendum, to which he occasionally resorted when faced with opposition on a major issue in parliament, the party or the National Congress. These devices were forged to preserve national unity as well as to concentrate power in Sihanouk's hands. But being always assured of popular support, Sihanouk did not have to act as a dictator. Factional rivalries persisted in the National Assembly and the Sangkum; nine governments fell from power between 1955 and 1958. The young élite rose in opposition, demanding positions of responsibility. The Pracheachon continued to function as an opposition party. But none of these factors forced Sihanouk into undertaking extreme dictatorial measures.

It was all plain sailing till 1959 when Sihanouk's neutrality (evolved through the inspiration of Nehru) began to irritate the Americans. The strings attached to American aid began to tighten. Sihanouk suspected a CIA–Thailand–South Vietnam conspiracy behind the unsuccessful plot of 1958 to overthrow his neutral government in favour of one which would associate Cambodia with the Western powers in a military alliance. With all his whims and vanity, Sihanouk was essentially a proud patriot. He resented being pushed around and bullied, especially by Americans who, he suspected, had no respect for Cambodia and Cambodians. When in 1965, despite his warnings, American planes violated Cambodian territory and dropped bombs on supposed communist sanctuaries, Sihanouk broke off diplomatic relations with the United States. But the crunch came in 1969.

Cambodia had always had a tiny communist Maquis, which Sihanouk had dubbed the 'Khmer Rouge'. In 1969, at the opening of the last act in the drama, it was perhaps not more than 5000 strong. But the Nixon–Kissinger policy of bombarding Cambodia resulted in an increase of strength for the Khmer Rouge to over 70,000. The occasion for this ruthless American intervention arose when the communists pushed increasing supplies through the Cambodian port of Sihanoukville or down the so-called Ho Chi Minh Trail to 'sanctuaries' inside the eastern borders of Cambodia, which were not more than thirty-five miles from Saigon.[35] President Lyndon Johnson rejected several requests from the US commanders in Saigon to mount a full-scale assault upon the communist sanctuaries. But the situation changed when Nixon took over the Presidency in January 1969. In February he allowed the US command in Vietnam to bomb

Cambodia. From March 1969 to 15 August 1973, when the ceasefire took place, more than half a million tons of bombs were dropped on Cambodia, killing, according to a US Senate estimate, half a million of Cambodia's seven million people.[36]

This ruthless measure achieved the opposite of what was intended. The North Vietnamese communists abandoned their eastern sanctuaries and moved west of the Ho Chi Minh Trail, deeper into the countryside of Cambodia. They became invisible and more powerful.

As critical of the American bombing as he was of the North Vietnamese infiltration, Sihanouk maintained his balance during the first year of the bombing, steadfastly holding to his neutral policy. Thus was hatched, as alleged by Sihanouk, the CIA plot to depose him.[37] The opportune moment came in March 1970 when Sihanouk left Cambodia on his Paris–Moscow–Peking visit. He was deposed in a bloodless *coup* carried out by his Prime Minister, Lon Nol, aided by Sirik Matat, the deputy Prime Minister. Sihanouk was told of the *coup* when travelling to Moscow airport in a car with Premier Kosygin.[38] When he arrived in Peking, Sihanouk was no longer neutral. He was now fully committed to the Khmer Rouge and solely dependent on Chinese and North Vietnamese support for his bid to liberate Cambodia.

From 1970 to 1975, civil war raged between Lon Nol's forces and the Khmer Rouge, the latter rapidly gathering strength with North Vietnamese–Chinese support. With all the American might behind them Lon Nol's forces kept on losing battles; by the middle of 1973 the Khmer Rouge had come to control over two-thirds of Cambodia. At the beginning of 1975 Lon Nol's forces had lost all except Phnom Penh. When the Khmer Rouge began its final onslaught Lon Nol relinquished all power and fled to America. The capital fell in April 1975.

★

Now we take up the last question and turn to Singapore, Malaysia and Sri Lanka to examine how and with what modifications democracy has functioned in these states. Formally these three fall into one category. They have preserved, with a few exceptions here and there, the basic ingredients of a democratic order: regular free elections, an independent judiciary, and a free press. Even though Malaysia and Sri Lanka each went through phases of emergency, in none of these was the entire opposition put into jail; a factor which distinguishes them from India.

SINGAPORE

On closer examination, Singapore stands apart. Here, since the island's independence, a restricted version of democracy has been functioning. The system has been 'amended', with its 'irksome restrictions' eliminated, and what we find functioning in this city state is an 'Asian version', or more appropriately Lee Kuan Yew's version of democracy. On paper, all the basic features of a parliamentary democracy exist: political parties are not banned, there is no censorship of the press, the judiciary is independent, elections have been held quinquennially. But in practice all these institutions have suffered from restrictions. Lee Kuan Yew has used his executive powers to limit the scope of the democratic institutions. And this he has done with a sense of conviction.

Lee has been the Prime Minister of Singapore since its independence. His ruling party – the People's Action Party – has not only won all the elections held over the last seventeen years, but in the last three elections of 1968, 1972 and 1976 it won all the seats in parliament. In 1971 the Indian *Statesman* remarked that a 'democracy' which succeeds in ensuring that all the sitting members in parliament belong to the ruling party is too perfect to be true.[39] Perhaps this miracle was achieved partly by pressure on and intimidation of the opposition parties. The opposition Barisan Sosialis was never banned – though every leader showing any potential, as alleged by the critics of Lee, was either jailed or exiled. Lee has thus succeeded in running a one-party parliament. Likewise, the press was never nationalised, but all the newspapers came to learn what not to publish the hard way. Judicial protection of individual liberty was considerably weakened by the abolition of the jury system, suspension of habeas corpus, and above all the introduction through the Internal Security Act of the 'democratic device' of imprisonment without trial. Pressure groups like trade unions had been suppressed earlier; the student insurgency of 1975 was stopped by making an example of Tan Wah Piow, the student leader of Singapore University, who was arrested, tried and sentenced to a year's imprisonment, and then conscripted into the army.

Not only on the political but also on the cultural side, Lee has introduced stringent restrictions and controls to prevent the spread, as it were, of the unhealthy habits and fashions of the West – crime, drugs, violence, long hair, sexual freedom.

Lee has no apology to offer for containing democracy. He believes that democracy had to be restrained not only in order to survive but, more importantly, to foster the stability and economic prosperity of the nation. Had democracy been allowed unrestricted play in Singapore, Lee would argue with some justification, the island would have been swallowed up by the communists. With equal confidence Lee could count the many economic achievements his city state has made under his paternalistic rule. Singapore has the highest *per capita* income in Asia after Japan, and a growth rate that should be the envy of every Western industrial power. Perhaps it is true that the people of Singapore support and trust him, and in voting for him overwhelmingly in December 1975 they made it clear that they are prepared to put up with authoritarianism in return for good living standards and a strong economy.

Has Singapore reached that mark of prosperity and stability when democracy can be unleashed? To this Lee would most probably say – NO. The communist threat to the stability of Thailand, Malaysia and Singapore has become more formidable since 1975. As communists follow an unscrupulous book of rules in knocking down their opponents once and for all, it is appropriate, Lee would argue, that a non-communist government should also play for keeps. He might even go further and say, perhaps with some justification, that old-style democracy has become cumbersome for even the most advanced countries of the Western world. It has overstrained the political fibres and made these nations vulnerable to terrorism and economic chaos. All authoritarians in Asia have used this line of argument. But whereas others have formally suspended the system, Lee has let it run.

★

Compared to Singapore, Malaysia and Sri Lanka have been far less prosperous and their stability more threatened by internal revolts. Yet, so far the system has run satisfactorily in these countries without sustaining many deep dents. Though different from each other in many ways, Malaysia and Sri Lanka have had in common one political feature which sustained democracy in each of them. In both the bulk of the political élite was power-sharing, hence contented and responsible. In other words, no single party monopolised power all the time. The two countries acquired this stabilising political phenomenon in different ways. We turn first to Malaysia.

MALAYSIA

In the decade preceding independence, the Malayan élitist leadership had evolved a non-communal approach to political problems. Dato Onn bin Jaafar founded the United Malays National Organisation (UMNO) and succeeded in expanding its base of support by opening its membership to non-Malays and by avoiding political postures which might antagonise the other important ethnic communities – the Chinese and the Indians. Dato Onn left UMNO but his non-communal approach came to form the backbone of the Alliance which emerged soon after. The Alliance formed between the three national parties – UMNO, the Malayan Chinese Association (MCA) and the Malayan Indian Congress (MIC) – was based on a multi-communal approach to politics. Nourished and strengthened by the able Malayan leadership of Tunku Abdul Rahman (Prime Minister from 1957 to 1970), Tun Abdul Razak (Prime Minister from 1970 to 1976) and Datuk Hussain Onn (Prime Minister since 1976), the Alliance has been in power since the country's independence, winning all the five general elections held since 1955. The Alliance has always kept its doors open for any important opposition party to step in. When in 1973 the most important Malay opposition party, the Pan Malayan Islamic Party, crossed the floor and joined the Alliance, the latter became a wide-based National Front of ten political parties. In the 1974 general election it won all but nineteen seats in the 154-seat House of Representatives.

Following the example and pattern of Alliance politics at the federal level, Alliance coalitions were formed in the federal states of Sabah and Sarawak. But they were different from the Malayan Alliance in the sense that they were dominated by the parties representing the non-Muslim native peoples. However, this has not caused any serious rift between the states and the federal government, mainly because the latter has always managed to find collaborators from the former. Also, as the federal government provides the bulk of the funds spent by the states, it has cleverly used this financial power to secure state compliance with federal policies and, at the same time, to improve the political fortunes of the state Alliance Organisation.[40]

The Alliance system has thus come to dominate the entire political life of Malaysia, providing almost all the politicians of the coalition parties with an opportunity to wield power at the federal or state level. The success of the system has so far depended on the non-existence of strong opposition parties. The opposition parties operating outside the Alliance do in fact have very little support. When a party in opposition becomes stronger it is most likely to be drawn into the Alliance. Malaysia's increasing prosperity has been another stabilising factor. The federation is the world's biggest producer of rubber and tin, and these products helped the country's exports to rise by 46 per cent to a value of £3400 million in 1976.[41] In the same year a growth rate of 12 per cent, in real terms, was achieved while inflation was held down to less than 3 per cent.

But it has not been plain sailing all along for democracy in Malaysia, although its basic features have not been interfered with. Elections have been held regularly, even during the long spells of emergency. The judiciary has continued to function independently and effectively. The domestic press has all along been free, though cautious. Two factors, however, have tended to overstrain the political order and force it into resorting to emergency measures: communist insurgency and racial riots.

The Malayan Communist Party (MCP), with an overwhelming Malayan Chinese membership, was a kind of nationalist party before the country's independence, agitating and fighting for the immediate withdrawal of colonial power from Malaya. In 1948 this moderate strategy was changed to armed revolution with a view to throwing the British colonial administration out of Malaya and replacing it with a communist People's Republic. This led to the declaration of emergency in June 1948; the MCP and its subsidiary organs were outlawed in the following month. The communists took to the Malayan jungles from where they continued to wage guerrilla warfare. Major successes against the communist guerrillas were won by continued military operations and greater co-operation from the public. The communists lost ground when Malayan independence came in 1957. By 1959 many of them had surrendered and been rehabilitated. Others remained with their leader, Chin Peng, and retreated to the most inaccessible dense jungle along the Perak–Thai border. From then on Chin Peng and his comrades were to play the waiting game. Taking inspiration from the example of Mao Tse-tung, they decided to wait until changes in the international or domestic scene would give them a new opportunity to seize power in Malaya.

The emergency was revoked in 1960 and the Emergency Regulations were replaced by the Internal Security Act, which empowered the government to detain suspects for indefinite periods. Since 1975, when the Indo-Chinese states fell into the communist fold, giving sufficient incentive to the Malaysian communists to renew their guerrilla warfare, the Malaysian government has brought into operation some additional security ordinances and also amended the Internal Security Act of 1960 to allow the death penalty for illegal possession of arms. Some of these regulations are harsh and seem to violate the liberty of the individual. The Universities and University Colleges (Amendment) Act of 1975, for example, prohibits students from joining or supporting any society, political party, or trade union, either inside or outside Malaysia, even if they are lawfully established.[42] Another Regulation of 1975 makes every member of a household above the age of fourteen responsible for the family's activities. Some Malaysian lawyers have felt alarmed over this clamp-down on civil liberties as part of an anti-communist drive. A few journalists have wondered whether the fear of a communist take-over was great enough to justify such erosions of democratic freedom. There is, however, no doubt that the communist guerrillas have posed an imminent threat to the Malaysian democratic order. The communists are supported by Malay Muslim secessionists in southern Thailand, so the communist sanctuaries on the border of these two countries have acquired great strength. Under the agreement reached between the Thai and Malaysian governments, in 1969, the armies of both countries have launched a joint offensive against communist strongholds in the border areas. There is also no doubt that a great majority of the Malaysian people are supporting the government in its war against the communists. From this it follows that the restrictions which have been imposed on some civil liberties have the approval and support of the people. Some innocent people are occasionally victimised, but the majority of those who are actually detained, punished or sentenced to death have been, in the eyes of the Malaysian people, the 'enemies of the nation'. The question is whether such restrictions on civil liberties, if imposed by a democratic government and approved by the people, can be technically construed as 'erosions of democracy'. By and large the Asians do not believe that they can be so construed unless it is shown that such restrictions were imposed, though ostensibly to strengthen a nation in its fight against an unidentifiable enemy, really to enable a particular individual or party to remain in power. In the Malaysian case, anyway, such a motive cannot be attributed to the Prime Minister, Datuk Hussein Onn, or to his party, the National Front.

The second problem which has agitated the democratic order in Malaysia is racial tension, prevailing mainly between the affluent Chinese community of 3·5 million and the majority community of Malays. This tension mainly comes from two factors. First is the government's economic policies, which are aimed at erasing the wealth gap between the two races. This involves giving preferential treatment to the relatively poor Malays, who on their own cannot compete with the rich Chinese. Allied to the economic policies was the government's decision in 1967 to make Malay the sole national language. This gave a decided advantage to Malays, at least for some years to come, in having access to jobs and political power. The second factor is the rise in recent years of new second-generation political élites. They are vernacular-educated élites, and whether Malay or non-Malay, they are all more intensely communal in their outlook.

These two factors have occasionally combined and caused communal riots; the one which occurred soon after the general election, in 1969, in which 143 Chinese were killed, led the government to declare a state of emergency. In consequence the federal parliament was suspended and the cabinet replaced by a military-style National Operations Committee. It may, however, be observed that the communal riots coincided with the communist uprising on the Malay–Thai border. The democratic order thus remained suspended until 1971 when the emergency was lifted and parliament recalled.

Thus, on account of the communist insurgency and racial riots Malaysia has been twice forced into declaring an emergency. In her case, anyway, it seems that these spells of emergency were invoked in order to protect democracy itself.

SRI LANKA

Democracy in Sri Lanka has survived thanks mainly to the effective functioning of the two-party system. Since its independence the country has been governed alternately by only two parties: the SLFP has ruled for seventeen years; the UNP, which in July 1977 came to power for the third time, had ruled the country for fourteen years from 1948 to 1956 and 1965 to 1970. Sri Lanka's electorate has displaced more governments since independence than any other country in Southern Asia. The bulk of the political élites of the island have thus had the opportunity of actually wielding power. Consequently, the party in opposition behaved quite responsibly, for it hoped to gain power at the next election. Sri Lanka was fortunate in being spared the major destabilising political feature common to most of the countries in their post-independence period – the proliferation of political parties.

This is not to say that Sri Lanka began its independent political life with only two national parties. In fact there were more than half-a-dozen important parties working in opposition during the first long spell of UNP rule from 1948 to 1956. Having won independence for the country, the UNP had come to acquire the same prestige as the Indian National Congress. None of the parties in opposition could hope singly to displace the UNP. At the time of the 1956 election, therefore, the opposition parties joined to form a single viable political party – the SLFP. This amalgamation was brought about by S. W. R. D. Bandaranaike, the leader of one of the component parties.[43] Consequently what happened in India and Pakistan (the alliance or merger of opposition parties) in 1977 had already taken place in Sri Lanka almost twenty years before. The SLFP won the 1956 election and displaced the nine-year-old rule of the UNP. However, the emergence of the two-party system did not bring about the total disappearance from the political scene of all other parties. Some leftist and communal parties have continued to exist. The July 1977 general election was, for example, contested, apart from the two main parties, by the United Left Front, the Tamil United Liberation Front and the Ceylon Workers' Congress, and though the results were pretty upsetting for the Left Front which gained not a single seat, the Tamil Front, by gaining more seats than the SLFP, for the first time became the leading opposition party. Sri Lanka has now three parties in the arena. But the Tamil Front, being a communal party and based on the support of a minority group, is most unlikely to replace the SLFP as a national party. It is possible that the SLFP may, in five years' time, regain its strength. However, if the SLFP fails to rise again, Sri Lanka might choose the Malaysian alternative of a coalition government.

Some other factors, too, have supported the functioning of the parliamentary form of democracy in Sri Lanka. Sri Lanka's electorate is more educated and has been more politically conscious than, say, that of India or Pakistan. Sri Lanka was the first Asian colony to have universal adult franchise introduced, as early as 1931. The country's literacy rate is among Asia's highest: 92 per cent of people aged under twenty-four can read and write. Newspapers are widely read. Since 1955 the poll has always been over 70 per cent, since 1965 over 80 per cent. Since 1956 the electorate has been conscious of its power to change government. But above all, Sri Lanka is the only country in Southern Asia to become a welfare state with free education and medicine, subsidised food and protective labour laws.

However, in spite of being in possession of such assets as a responsible political élite and a politically conscious electorate, Sri Lanka had to resort to a state of emergency many more times than any other state in South and South-east Asia. Leaving aside the first state of emergency imposed on the island during the Second World War, the country has passed through five states of emergency since independence, the last being the longest, from 1971 to 1977. The first emergency, of 1958, was caused by the violent communal riots between the Tamils and Sinhalese, the second, of 1959, by the assassination of Prime Minister Bandaranaike by a Buddhist monk; the third, in 1961, again by the Tamil–Sinhalese riots; the fourth, in 1962, by the discovery of an army–police conspiracy to overthrow the government; and the fifth, in 1971, by a revolution organised by a party of rural Buddhist youth, who for a while succeeded in running their own form of government in some villages of Sri Lanka.

Of all the different factors which caused these emergencies, the Tamil–Sinhalese conflict has been the most formidable. It has

THE CRISIS OF DEMOCRACY 63

continually threatened the unity of the island. The Hindu Tamils form the largest single minority community in Sri Lanka. They account for about 21 per cent of the island's total population of over 14 million. Their language and religion are different from those of the majority community, the Buddhist Sinhalese, who constitute 70 per cent of the population. But what has facilitated the Tamil separatist movement most is the predominance of this community in the northern and eastern provinces of the country. These provinces thus constitute Sri Lanka's potential Ulster.

Though the Tamils have had a long list of grievances, their separatist movement was fairly moderate until 1972. But when the republican constitution of 1972 renamed Ceylon as Sri Lanka and reaffirmed Sinhala as the sole official language, the movement became more aggressive. After the July election of 1977, the demand for an independent, sovereign state, to be called Eilam, was boldly put forward by the Tamil United Liberation Front. The Sinhalese reacted violently. About 200 people were killed in August 1977. J. R. Jayewardene's UNP government had to impose curfews and use the army to restore law and order. By the beginning of September the situation was brought under control. The island was not subjected to yet another spell of emergency.

Like Malaysia, Sri Lanka too had to resort to emergencies in order to fight forces that threatened its integrity. All the emergencies except one seemed to have had national support while they lasted. Mrs Bandaranaike's emergency of 1971 turned out to be the controversial one. There was justification for its coming into being when it did. But was she justified in prolonging it for nearly six years and postponing the election, due to be held in 1975, until 1977? Like Mrs Gandhi of India, Mrs Bandaranaike is suspected of misusing the state of emergency for personal ends. On the surface the parallel between the two seems obvious. Mrs Bandaranaike gagged the press by nationalising the Associated Newspapers of Ceylon, curbed the independence of the judiciary, banned demonstrations here and a party or two there, locked up nearly a dozen members of the UNP, groomed her son Anura Bandaranaike as a leader of the youth movement, and disengaged her party from an alliance with the pro-Moscow communist party. All this she did, it is alleged, to remove obstructions in her way towards keeping herself and her party in power. However, Mrs Bandaranaike did not go as far as Mrs Gandhi. She did not put the entire opposition in jail. Unlike his Indian counterpart, Morarji Desai, the opposition leader Jayewardene was, throughout the emergency, at liberty to keep on agitating against the postponement of the election. Neither did Mrs Bandaranaike amend the country's constitution so drastically as Mrs

Gandhi. The fact that the people had ceased to support the emergency Raj and turned against Mrs Bandaranaike's government is proved by the 1977 election results. In the 168-member parliament the SLFP secured only 8 seats; in the 1970 election it had won 91 seats. Mrs Bandaranaike, however, was fortunate in retaining her own seat.

In July 1977, democracy was thus fully restored in Sri Lanka. Jayewardene, however, was convinced that the country's grave economic problems, with 10 per cent of its population remaining unemployed, could not be resolved by a weak, parliamentary form of government. A change-over to a strong, French-style presidential form of government was thus considered a necessity. Accordingly, the constitution was amended, and on 5 February 1978, the seventy-two-year-old Jayewardene became the President. Under the new constitution, the President has sweeping executive powers, including the right to dissolve parliament, to address it whenever he wants, to preside over the Cabinet and to 'assign any Ministry or ministries to himself'. As a curb on the power of the President, it will be possible by a simple two-thirds majority of the parliament to vote him out of office.

3   The Authoritarian Alternative

In 1976, 1000 million of the 1100 million people of South and South-east Asia lived under authoritarian rule. 1976 was in fact a lean year for democracy. A world survey showed that only 19·6 per cent of the world's inhabitants then lived in free countries.[1] The retrieval of India from authoritarianism in March 1977 changed the picture. Today only about 460 million people live under dictatorial systems in this region of Asia. In terms of countries, however, ten out of fourteen presently remain lost to democracy. Of these ten, Laos, Cambodia and Vietnam have fallen into the communist fold. In the case of Thailand military dictatorship has been the rule and democratic government the exception. In Bangladesh the dictatorship of General Rahman is now five years old. But unlike other authoritarians, the rulers of both Bangladesh and Thailand have not so far ventured into the problems of evolving any indigenous surrogates for democracy. General Rahman had promised to hold general elections in February 1977. But they were postponed on the grounds that party leaders had not yet sunk their past differences and, consequently, over fifty political parties had sought recognition. Instead, in May 1977 Rahman held a referendum. Over 98 per cent of the votes cast went in his favour. In the same year elections to local bodies in rural and urban areas were held and democracy was modestly revived at that level. In February 1978 Rahman went on record promising general elections in December. Nineteen political parties were registered, including a new one – the Nationalist Party – in which Rahman was expected to be a key figure. In order to acquire democratic legitimacy for himself and approval for a French-style presidential system of government, Rahman held the first direct presidential election in June 1978. He won the election with a large majority; the opposition complained that the election was rigged. The promised general election was held in February 1979. Rahman's Bangladesh Nationalist Party won a two-thirds majority in parliament, capturing over 200 of the 330 seats. The leaders of the twenty-nine political parties in opposition alleged that the election was rigged, and that the media and other government resources were used by Rahman to influence the electorate in favour of his party. Rahman, however, took his victory as a firm mandate from the electorate to establish a presidential form of government as opposed to the parliamentary systems demanded by the other political parties.

Bangladesh and Thailand have so far had straightforward military rule with perhaps only one difference – whereas in the former the supreme power is exercised by General Rahman (who assumed the presidency under the 1975 constitution), in the latter the absolute power appears to be vested collectively in the National Policy Council of twenty-three senior military and police officers. Admiral Sangad Charloryu, the author of the October 1976 *coup*, remains the Chairman of the National Policy Council, while another respected military officer, General Kriangsak Chamanand, was in November 1977 appointed Prime Minister by the Council. In some degree, this division of power insures the military regime against in-fighting and counter *coup*. Thailand's military junta, however, is still formally committed to bring back democracy. In October 1977, when the civilian administration of Prime Minister Thanin Kraivichien (set up by the military council after the *coup* of 1976) was replaced by direct military rule, General Kriangsak Chamanand said: 'We have got to start learning about democracy by practising it.'[2] A general election was actually held in April 1979, but under a constitution which carefully circumscribed the powers of the elected representatives.[3]

This chapter will, therefore, focus mainly on the remaining five of the present ten 'unfree' countries – Pakistan, Nepal, Burma, Indonesia and the Philippines – as well as on India's brief experiment with authoritarian rule, and the revival and functioning of the democratic order since March 1977.

Though each authoritarian system has its own peculiarities, yet all or most of them broadly display some common features. First, all claim to have emerged out of chaos. In physical terms, all the dictatorial regimes, except those of Nepal (1955) and Burma, came into being through the instruments either of martial law or emergency; in Nepal and Burma the take-over was so smooth that the need to resort to either of the two devices did not arise. The device of 'internal emergency' was used only in India and Pakistan by Mrs Gandhi and Mr Bhutto respectively. When compared to martial law emergency was a weak device, for it technically left intact the legislative and judicial organs of the state. The emergency regime, therefore, had to resort to constitutional amendments in order to acquire powers to override the judiciary and legislature. The martial law regimes, by dispensing with legislature and judiciary from the very beginning, were less encumbered by constitutional restrictions and therefore more dictatorial and repressive than the emergency regimes.

Secondly, almost all regimes decried liberal democracy particularly for fostering the politics of opposition. Some regarded the system as out of date, some believed it was unsuited to the genius of their particular country. Hence, each regime strove to evolve its own version of a democratic system. As a result five different Asian surrogates for liberal democracy emerged; each differed from the other in detail but all tended to concentrate powers in one person and to stifle the politics of opposition.

Thirdly, each regime was driven by a compulsive need to acquire 'legitimacy', and each came to claim that it had the people's support; the aspiring political élites were of course excluded from the category of 'real people'. Direct appeal to the mute, illiterate millions characterised the style of all authoritarians. Like monarchs of old, these dictators came to believe that they represented the conscience as well as the consensus of the people.

Fourthly, all regimes, though formally claiming to be socialist, were essentially anti-communist. None introduced any radical economic or social reforms. Consequently, none has so far shown any rapid economic growth. The achievements of authoritarian governments lie in the political field. Each succeeded in restoring, for a shorter or longer period, a certain degree of stability and security in its territory. Secessionist, regional and subversive movements were subdued. Industrial disputes, strikes, demonstrations and rallies were banned. This provided favourable conditions for economic progress. But these conditions were not fully exploited.

Lastly, each authoritarian ruler, though armed with supreme power, betrayed a sense of insecurity. As none of the regimes carried any provision for a smooth transfer of power, the fear of a counter *coup* or communist insurgency always haunted the dictator's mind. The danger was real in most cases. The diverse opposition forces in each country under authoritarian rule joined hands and the underground movement against the regime continued to grow. For example, today the most serious threat to Marcos's regime in the Philippines is posed by a combination of opposition forces – the Catholic Church, the Muslim secessionists and the communist rebels. Likewise, against Ne Win's regime in Burma are arrayed the communist guerrillas as well as the various warring ethnic minorities united in the National Democratic Front.

PAKISTAN

Pakistan was the first country to send packing its long-staggering democratic order. General Ayub Khan was also the first leader seriously to evolve a Pakistani surrogate for the Western form of democracy. He was to inspire King Mahendra of Nepal and Ferdinand Marcos of the Philippines when they devised their own versions of democracy. An upright, Sandhurst-trained Pathan, Ayub, while a cabinet minister from 1954 to 1958, acquired an intense dislike for politicians and a pity, almost verging on contempt, for the 'down-trodden' race of Bengalis who inhabited East Pakistan and formed the majority of Pakistan's total population. His dislike for the Pakistani politicians, who excelled in 'baseness, chicanery, deceit, and degradation', led him to believe firmly that Western democracy was unsuited to the genius of his country. How could one, he argued, run a parliamentary democracy in a country which was infested with feudal lords, religious leaders, and more than a dozen political parties, none with any programme whatsoever, and all determined to exploit and influence the population, which had not yet reached the level of primary education.[4] His case against liberal democracy rested on classical arguments and it was set in the same language which the colonial masters used when denigrating the nationalist demand for representative government.

Bengalis being what they were in Ayub's analysis – a race of suspicious, aggressive, and intriguing people who had been ruled from time immemorial until the creation of Pakistan by caste Hindus, Mughals, Pathans or the British – needed to be tutored and disciplined.[5] It was obvious that in Ayub's system they were not going to carry any weight merely on the ground of their numerical strength.

The system of 'Basic Democracy' which Ayub imposed upon the nation on 27 October 1959 was essentially paternalistic and 'tutorial'. Under this system the country was initially divided into 80,000 constituencies which were equally shared by the two provinces of Pakistan – East and West. Each constituency, with an average population of 1000 to 1500, elected on the basis of universal suffrage a representative who was called a Basic Democrat. About ten such Democrats formed a primary body – called a union council (it was called committee in towns and cities). Each primary body was to have in addition to its directly elected Democrats some government-nominated members, mostly officials, who were to exercise controlling authority over the council committee. These primary bodies were entrusted with the development programme in their respective areas. They were also to elect members from amongst themselves to the higher bodies at sub-divisional, district and divisional levels. And later, under the constitution of 1962 – Pakistan's second constitution which Ayub promulgated on 8 June 1962 – the 80,000 or so

Basic Democrats of the country were to elect the President, the members of the National Assembly and the provincial legislators. The Basic Democrats, the President, the central and provincial legislators were all to be elected for a term of five years.

Prior to introducing Basic Democracy, President Ayub had taken measures to ensure that his 'home-grown' system was not contaminated by politicians and political parties. Political parties were banned at the beginning of the martial-law regime. Then two orders were promulgated, in March 1959 the PODO (Public Offences (Disqualification) Order) and in August of the same year the EBDO (Elective Bodies (Disqualification) Order), which together ensured that politicians suspected or found guilty of corruption kept themselves away from political activity.

The election of Basic Democrats was completed in January 1960. In February a referendum was held: the Basic Democrats were asked to register by secret ballot whether or not they had confidence in President Ayub Khan. Over 95 per cent of those casting ballots registered their confidence in Ayub. Consequently, Ayub officially took the oath as the first elected President of Pakistan.

All Ayub's political thinking, and the institutions like Basic Democracy which he had already created, were embodied in the constitution of 1962. The constitution created a strong centre and invested the President with powers to override the central legislature (the National Assembly – 156 seats of which were equally divided between the two provinces). Through his provincial governors the President could exercise similar control over provincial executive and legislature. The main characteristics of the authoritarian system which thus emerged were that it suppressed the politics of opposition, restricted universal franchise, and brought East Pakistan firmly under the West-Pakistan-dominated national fold. Naturally the most implacable opponents of the system were the Bengali élites who had so far striven to achieve the liberation of their province from its economic, linguistic and political bondage to West Pakistan. Only through such political artefacts as power-sharing at the centre in accordance with their numerical strength, or provincial autonomy in a loose federal structure, could the Bengalis have achieved their liberation. Ayub's system seemed to put an end to such prospects.

Though the constitution turned him into a constitutional dictator Ayub came to believe, especially in the light of the February 1960 referendum, that he derived his powers from the people and that the constitution, far from being dictatorial, brought into being 'all the elements of democracy' and suited the conditions, the requirements, and the genius of the people'.[6] In other words, Ayub genuinely believed that the constitution, by virtue of its giving to the people what was in their best interest and what they really wanted, had acquired their approval.

It has been the common failing or virtue (depending on how one is disposed towards dictatorship) of the non-communist authoritarians in South and South-east Asia to seek legitimacy for their regimes in 'people's approval'. This approval has been elicited or gauged in many different ways but never sought, except in the singular case of Mrs Gandhi of India, through a free election based on universal franchise. This practice of seeking people's consent or acquiescence implies that non-communist authoritarianism, whether military, civilian, or monarchical, having no ideological structure of its own, tends to justify itself by the norms and standards of the very democratic system it has displaced. Straightforward and ruthless dictatorship is considered unfashionable and even risky by the dictators themselves, particularly those of South and South-east Asia. No practising dictator of this region has ever in principle conceded that his or her regime was thoroughly dictatorial. Even though it was within their power, the authoritarians have compulsively refrained from utterly ignoring or defying 'people', 'freedom' and 'election'. In practice they have controlled and redefined them, but the fact that they have in theory continued to pay homage to the triumvirate of democracy has weakened their regimes more than any other factor, and given them the appearance of impermanence, of makeshift arrangements, which essentially they are.

Ayub was no exception. The more 'support' he acquired for his system the more democratic he claimed it to be. Soon after the implementation of the constitution it was realised by members of Ayub's coterie that support for his regime in the National Assembly could best be manipulated through the revival of party politics. Ayub himself needed his power to be based on party support. It was not easy for an erstwhile opponent of party politics to endorse the Political Parties Act of 1962. But his supporters convinced him that this measure, though ostensibly liberal, might open for the regime the best prospect of breaking the strength of the lurking opposition. For a political party headed by President Ayub, they argued, it would be a downright easy job to overpower all opposition parties, which would anyway be run in the absence of the old hands (put out of action by EBDO and PODO) by political dwarfs. The Political Parties Act permitted the formation of political parties. At the same time one of its provisions banned the practice of 'crossing the floor' or the politics of defection. If a person, elected to the National or to a Provincial Assembly as a candidate or nominee of a political party, withdrew from that party, he would, from the date of withdrawal, be disqualified from being a member of that Assembly for the unexpired period of his term as a member. The significance of this ban on defections was lost on the regimented and authoritarian policy of Pakistan. But in India, which reached the world's highest record in defections from 1967 to 1974 and where this kind of legislation might have uplifted the falling political standards, it would have been most probably declared *ultra vires*, by the Supreme Court as abridging the fundamental rights guaranteed by the constitution.

With the revival of political parties began the gradual decline of Ayub's system. In May 1963, Ayub himself adopted a party – the Pakistan Muslim League or a faction of it – and became its President. Five opposition parties, each with only a modicum of national stature, and all sharing nothing in common except the resolution to oust Ayub from power, joined hands on the eve of the 1965 elections for the presidency and for the central and provincial legislatures. The nine-point election programme of the Combined Opposition Parties included the restoration of democracy. They put up Miss Fatima Jinnah, sister of Mohammed Ali Jinnah, for the presidency. Ayub, however, won the election, acquiring 73 per cent of the votes of the electoral college in West Pakistan and 53 per cent in East Pakistan. Also, Ayub's Muslim League won 120 of the 150 seats of the National Assembly. Ayub had every reason to assume that he had beaten the politicians at their own game. He interpreted his victory as meaning that the 'country had chosen stability against chaos, security against disintegration, progress against stagnation'.[7] He felt confident, and benignly thanked those who had differed with him, for 'they too had served the cause of democracy'.

There was now no turning back from the liberal path Ayub had willy-nilly set for his authoritarian regime. The regime began heading, almost helplessly, towards its total collapse. It was perhaps inevitable. But three factors seem to have hastened the process: Zulfikar Ali Bhutto's persistent and unscrupulous opposition to Ayub; East Pakistan's movement for regional autonomy under the leadership of Sheikh Mujibur Rahman; Ayub's illness from March 1968 to March 1969.

Bhutto had served in Ayub's Cabinet since 1958, and as Foreign Minister from January 1963 to June 1966, when he resigned on account of his disagreement with the President particularly over the peace terms embodied in the Tashkent Declaration (January 1966) following the seventeen-day Indo-Pakistan War of September 1965. Bhutto left the government with injured feelings, and personal bitterness towards Ayub. This, combined with a fair measure of popularity he had come to acquire among the Pakistanis on account of his performances abroad as Foreign Minister, impelled him into a relentless struggle for power.[8] He soon gathered around him all the anti-Ayub elements including industrial labour, unemployed college graduates and urban professionals, who had not benefited, economically and politically, from Ayub's regime. In December 1967 he formed his own political party – the Pakistan People's Party. The expiry at the end of 1966 of the ban under the EBDO on certain politicians participating in political activities further liberalised the political atmosphere. The old guard was back in the race. Bhutto joined the scramble for power with a princely hauteur but with few if any scruples, for in his bid to mobilise opposition against the regime he went as far as to support Mujibur Rahman's demand for East Pakistan's regional autonomy. So far he had always been opposed to Bengali separatism, and was to resume his opposition to it soon after Ayub's fall.

Bengali political élites were the most frustrated under Ayub's system. Basic Democracy had cheated them of what they considered their legitimate role in the selection of their rulers and legislators. They could neither participate effectively in the system, nor were they drawn into Ayub's military and civil bureaucratic order. The corridors of power lay in West Pakistan and their growing sense of isolation from them became more tense during the Indo-Pakistan War of 1965, when East Pakistan was virtually cut off from the West and left on its own to defend its 55,126 square miles of territory and 75 million people with barely 10,000 soldiers. Their failure to enter into the system during the elections of 1965 had considerably influenced the élites in deciding to take to the politics of regional autonomy. In 1966 Sheikh Mujibur Rahman gave a regional colour to his party – the Awami League – and put forth his six-point programme, which asked for East Pakistan's full regional autonomy (financial, military and political), confinement of federal responsibility only to matters of defence and foreign affairs, and direct election to legislatures on the basis of adult franchise. For President Ayub this was a 'horrid dream' which would spell disaster for the country and turn the people of East Pakistan into slaves. Ayub resorted to some repressive measures, mild by authoritarian standards. Mujibur Rahman was arrested, and later, during the course of the maelstrom which swept over the whole of Pakistan in 1968 and early 1969 and was characterised by general strikes, looting and burning of public properties, a few more leaders (Bhutto, Abdul Wali Khan, Maulana Bhashani) were arrested. Parties were not banned, nor were political leaders arrested wholesale.

Ayub fell seriously ill with a pulmonary embolism early in 1968. His illness gave rise to speculations about his successor, and at the same time infused more purpose and vigour into the political warfare.

By February 1969 Pakistan had fallen back into the state it was in immediately before the declaration of martial law in 1958. The whole country was almost paralysed by the general strikes called by the opposition parties. Administration had virtually collapsed in East Pakistan, where mobs of people roamed the streets looting and burning houses, and killing prominent supporters of Ayub. On 10 March 1969 Ayub made his last attempt to save the country from falling to pieces. He met the opposition leaders and conceded their demands for a federal parliamentary system of government with regional autonomy, and the election of legislatures by direct adult franchise. But he was quite adamant, even at this late hour, against conceding Mujibur Rahman's demands, which would have not only given more autonomy to East Pakistan but also have enabled the Bengali élites to dominate the federal government. The long-drawn-out war between West Pakistani and Bengali élites could not be resolved. As Ayub put it, he would on no account 'preside over the destruction of my country'. However, he was not prepared to hand his country back to the politicians. On 25 March 1969 Ayub stepped down from the Presidency, handing over power to the army's Commander-in-Chief, General Yahya Khan, who forthwith abrogated the 1962 constitution, declared martial law, and appointed himself as the chief martial-law administrator. On 31 March Yahya also assumed the presidency.

The main task of Yahya's regime was 'to seek a new political order which could maintain the status quo', although granting concessions to the Bengali counter-élite.[9] It thus began on a conciliatory note. Yahya projected the image of an unambitious military ruler determined to leave the affairs of the country in the hands of politicians when law and order was restored, elections held, and a constitution adopted; though he had good reasons for believing that this might not happen for quite some time to come. In the meantime, Yahya decided to play the role of an arbitrator among the conflicting and perhaps irreconcilable political groups. In November 1969 he announced his policies: election on the basis of universal franchise to be held in October 1970; the province of West Pakistan to be dissolved into its old four constituent provinces; East Pakistan representation to the National Assembly to be apportioned on the basis of population rather than parity with West Pakistan. The last was the most important concession Yahya made to the Bengali political élites. It held out to them the prospect of controlling the central structure of Pakistan. Their demand for full autonomy, however, was to be considered at a later stage by the newly constituted National Assembly. These policies were embodied in the Legal Framework Order (LFO) which Yahya promulgated on 30 March 1970. The LFO laid down the principles on which the constitution was to be based and also the distribution of the National Assembly seats among the five provinces of the country; of the total of 300 general seats in the National Assembly East Pakistan was allotted 162.

The elections scheduled to be held in October were postponed to December because of a severe cyclone disaster which struck East Pakistan. On 7 December 1970 Pakistan went to the polls for the first time since its independence. Mujibur Rahman's Awami League won the election, capturing 160 (over 53 per cent) of the seats. Bhutto's People's Party came second, capturing 81 (27 per cent) of the National Assembly's general seats.

Yahya Khan had tried to devise what one may call an arbitral (or mediatory) form of dictatorship. Its smooth operation depended on divisions and irreconcilability among the political élites. The election results were thus a disappointment to him, and of course a threat to the West Pakistani ruling class to which both he and Bhutto belonged. If the unity of Pakistan was to be maintained, then the situation which emerged out of the election demanded the immediate termination of military rule and transfer of power to Mujibur Rahman and his Awami Party. If Bhutto had reconciled himself to the situation, and submerged his personal ambition into the larger interest of his country, Yahya would have had no option but to make way for the succession of the Bengali élite to power. But mercifully for Yahya, Bhutto was not at all willing to abide by the verdict of the people. Bhutto could very well argue that it was not a 'national' verdict. Bengalis had voted virtually *en bloc* for Mujibur Rahman; his party had not acquired a single seat in West Pakistan. Bhutto had acquired all the eighty-one general seats for his party from West Pakistan. In effect it appeared that two nations had voted separately for their respective national parties. Must then one nation be 'swallowed' by the other merely because the latter happened to be more populous?

Bhutto thus stood for power-sharing at the centre. He would not give away the whole to Mujibur Rahman. Mujibur Rahman saw no reason for negotiation. He claimed the headship of the government. If that was withheld from him he threatened to opt for an independent Bangladesh. Yahya sought the last hope for his mediatory dictatorship in this growing polarisation of opposite forces. The period from December 1970 to March 1971 was marked by the postponement of the inauguration of the National Assembly, negotiations between Yahya, Bhutto and Mujibur Rahman, and deadlock. Yahya's personal interest induced him at one point in the negotiations (20 March 1971) to concede powers to Mujibur Rahman and Bhutto in the provinces, while retaining the federal powers in his own hands until a final settlement was reached. This was attacked by Bhutto as a 'massive betrayal of West Pakistan'. Mujibur Rahman could wait no longer. The Civil Disobedience Movement which he had started on 1 March was losing steam and becoming violent. On 23 March he then delivered an ultimatum asking for autonomy for East Pakistan within forty-eight hours. On 25 March Yahya resorted to a military solution. On that day Mujibur Rahman was arrested, the Awami League was banned, press consorship imposed, and a large number of Bengali civilians were killed. The following day the Awami League launched its resistance to the Pakistani army and declared the independence of Bangladesh.

Bangladesh, though theoretically conceived on 26 March, became a reality only on 16 December 1971 when the Pakistani army unconditionally surrendered to the Indian forces at Dacca. Even though the Bengali resistance (or liberation) forces – the Mukti Bahini comprising the Bengali elements in the Pakistani armed forces stationed in East Bengal, and the student guerrillas – fought relentlessly during those nine months from March to November, they would have made little headway on their own against Yahya's well-armed regular military forces, which by May had reoccupied all the major cities of East Pakistan. Indian intervention became imminent when India faced the problem of supporting about ten million East Pakistani refugees. If India was looking for a tenable excuse to intervene it was, on 3 December, mercifully provided by Yahya Khan himself, who to the utter surprise of India, first began the offensive by ordering the bombardment of a few Indian airports in the Punjab–UP region. That very day India declared war on Pakistan.

With the defeat and distintegration of Pakistan the second authoritarian phase in the country's history came to an end. Even to the last moment Yahya and his generals were reluctant to hand over power to the politicians. But the army was now very much discredited in West Pakistan (now Pakistan), and the middle-rank military officers supported a civilian take-over. On 20 December 1971 Yahya Khan handed over power to Bhutto.

One might have expected that after the breakaway of its eastern wing and the restoration of a civilian government, Pakistan would once and for all be free from regional strife, and progress steadily on democratic lines. But this was not to be. Regionalism raised its head in Baluchistan and the North West Frontier Province. It was directed against the dominance of the Punjab and against Bhutto, whose power was based in this most populous and prosperous of the four provinces of Pakistan. The National Awami Party (one of the opposition parties in the National Assembly and the dominant party in the provincial legislatures of Baluchistan and the North West Frontier Province) and its leader Abdul Wali Khan championed the cause of regionalism.

In the beginning the regionalists stood for more provincial autonomy and freedom from the Punjab–dominated centre, but in due course they became frustrated and desperate at the assumption by Bhutto of increasing powers for himself and the central government, and consequently they began agitating and plotting for independent states. It was in this way that Wali Khan and his party came to be associated with the demand for an independent Pakhtunistan state comprising the North West Frontier Province and perhaps the Pashto-speaking areas in Baluchistan.

Faced with an 'anti-national' opposition from the very beginning Bhutto abandoned whatever idea he may have had of reviving democracy. Instead he brought into being yet another variety of authoritarianism – constitutional autocracy. It was the same variety which Mrs Gandhi was to evolve in India during her emergency rule. What made it 'constitutional' was that almost all the authoritarian measures of the government, including the implementation of a new constitution or amendment of the existing one, were endorsed by a rubber-stamp parliament.

Though Bhutto lifted the martial law which had been in existence since 1969, he continued to govern the country under the emergency which had been declared at the outbreak of the 1971 Indo-Pakistan War. The ostensible reason he gave for its continuance was that it enabled him to carry out the 'revolutionary reforms': a ceiling on land ownership, quasi-nationalisation, remedying of some educational inequalities, and so on. Such reforms scarcely deserve so radical a description. In fact the emergency was continued to enable Bhutto to suppress opposition and regionalism.

While the emergency gave Bhutto enough room to out-manoeuvre the 'anti-national' forces, the constitution of 1973 (Pakistan's third constitution adapted by the National Assembly in April) vested him with almost absolute power. This constitution turned Pakistan into a federal system of parliamentary democracy (with a bicameral legislature and a figurehead president) and vested the Prime Minister with the supreme executive power. The Prime Minister was to be elected by the National Assembly through an openly recorded vote. This, together with certain other provisions of the constitution and the Political Parties Act of 1962, made it almost impossible for a motion of no confidence to be carried against Prime Minister Bhutto. In this respect the Pakistan constitution was very similar to Ferdinand Marcos's constitution of the Republic of the Philippines which appeared in the same year. In both constitutions the office of Prime Minister was made supreme and secured against any likely encroachment on its powers by the nominal President. Bhutto held his constitution as the culmination of 'Pakistan's long quest for a new identity'.[10]

However, with the increase in Prime Minister Bhutto's powers the opposition grew more restless, violent and united. Bhutto had to use additional devices. In February 1975 he banned the National Awami Party on the grounds that it had been attempting to establish an independent state of Pakhtunistan through large-scale insurgency, terrorism and sabotage. In October of the same year the Supreme Court upheld the ban as justified. This was by no means a case in point of the judiciary playing second fiddle to the government. In fact the judiciary asserted its independence against the government in a number of cases. As a result in September 1976 the constitution was amended, for the fifth time, in order to curb the independence and power of the judiciary. Bhutto said that the amendment was necessary to stop superior courts allowing bail to people involved in delicate cases of national security.[11] The constitution which had been originally framed with all-party agreement, had now had amended one-fifth of all its provisions, giving it a definite partisan character.

His need to acquire legitimacy for his regime, his belief that 'he was needed by the people',[12] and his conviction that the opposition was too weak to pose any serious challenge to his party at the election – these were the three main factors which urged Bhutto to go to the polls. Early in January 1977 he announced that elections to the parliament and provincial legislatures would be held respectively on 7 and 10 March. (It was sheer coincidence that Mrs Gandhi having done her own calculations made the announcement, on 18 January, two weeks or so after Bhutto's, of the Indian parliamentary election on 16 March. It is most unlikely that she took this decision merely to keep pace with Bhutto, as the latter claimed.[13]) Nine right-wing opposition parties united and formed the Pakistan National Alliance to contest the election. Their joint programme seemed reactionary and anti-modern. It demanded, for instance, that women must not be allowed to vote and that affairs of state must be run according to the Holy Koran. Without Abdul Wali Khan, who was in prison, and his banned National Awami Party, the opposition seemed poor and ineffective by comparison with Bhutto's Pakistan People's Party. For the thirty million voters, involved in this second general election since the country's independence, authoritarianism had been the rule of their political life, democracy an exception. Bhutto's party won the election, acquiring 155 of the 200 seats in the National Assembly and a majority of seats in each of the four provincial legislatures.

The opposition, however, did not take its defeat in good part. It attributed its defeat to alleged widespread rigging organised by Bhutto. Consequently, it launched a nation-wide civil disobedience movement against Bhutto's government. The religious and chauvinistic programme of the opposition appealed to some disgruntled and 'alienated' members of the urban middle class. The confrontation between the government and the opposition resulted in several riots and the loss of many lives. In April 1977 martial law was imposed on three of Pakistan's main cities, and from then onward Bhutto began relying on the army for the restoration of law and order.

We cannot answer with any degree of certainty the question why Bhutto did not become ruthlessly dictatorial at this point and use all his powers to crush the opposition. 'Suffocating, though mercifully inefficient dictatorship' – is the verdict an Indian journalist cast on the rule of Bhutto as well as of Mrs Gandhi and Mrs Bandaranaike – all of whom lost power within a space of five months from March to July 1977.[14] But then this does not answer the question why they had to be 'inefficient' or 'liberal'. Was it the British legacy of parliamentary democracy, or President Carter's campaign for the protection of human rights and political freedom, or the upbringing and education of the individual rulers which, separately or jointly, inhibited the authoritarians from forsaking the need to legitimise their regimes and becoming ruthless and indifferent towards their people? Leaving aside these factors, who impact on the psyche of these authoritarians cannot be precisely assessed, there was always this fear of being eventually ousted by the generals which prevented the civilian authoritarians from severing their link with the people and relying heavily on the military. Particularly in the case of Pakistan, where the military had become involved in politics during the regimes of Ayub and Yahya Khan, there was a real danger to Bhutto in liberally using the armed forces to crush the opposition.

Bhutto seemed to be aware of this, for in order to avoid this happening he tried to propitiate the opposition. In May he proposed to hold a referendum to decide whether he should continue as Prime Minister. When this was rejected by the opposition, Bhutto went so far as to agree, in June 1977, to hold a fresh election in the autumn of the same year. On 3 July the opposition (PNA), objecting to certain provisions in the agreement, rejected the offer. This by no means looked like a final breakdown of the negotiations. But for the military it seemed the right moment to intervene. On 5 July 1977 General Muhammad Zia-al-Huq, the Pakistan Army Chief-of-Staff, overthrew Bhutto's government, suspended the constitution, dissolved national and provincial legislatures, and began his martial-law regime.

Like General Yahya Khan, General Zia projected the image of an unambitious soldier of Islam. The very day he took over the government he said that his martial-law regime intended to restore democracy to Pakistan in the space of three months. He announced that fresh elections would be held in October. After spending a few weeks in 'protective custody' the political leaders, including Bhutto, were released to commence their election campaigns.

During August when Bhutto began electioneering he drew large crowds. General Zia realised that Bhutto was still a great political force. Holding the election thus became too risky for General Zia. For his personal security he would have liked the Pakistan National Alliance to win the election. For if Bhutto won he was sure to bring high treason proceedings against the General for deposing the Prime Minister. Zia thus resolved first to destroy Bhutto as a political force and then to hold the election. Bhutto must be proved to be an 'evil genius' and thoroughly discredited in the eyes of the people. On 3 September 1977 Bhutto was arrested in connection with a political murder which had taken place in 1974. Zia argued that it was essential that the electorate be made fully aware of 'the true face of all candidates'. On 26 September, when the Supreme Court intervened to examine the propriety of the martial-law order under which Bhutto was arrested, Zia reacted by dismissing the Chief Justice of the Court. Bhutto began to acquire the air of a martyr. On 1 October 1977 Zia postponed indefinitely the election scheduled for 18 October. He announced that a new election date would be arranged only after Bhutto had been tried on all the criminal charges he faced.

The promise which Zia made at the time of the *coup*, that his regime would be only an interregnum, he has so far failed to fulfil for reasons which, as he has tried to induce the people to believe, are beyond his control. In November 1977 the Supreme Court blessed his *coup* by upholding the view that the imposition of martial law was an 'extra-constitutional step necessitated by the complete breakdown and erosion of the constitutional and moral authority of the Bhutto Government'.[15] In January 1978 the prospects for elections in Pakistan further receded with the appointment by General Zia of a council of sixteen advisers, comprising generals, senior civil servants and a few retired politicians. Zia has not yet evolved any political system of his own except for expressing his preference for a presidential system of government (which of course would enable him to move easily into the presidential chair), and his opinion that the future constitution of Pakistan must provide constitutional rights for the armed forces to intervene in political crises.

On 19 March 1978 the Punjab High Court found Bhutto guilty and sentenced him to death. The Supreme Court of Pakistan commenced hearing the appeal in May. A week or so before the Supreme Court judges were to deliver their judgement on Bhutto's appeal, General Zia's administration published a few White Papers in which Bhutto was accused of having misused his powers, while in office, to subvert parliament, undermine the judiciary, and cripple the economy of the country for short-term party political gains. The timing of the publication of the White Papers suggested that Zia was trying either to influence the judges, or to prepare the people of Pakistan to accept the fate which was to befall Bhutto. General Zia had been in a great dilemma. He would be risking his own personal safety by letting Bhutto live, for whether in prison or exile Bhutto was most likely to come back into power, if and when the election was held. Even if Bhutto was disqualified from contesting any election, his wife, the leader of her husband's People's Party, could successfully contest the election, capture power and re-install Bhutto on the throne. Hanging Bhutto might shock foreign powers and possibly plunge Pakistan into a state of anarchy, but keeping him alive augured personal disaster for Zia and his collaborators.

On 6 February 1979 the Supreme Court judges gave their verdict on Bhutto's appeal; four of the judges upheld his death sentence, the remaining three, disagreeing with the majority, held the view that the prosecution had completely failed to prove its case. This division among the judges raised a ray of hope for Bhutto's life. Many heads of governments appealed to Zia to show mercy and spare Bhutto's life. Bhutto's lawyers filed a review petition to the judges. The judges were this time unanimous in rejecting the review petition, but at the same time they indicated that arguments for a lighter sentence were 'relevant for consideration by the executive authorities in the exercise of their prerogative of mercy', suggesting there were grounds for following that course. The court announcement meant that for the second time a decision on Bhutto's life came to rest with General Zia. But the General was determined to go ahead, rather stealthily, with the execution of the former Prime Minister of Pakistan. In the early hours of 4 April 1979, death came to Bhutto, not with the due panoply of justice, but like a thief in the night.

In March, just before the hanging of Bhutto, General Zia had gone on record promising a general election to be held on 17 November 1979. The execution did not cause any widespread furore or riots, mainly because of the fear of ruthless suppression the martial law regime held out to those who publicly displayed any grief and anger. But the wife and daughter of Bhutto at once became the subject of people's silent support and sympathy. As the leaders of the Pakistan People's Party, Mrs Nusrat Bhutto and the twenty-seven-year-old Miss Benazir Bhutto now became a threat to Zia. The Pakistan

People's Party seemed bent on gaining a landslide victory if an election were to be held. In August, Zia amended the Political Parties Act of 1962 in order to make it compulsory for all political parties to register with the Pakistan Election Commission. Any party which received money from abroad, worked against the Islamic ideology, propagated violence, or created hatred against the armed forces or the judiciary was to be disqualified from contesting the national election. Members of such a party were also to be debarred from contesting elections in their individual capacity. Zia then ordered the local elections to be held in September. Political parties were not allowed to contest these elections. It was not, however, difficult for the voters to identify the political affiliations of the candidates. As a result, candidates having clandestine support from the Pakistan People's Party won sixty to eighty per cent of the seats. The election results were thus discomforting to Zia.

If the law requiring the political parties to register with the Election Commission was in any way intended to be a trap for them, then here lay a further disappointment for Zia. Of the eighty-odd political parties, not more than fifty applied for registration. The two major national parties of Pakistan – the PPP and the PNA – did not comply. The PPP of the Bhuttos was indeed Zia's main target. Proceedings had already been launched against Mrs Nusrat Bhutto to disqualify her from politics. When Benazir Bhutto decided to contest the elections, even without her Pakistan People's Party having become duly registered, she was banned from doing so. Zia was rid of the Bhutto ladies and the PPP, but to proceed with the election, that is if he ever intended to hold it, without the participation of the national parties would have looked undemocratic and almost phoney. In the first week of October, Zia relaxed his rigid restrictions on political parties in an attempt to bring the Pakistan National Alliance into his fold. Perhaps it was the last of Zia's performances devised to assure the Pakistanis, and possibly the outside world, that in spite of the circumstances most unfavourable to the revival of democracy in Pakistan he was determined to hold the election and let himself and the military return to the barracks.

However, in less than ten days after this last performance, Zia's 'faith' in the Western-style democracy and his determination to hold the elections suddenly flagged. On 16 October 1979, Zia cancelled the general elections, banned all political parties, imposed strict censorship on the press, tightened the martial law control, and imprisoned a few hundred politicians including Nusrat and Benazir Bhutto. A few days after, on 21 October, Zia declared that he would create an Islamic state which would have no room for the secular democratic system of the West and the Western-type elections based on universal franchise. In Zia's Islamic state only practising Muslims were to be nominated as election candidates and not everyone was to have the right to vote, certainly not the majority of Pakistani women. Whether or not this projected Islamic state would create conditions in which, as Zia hopes, 'investors will not be afraid of investing, parents will not be afraid of sending their children to school, and voters will not be afraid of politicians coming to power', this state might at least succeed in destroying the prospect of a woman becoming the ruler of Pakistan. President Zia may find in this Islamic order his personal security and salvation but it is doubtful whether Pakistan, which has so far alternated between nights of the generals and brief dawns of democracy, will find in this system its stability, purpose and identity.

NEPAL

The suspension of democracy in Nepal for the second time in December 1960 has been called by some the royal *coup*, suggesting that it was unnecessary and unjustified, if not down-right illegal. This second royal take-over was accompanied by a declaration of emergency under the constitution of 1959, which vested the King with the powers to suspend or abrogate, both in times of peace and war, part or whole of the constitution. This time King Mahendra made it very clear that his direct rule was not going to be a temporary affair. The Western form of democracy was now finally rejected as alien, wasteful and unsuited to the Nepali genius. All political parties were banned and the Prime Minister, B. P. Koirala, among others, was put into prison.

However, the days had passed even for a king to use no fig leaf to conceal his autocratic rule. It had in fact become a common practice among the authoritarians to seek some security for their system by disguising it in the veil of a people's Raj. Besides, King Mahendra had a special factor to reckon with. His next-door-neighbour Nehru was shocked and aggrieved at this royal *coup*.[16] And it would not have been for the first time if Nehru had decided to intervene in the internal affairs of Nepal. King Mahendra was thus obliged immediately to acquire a viable legitimacy for his Raj. This he did by evolving his own brand of 'purest democracy' – the Panchayati Raj. Though very much like Ayub's Basic Democracy it was by no means an importation. It had its rudiments in the Nepali constitution of 1948, in which the Rana regime had tried to revive the traditional local bodies called *Panchayats*. However, President Ayub (head of an Islamic state) and King Mahendra (head of a Hindu state) met in September 1961 and praised each other's systems. They had come to have in common a home-grown system and, of course, were both feared by India, which carried the largest democratic structure in the world.

Panchayat democracy was established by means of various acts and the new constitution of 1962. The system came to be based on two separate pillars, each with village to national level organisation. Panchayat structure was one pillar and class organisation the other. The four-tier Panchayat framework consisted of the village Panchayat, the district Panchayat, the zonal Panchayat, together with their respective assemblies or *sabhas*, and the Rastriya Panchayat (the unicameral National Legislature) at the highest level. As in Ayub's Basic Democracy so in Mahendra's Panchayat Raj, universal franchise was relegated to the bottom level; only the village and town assemblies, comprising the adult population of their respective areas, directly elected the members of their respective councils or Panchayats. Members of the three higher bodies (district, zonal and national) were to be indirectly elected. About 4000 village and town Panchayats, with a total of about 40,000 directly elected councillors, were brought into being. The members of all village and town Panchayats in a district formed the district assembly, which in turn elected from among its members an 11-member district Panchayat. Likewise, members of all district Panchayats in a particular zone constituted the zonal assembly and elected the zonal Panchayat. The national legislature (Rastriya Panchayat) was to consist of 125 members, of whom 16 were to be nominated by the King. Of the 109 elected members, 90 were to be elected by the 14 zonal assemblies (each of the 75 districts of Nepal was to have at least one representative in the national legislature), 15 to be elected by the class organisations, and 4 by the constituency of registered university graduates.

Five class organisations, each with a Panchayat type four-tier pyramidal structure, were constituted. They were peasants, youth, women, ex-servicemen and labour organisations. Official control here was more pronounced than in the Panchayat sector. It was the government which appointed the fifteen-member Central Committee for each of these class organisations. Whereas the Panchayati system was designed to foster a partyless political system, the class organisations were intended to crush class conflicts. The class organisations were given organisational monopoly in their respective spheres, as parallel unofficial organisations were not permitted to function. At the same time the King impresssed upon the five official class organisations that in the course of national advancement each of them must, to a certain extent, renounce its class interests.

Over and above the Panchayati and class organisations, which lent a representative character to royal despotism, the King created a

Council of National Guidance with himself as its chairman. The Council was to guide and co-ordinate the activities of the Panchayats and class organisations. In 1967 this was to be replaced by the 'Back to the Village' National Campaign, with a Central Committee of eight members. The objectives of the National Campaign covered all aspects of the country's life. It was King Mahendra's version of Mao Tse-tung's Cultural Revolution, with the difference that the National Campaign was intended to preserve rather than destroy the old order.

The constitution of 1962 vested all powers – executive, legislative and judicial – in the King. The King could amend or suspend all or any of the articles of the constitution. Under the constitution the National Panchayat came to occupy the position of an advisory rather than a sovereign assembly. The King was to appoint the Prime Minister and ministers from amongst the members of the National Panchayat, but the ministers were not to remain responsible to the legislature. The constitution also imposed a number of restrictions on the independence of the Supreme Court, which was virtually debarred from enquiring whether the substance of any particular law, passed by the King 'in the public interest', was *ultra vires* of the spirit of the constitution.

The first elections to village and town Panchayats were held between February and May 1962. Elections to the higher Panchayati bodies were completed by March 1963. On 14 April 1963 King Mahendra formally inaugurated the 125-member National Panchayat. In October of the same year he proudly asserted that his Panchayat system was 'more progressive than communism and more democratic than the parliamentary system'. At any rate, the King succeeded in giving to his regime the appearance of a representative government – 'a government by villagers, for villagers, and of villagers', as one of his loyal ministers described the system. However, in theory as well as in practice, none of the various bodies the King erected from the village to the national level handled any real power. They were created primarily to absorb the aspiring élites and make them ineffective. The very proliferation of political bodies at national level, a ploy used by other authoritarians as well, was designed to balance them against each other and consequently to ensure the continuation of the monarch's supremacy and dominance over the Nepali polity.

In January 1972 King Mahendra died and was succeeded by his son Birendra, who soon affirmed his commitment to his father's party-less Panchayat system. A growing demand among the intelligentsia for the restoration of democracy, together with a threat of armed insurrection as occasionally posed by Nepali political exiles in India, led the King to appoint a constitutional commission. In 1975 the commission came out with its report, which among other things criticised, to the King's chagrin, the present system and recommended such liberal measures as the widening of franchise, the appointment of the Prime Minister by the National Panchayat, and the formation of political parties. The collapse of democracy in India in the same year, however, turned the tide against liberalism, enabling King Birendra to ignore the commission's recommendations. The constitutional changes the King eventually introduced in December 1975 did in fact betray his uncompromising attitude towards liberalism. Through this second amendment to the 1962 constitution the King abolished the four seats hitherto reserved for graduates in the National Panchayat.[17] Candidates standing for these seats were the only ones who could issue election manifestos, which often demanded sweeping liberal reforms in the constitution. At the same time he turned the 'Go to the Village National Campaign' committee into a constitutional body with immense powers. From now on it was to act as a political watchdog and virtually became the politburo of the Panchayat system. The same year, following Mrs Gandhi's example, the King imposed stricter control on press and banned a number of newspapers.

With the restoration of democracy in India in March 1977, King Birendra's complacency was slightly ruffled. But his response to the call of the times was not to move, beyond slightly increasing the role of direct elections in the political process, releasing political prisoners and allowing several banned newspapers to appear. These liberal measures, however, enabled Nepal to advance early in 1978, from the category of 'not free' to 'partly free' nations.[18] The King, none the less, continues to reign as well as rule, refusing to recognise the obsolescence of monarchy, and as determined as ever to play a dynamic role in the politics of the country.

BURMA

Territorially Burma is the fourth largest country in South and South-east Asia, after India, Indonesia and Pakistan. The country has its fair share of mountainous regions, which on the one hand isolate it from its neighbours and on the other provide safe hide-outs for insurgents and guerrillas. Here in Burma the secessionist movement among the ethnic minorities has been the strongest. The Shans and Kayahs, for example, had been given the right under the 1947 constitution to secede, if they still wished, after ten years. The occasion for the March 1962 *coup* was in fact the Shans' threat to secede if their demand for a further measure of independence was not conceded.

The system of socialist democracy or democratic centralism,

which the military rulers of Burma evolved between March 1962 and December 1973, was distinguishable from other authoritarian systems in that it had a definite flavour of communism. And yet it was by no means a communist order. In fact one of the main objectives of the regime throughout has been to suppress communist insurgency. As Ne Win declared in July 1971, his government was to steer, in the Buddhist fashion, the middle path between the rightists (as represented by the deposed Prime Minister U Nu) and the leftists (comprising Burma's two communist parties – the pro-Peking 'white flag' and the Stalinist 'Red Flag'). Ne Win's system resembled a communist order only in the structure of its one-party rule, its excessive nationalisation of the means of production, and the verbal homage it paid to Marxism. Like the ancient Hindu religious leaders of India who adopted Buddha as one of the Hindu gods in order to annihilate Buddhism, Ne Win strove to neutralise the communist challenge by dressing his system in the style of a communist order.

The evolution of Burmese socialist democracy was marked first by the declaration of a political philosophy, then by the foundation of an official political party and finally by the adoption of a constitution. It took over ten years for the system finally to emerge. The process started with an explicit denunciation of parliamentary democracy. The military junta affirmed that Western democracy was full of flaws and loopholes and its working in the emergent countries had only led to an internecine struggle for power between political élites. In some countries, it was further averred, the parliament had been so abused as to have become only the means by which opportunists and propertied people deceived the simple masses. The same document (issued on 30 April 1962 by the Revolutionary Council and entitled *The Burmese Way to Socialism*), which decried Western democracy, committed Burma to the traditional Marxist socialism. The Revolutionary Council, however, conceded that Marxism needed to be modified in order to suit the circumstances of Burma. While some private enterprise was to be allowed, all the vital means of production were to be nationalised. By the end of 1965 the Burmese Revolutionary Government had in fact succeeded in nationalising the entire oil industry, banking, foreign trade, domestic wholesale trade, the timber and tobacco industries, and most of the mining industry.

The system was to be based on the support of the peasants and workers, who were described as 'the vanguard and custodians' of a socialist democratic state. At the very outset of his rule General Ne Win had promised that he was eventually going to transfer power to the 'revolutionary party' of the working people. As a first step towards this, the Revolutionary Council constituted the Burma

Socialist Programme Party (BSPP) on 4 July 1962. During the 'transitional period' this official political party, with its three central committees, was to be tightly controlled by the Revolutionary Council. Candidate members had to pass through a two-year probationary period before attaining full membership of the party. All membership applications had to be supported by two members. Since the only members were the Revolutionary Council, the initial membership was hand-picked from the armed services and closely identified with the *coup* members. Power was to be transferred to this party when it had fully blossomed with its units stretching downward to village level. In March 1963 the BSPP began to enrol members. Continuing opposition to the government, particularly from the ethnic minorities, was finally destroyed in March 1964, when the Revolutionary Council banned all political parties other than the BSPP. By mid-1971 the BSPP attained maturity. It had by then acquired 73,369 full members, 42,359 of whom were members of the armed forces.[19] Accordingly, in July 1971 the BSPP was officially transformed into a people's party. At the same time the party's first Congress was convened. The Congress constituted its 150-man Central Committee. Further, it constituted the fifteen-man Revolutionary Council headed by Ne Win, who also remained the Chairman of the BSPP. The Revolutionary Council in turn appointed an eleven-man all-military government with Ne Win as Prime Minister. Ne Win and his colleagues thus came to acquire legitimacy for their government from the 'people's party', which was essentially created and controlled by them. Emboldened by this symbol of people's support, Ne Win resigned his military rank, in April 1972, and became a civilian Prime Minister. He dropped 'General', adopted U (the Burmese title of respect used before a man's name) and henceforth became U Ne Win. But in fact the new 'civilian' government was essentially military without uniforms. There were only two real civilians in the Cabinet. The army dominated all levels of administration, from the Secretariat in Rangoon down to the villages. This was done through the Security and Administration Committees (SACs) which functioned at all levels with army officers as their chairmen.

The decision to draft a constitution was taken by the BSPP in June 1971. Technically the 1947 constitution still existed because the *coup* government had neither repealed nor suspended it. But in practice the old constitution had been substantially eroded by new rules, regulations and ordinances of the Revolutionary Government. As the chairman of the Revolutionary Council, General Ne Win exercised all legislative, judicial and executive powers which under the 1947 constitution were vested in the President and Prime Minister.

As a result, Ne Win had succeeded in introducing a number of radical changes including the abolition of the Supreme and High Courts and the creation in their place of a new Chief Court of Burma. A new constitution was thus overdue. By March 1973 its drafting was completed. In December of the same year it was put to a referendum. It acquired an overwhelming majority of 'yes' votes from the people. Accordingly, on 4 January 1974, the day of the twenty-sixth anniversary of the country's independence, the new constitution was inaugurated.

The constitution created a unicameral central legislature – the People's Assembly – of 450 members to be directly elected by the people every four years. Councils were also created for states, divisions, townships and villages. The highest organ of the state, however, was to be the twenty-nine-member State Council to be elected by the People's Assembly. The State Council was to be responsible for policy-making and was to exercise judicial and executive powers. The Chairman of the State Council was to be the President of the Republic of Burma. The People's Assembly was also to elect an eighteen-member Council of Ministers, which was to exercise executive powers under the supervision of the State Council. For administrative purposes the country was divided into seven states inhabited by national minorities, and seven administrative regions inhabited by the Burman population. The BSPP was constitutionally recognised as the only political party leading the state. Finally, the constitution declared that all natural resources, including land, were the property of the state.

From 27 January to 10 February 1974, the first elections under the constitution were held. 288,681 BSPP-nominated deputies were returned, 450 of them to the People's Assembly, 960 to the state and division Councils, over 20,000 to town councils and the rest to ward or village Councils. The People's Assembly met on 2 March 1974. It elected the State Council with Ne Win as Chairman and ex-officio President of the nation. It also elected the Council of Ministers with U Sein Win as Prime Minister. On the same day it was officially declared that the revolution that began on 2 March 1962 had ended and the power was now transferred to the people. Ne Win dissolved the Revolutionary Council. In reality, however, Burma continued to be ruled by the military junta which he headed. The ritual of electing the People's Assembly was to be repeated, after four years, in January 1978.

Burma's military authoritarian rule has seemed stronger and more stable than that of Pakistan, Bangladesh, even Thailand and Indonesia. The country's image of political strength has partly been nurtured by the isolationist policies it has rigidly followed since the *coup*. Of all the non-communist countries in this region of Asia Burma has been the only one to appear unconcerned about the West and Western values. It has pursued economic, social and political self-reliance to a chauvinist extreme. The country's strength might have also lain in the fact that of all the non-communist regimes hers has been the most ideologically oriented. However, Burma's strength, whether a reality or fiction, has not enabled her yet to resolve her basic problems. In the economic field excessive national-isation failed to satisfy the country's social and economic aspirations. In February 1977 General San Yu, General Secretary of the BSPP, told the party's congress that economic self-sufficiency could not be attained without capital investment and technical assistance from abroad.[20] In September of the same year the tempo of nationalisation was relaxed. President Ne Win promulgated the Private Enterprise Law which opened six avenues to private entrepreneurs – agricul-ture, fishing, forestry, mining and industry and transport. Foreign co-operation and aid, and expansion of private enterprise might make inroads into the Burmese way to socialism and bring the country into line with other authoritarian countries of South and South-east Asia. In the political arena, opposition to Ne Win's democratic centralism has throughout persisted among the national minorities, communist guerrillas have been operating on Burma's exiled in Thailand. The National Democratic Front of various warring ethnic minorities has been operating from its hide-out on the Burma–Thailand border. More formidable than the national minorities, Communist guerrillas have been operating on Burma's north-eastern border with China. In November 1977 the Burmese army killed over 500 of them but the communist threat has by no means been overcome. When in 1976 the Chief-of-Staff and Defence Minister, General Tin U, was sacked, and together with fourteen other young army officers brought to trial for conspiring to assassi-nate President Ne Win and overthrow the government,[21] the Bur-mese system appeared to be denuded of its only distinguishing feature – its security.

INDONESIA

The Indonesian substitute for liberal democracy – Guided Demo-cracy – was evolved by Sukarno. In 1968, General Suharto inherited the system and has since then made 'improvements' upon it.

For personal as well as objective reasons, Sukarno had become a detractor of parliamentary democracy while it operated in In-donesia, rather precariously, between 1949 and 1959. Indonesia's constitution of 1945 (framed by the nationalists within weeks of the

Japanese surrender on 15 August 1945) had been superseded by the constitutions of 1949 and 1950, both of which placed effective power in the hands of the Prime Minister and a cabinet dependent on parliamentary support, and which assigned a mere figurehead role to the President. President Sukarno resented the limitations imposed upon him. If he had wished he could have become Prime Minister and exercised effective powers. But he wanted to remain high above political parties, hold the highest office of the nation, and at the same time exercise general leadership and power. This was not possible in a parliamentary form of government.

Sukarno, however, attacked the system on objective grounds. Being based on the principles of conflict and competition, Western democracy, he argued, encouraged on the one hand the divisive forces in society and on the other the coercion of minorities by mere majorities, and was, therefore, essentially unsuited to the consensual mode of life which characterised the Indonesian tradition.[22] Western liberalism and individualism, he alleged, had poisoned the social consciousness, broken the unity and cohesion of Indonesian society and bred the cancer of regionalism, groupism and multipartism. Sukarno particularly attacked the three 'malignant' features of parliamentary democracy – party politics, the rule of majority, and territorial representation. This Western import, therefore, had to be replaced by something Indonesian or Eastern.

In his Guided Democracy, therefore, the importance of political parties was to be undermined, the Western mode of arriving at decisions by majority votes was to be replaced by the Indonesian alternative (as practised by the old village assemblies) of reaching consensus by deliberation and consultation, and territorial representation was to give way to functional representation. This system was to be headed by an all-powerful leader who would guide and discipline the people in making unanimous decisions and living a harmonious life.

Between July 1959 and August 1960 the structure and ideology of Guided Democracy were evolved. Each stage in the evolution of Guided Democracy was marked by the destruction or mutilation of a liberal institution. The beginning was made in July 1959 when Sukarno dissolved the Constituent Assembly and declared the constitution of 1945 operative by decree. Undoubtedly the decree was unconstitutional. The 1950 constitution gave no such power to the President. But Sukarno acted in accordance with the 'wishes of the people'. The army and the cabinet, anyway, had expressed their preference for the 1945 constitution. But the Constituent Assembly, which had led an ineffective existence since its formation in 1955 at the double elections (for a parliament and a constituent assembly), voted against the adoption of the 1945 constitution.

Soon after the promulgation of the 1945 constitution, Sukarno, now holding the offices of both President and Prime Minister, formed the cabinet. None of the major party leaders was included. The armed services' representation in it rose to eleven. Members of the cabinet, high civil servants and senior men in government enterprises were instructed to renounce political party membership. Members of the existing parliament were required to take an oath of loyalty to the new constitution. Parliament itself was deprived of its rights of enquiry and interpellation. Party politicians accepted their humiliation in silence. However, when in March 1960 the parliament unexpectedly showed its independence by rejecting the government budget, Sukarno immediately dissolved it and enacted the budget by decree. In June 1960 he nominated a new parliament – a *gotong royong* (mutual help) parliament as he called it – which was to sit until new elections were held. This appointed parliament consisted of 283 members, of whom 130 were party representatives and 153 were representatives from functional groups – army, navy, air force, police, workers, peasants, Islamic authorities, youth, women, intellectuals and educators. The new parliament was required to legislate by unanimity. If this proved impossible it was required to refer the particular matter back to the President.

Sukarno banned only two political parties – Masjumi and PSI (Socialist Party) – on the ground that they were involved in the 1958 separatist Sumatra rebellion against the central government. Other political parties were allowed to function but under such conditions as denied them any effective role. By decree President Sukarno set out various ideological tenets to which parties were required to assent. Further, all parties were required to submit membership lists to the government. A party with less than the prescribed minimum of 150,000 members was not allowed to exist. A further blow to party politics was administered when, in the years 1960 and 1961, Sukarno appointed new regional assemblies to replace the elected ones. Governors as heads of first-level regions (roughly equivalent to provinces) were appointed by the President and were to be solely responsible to him. Each region came to be ruled by a triumvirate of the regional military commander, the governor and the police chief. A combination of low-ranking military, civil and police officers ruled at sub-regional and village levels. To undermine further the importance of political parties as well as to acquire a direct link with the people President Sukarno appointed a fifty-eight-man Central Board of the National Front. All functional group candidates for central and provincial assemblies were to be chosen through the National Front. The National Front was virtually a government party. Sukarno did not go too far in turning it into a strong party; he feared that it might come under army control. Besides, some of the political parties (PNI, NU and PKI) were functioning more as his allies than as his opponents. Sukarno was content to base his personal autocratic rule on the balance of power between the armed forces, the Communist Party (PKI) and the National Front.

The main feature of the 1945 constitution was the provision for a strong executive president who was to be responsible not to parliament but to a larger body of 616 members – the People's Deliberative Assembly or Congress (MPR) – formally the highest organ of the state under the constitution. The MPR was to consist of all the members of parliament and others chosen as representatives of regions and groups. It was to meet at least once in five years and elect the President. In 1960 Sukarno appointed the provisional MPR. Since the MPR was a large body and met once in five years, the 1945 constitution provided for another deliberative body – the Supreme Advisory Council, DPA – which was to meet frequently and which was intended to provide for the President an alternative source of advice to that available from his cabinet. Sukarno formed the DPA of 43 members with himself as its chairman; 12 seats in the DPA were given to the leaders of 10 political parties, 8 to representatives of the regions, and the remaining 23 to representatives of functional groups.

These were thus the main institutions of Guided Democracy. The main component of each of these institutions was formed of functional representation. Unanimity or consensus was the main code of conduct set for both the central and regional bodies. Ten political parties were allowed to function but under conditions which took away competitiveness from them. The Civil Service went through the process of 're-tooling', by which civil servants of doubtful loyalty were replaced by others who were sympathetic to the regime. Critics of the regime were placed under house arrest. Indoctrination courses were adopted at the universities; university dons still showing the signs of 'lingering liberalism' were removed. The press was brought under strict control. Legal institutions were deprived of their autonomy. In February 1960 the Chairman of the Supreme Court was made a member of the cabinet and later in the year Sukarno denounced the very principle of the separation of powers. In fact the administration of justice became 'an ancillary aspect of the maintenance of government power'.[23] However, Sukarno's regime did not become harshly coercive. There was no brutal elimination of opposition, and there were no concentration camps.

There was much sincerity and some faith involved in Sukarno's rejection of the alien liberal democracy and his 'returning to our own national personality '. His speech entitled 'The Rediscovery of Our

Revolution', which he delivered on 17 August 1959, became the manifesto of Guided Democracy. It consisted of five ideas – the 1945 constitution, Socialism à la Indonesia, Guided Democracy, Guided Economy and Indonesian Personality – and the first letters of these five phrases were put together to make the acronym USDEK.[24] With 'Political Manifesto' shortened to 'Manipol' the new creed became known as Manipol–USDEK. Though vaguely conceived and incoherently expounded, the emphasis of the creed, as can be discerned, was on all pulling together, on national interests being put above group interests, and on the possibility of coming to unanimous agreement through patient consultation.[25] These constituted in Sukarno's thinking a return to Indonesia's own national personality.

The political apparatus which Sukarno forged has since his fall in 1966 been operative under President Suharto's regime. Suharto introduced only a few changes, which were by no means fundamental. For example, he raised the membership of the parliament to 460 and of the MPR (People's Congress) to 920. This was done partly to enlarge military representation and consequently presidential control over these bodies. Further, Sukarno's National Front was turned into Sekber Golkar (Joint Secretariat of Functional Groups) in 1968 and brought under government control. This was done to provide President Suharto's regime with a civilian basis. Golkar became a federation of 260 trade, professional and regional organisations, ranging from civil servants, teachers, journalists and students to village chiefs, farmers and fishermen. Though virtually a government party, Golkar is technically not a political party because civil servants, who are not allowed to join political parties, can be its members. Like Sukarno, President Suharto insisted, rather obsessively, on consensus, unanimity and harmony. However, one may bear in mind that insistence on consensus gave some practical advantage to the President. All the matters on which no consensus could be reached in any of the various rubber-stamp assemblies had to be referred to the President.

Suharto's regime differed from Sukarno's in some ways. Suharto did not have to balance his power on continuing rivalry between the communists and the armed forces. The communists ceased to be a force in Indonesian politics after the *coup* of 1965. Those who survived the great massacre which followed the abortive *coup* were put into prison. The Communist Party was banned and its members disqualified from voting in the country's general elections. The military thus became the only effective political force, and here Suharto succeeded in integrating the hitherto separate and divided services under a single command. The archipelago was divided into seventeen military Area Commands (KODAMs) and each KODAM had similar commands at various administrative levels, down to the village, where the army was represented by a non-commissioned officer. But the KODAM commanders were stripped of their former non-military powers and responsibilities, and consequently they no longer had the same opportunities to establish themselves as 'war lords'.[26] On the debit side, however, Suharto lacks the charisma with which Sukarno abounded. Suharto is restrained, very traditional and cautious. He is often characterised in the Indonesian press as one who 'makes haste slowly' and avoids the 'spectacular'.[27] In the beginning his was a welcome change from the theatrical and slogan-charged regime of Sukarno. But after a time the people began to miss the charisma and came to regard Suharto's regime as lacking in a 'national purpose' and leadership. Though there has been no continuing resistance to his rule, in 1976 two separate plots to assassinate him and his family were discovered. Yet, looking at the decade of Suharto's rule from 1968 to 1978, one draws the impression that it has been smooth sailing throughout for him, and he has over the years acquired more of self-confidence, and a sense of personal security.

It was on 27 March 1968 that the People's Congress conferred the Presidency on Suharto unanimously, and he was accordingly sworn in as the country's second President for five years. He had been acting as President since March 1967. At the same time it was decided to hold general elections in July 1971. In January 1970 the government framed rules for the 1971 election. The President appointed the election committee of 20 members. Of the 460 members of parliament 360 were to be elected and 100 appointed by the government. All candidates for the election had to be approved beforehand by the Election Committee. During the election campaign all political parties were forbidden to criticise the government, discuss religious questions, or spread the ideas of the late Sukarno.

The July 1971 election was the second (the first being the 1955 election) in the country's history. Elections were held simultaneously for 360 seats in the parliament (House of Representatives), 884 seats in the 26 Provincial Assemblies, and 80 per cent of the seats in 281 Regency (District) Assemblies. Apart from appointing 100 to the parliament and a total of 221 to the Provincial Assemblies, the government was to fill by appointment 20 per cent of the seats in the Regency Assemblies. The elections were contested by 9 political parties (28 political parties had contested the 1955 elections) and the government-controlled Sekber Golkar. The government exercised much pressure on the electorate to support Golkar. As was expected, Golkar won all along the line, gaining 227 of the 360 elective seats in

the parliament.[28] In March 1973 the People's Congress re-elected
Suharto as President for another term of five years. There was of
course no other candidate for the presidency. The merger between
political parties continued, and the country's third general election,
held in May 1977, was contested by only 3 parties – the government-
sponsored Sekber Golkar, the United Development Party (PPP)
which had been formed in 1973 by the merger of 4 Islamic parties,
and the Indonesian Democratic Party (PDI) formed in 1973 by the
merger of 5 nationalist and Christian parties. As was expected again
Golkar won the elections, gaining 232 of the elected seats in the
parliament. The PPP gained 99 and PDI only 29. Both the opposition parties (PPP and PDI) alleged that the government exercised
pressure on the electorate to vote for Golkar. The People's Congress
(consisting of 460 members of the parliament and about 500 delegates appointed by the President) met in March 1978 and unanimously re-elected Suharto as President for another term of five years.
This time, however, there was some opposition to Suharto's re-
election among the students and journalists. Just before the People's
Congress meeting the government clamped down on the press,
temporarily closing six leading newspapers.[29] Also over 200 students
were taken into custody for interrogation.[30] There was also opposition from the PPP. In March 1978 the PPP, hitherto a junior partner
in the government, voiced strong opposition to some items of
government policy being drafted for the next five years, and its
members walked out of two committees and forced votes on at least
five issues. Such action had not been taken by any faction in either
the Parliament or the People's Congress since Suharto took over as
head of state in 1967.

The PPP, however, had to pay the price. In the last week of March
1978 when Suharto reshuffled his cabinet, he excluded both the PPP
and PDI representation from the cabinet. Both these parties had held
one ministry each in the former cabinet. At the same time Suharto
increased military representation to almost half, the military group
in the cabinet consisting mainly of generals who had actively helped
him crush the communist *coup* attempt of 1965. In the previous
cabinet less than a quarter of the posts were held by the military.

Now 57 (the usual age of retirement from the army being 55),
Suharto for the first time projected the image of a civilian President
by relinquishing his post of commander of the all-embracing Command for the Restoration of Security and Order (Kopkamtib) and
appointing Admiral Sudomo in his place. This was in keeping with
the style common among the military rulers, the generals of Thailand excepted. The same pattern, as established by General Ayub of
Pakistan in 1965 and General Ne Win of Burma in 1974, was adopted

by General Suharto in 1978. As a military Raj smacks of impermanence, the generals by discarding their uniforms and forging the
semblance, if not the reality, of a direct link with the masses, were in
effect trying to gain for their regimes stability, respectability and
security. President Ayub was carried away by his own image of
being the people's choice. Suharto is more cautious and restrained.
He is also the most fortunate among the authoritarians of South and
South-east Asia in the sense that there is no strong opposition to his
rule. In December 1977, 10,000 'communist' prisoners were released
after twelve years of detention without trial. A further 20,000
political prisoners remain in camps throughout the country, but the
government has promised to release them within two years. The
released prisoners had been thoroughly broken, all pledging loyalty
to the government of President Suharto and denouncing communism. It is unlikely that they will ever become subversive.

The achievements of Indonesia's authoritarian government are
few and all confined to the political sector. Political stability has been
achieved by suppressing regionalism, which was a strong force in
this country of 13,600 islands. The country is free from strikes,
separatism and insurgency, which elsewhere in this region continue
to undermine the strength of democratic governments. But the
government itself has become probably the most corrupt government in the world. The army is corrupt and it runs the economy as
all-powerfully as its politics. Of the 270,000 in the forces 20,000 have
civilian jobs, including 100 of the 300 generals.[31] The President's
own family is suspected of corruption. Rumour has it that his own
son runs an airline which has no aircraft. This reminds one of
Mrs Gandhi's son, Sanjay, who ran a car factory which never
produced a car. The President's younger brother has the clove
import monopoly. And the President's wife, Madame Tien Suharto,
is known as 'Madame Tien Per Cent'. She needs money to build a
mausoleum for her family. The President himself in a way acknowledged the prevailing corruption in his government when, in March
1978 at the time of setting his new twenty-four-member cabinet, he
pledged to take the initiative towards building a clean government in
the next five years.[32]

THE PHILIPPINES

Like Ayub of Pakistan, Ferdinand Marcos of the Philippines held the
view that unfettered Western democracy could not be operated in
the developing societies of Asia. Democracy had a restricted beginning in the West and the Western democracies were in those early
days as 'despotic' as the present Asian democracies appear to be, with

one-party authoritarian rule, weak assemblies, press censorship and militarism.[33] A Western observer would therefore be wrong in dismissing such a democracy as fraud. He should 'go back to the experience of his country at a similar period', Marcos argued, and 'he will understand that the militarism of some new nations is as much the instrument of national unification as it was for the then developing Western countries'. Marcos further argued that even the advanced form of democracy as practised in the West was presently in a state of crisis brought about by bureaucratisation, the rise of technocracy, the increasing complexities of modern life, and the acceleration of technologies and their cost, especially in mass communication.[34] As a result the ordinary citizen in the Western democracies 'has lost the sense of control over his government'.

The message which Marcos wished to convey through his arguments was that the developing countries must of necessity control 'the revolution of rising expectations' by putting into operation a restricted form of democracy. Endorsing Ayub Khan's thesis, Marcos upheld that the kind of democracy suited to the developing societies was basic or guided democracy which would be simple to understand, easy to work, and cheap to sustain.[35] In such a system only those questions should be put to the voters which they could answer in the light of their own personal knowledge and understanding. The system should ensure the effective participation of all citizens in the affairs of the country up to the level of their mental horizon. This system should be able to produce a strong and stable government.

Marcos was not as systematic as Ayub Khan in structuring the Philippine surrogate of Western democracy. He called it 'the participatory democracy'. The basic units in the system were the village or citizens' assemblies, the modern form of the ancient Filipino *barangays* or groups of families. More than 35,000 *barangays* were created all over the country. They were of course controlled by the government. From these *barangays* were to emerge higher assemblies for the 72 provinces and 1500 municipalities of the Philippines. In the absence of any central legislature, Marcos started the practice of consulting the *barangays* on political issues by means of plebiscite and referendum. All Filipinos aged fifteen and above were franchised to vote through *barangays* in the referendums and plebiscites – of which five were held between the advent of the martial-law regime in 1972 and December 1977. Marcos called the first plebiscite in January 1973, in which the *barangays* rectified the new constitution of 1973. In July of the same year he called a referendum on a single question. Did the people want him to continue as President beyond 1973, the year in which his term expired under the old constitution? Ninety per cent of the voters said 'yes'. The third referendum was held in February 1975. This time the people were asked if they wanted martial law to continue. Having secured a modicum of success against the Muslim and communist insurgents, Marcos needed new justification for the continuation of the martial law, for the 'threat to the security of the nation', the initial ground for the declaration of martial law in 1972, no longer seemed valid. The people were now tutored to believe that the country suffered from economic dislocations caused by world recession. They duly endorsed the proposition that the martial-law government be continued as 'crisis government'.

In 1975 Marcos formed another people's assembly called Sangguniang Bayan. It consisted of 3600 members, representing *barangays*, youth associations, provincial and municipal governments, and the labour, farming and professional sectors. To some extent this assembly resembled Indonesia's National Front or Sekber Golkar. It was controlled and appointed by the government. In January 1976 this body met in Manila and overwhelmingly approved Marcos's proposal to form a Legislative Advisory Council. The absence of any central legislature (the Interim National Assembly, as provided in the transitory provisions of the 1973 constitution, had not met so far), had begun to irritate the Americans, and prove embarrassing to Marcos himself. In September 1976, at the fourth anniversary of martial law, the Legislative Advisory Council, comprising the members of Marcos's cabinet and ninety-one members of the government-controlled people's assemblies, was inaugurated. Even though it was Marcos's creation, the Legislative Advisory Council was given no real powers. It was to meet once a year when called by the President. It had the power only to pass resolutions.

In its very first meeting the Legislative Council suggested major constitutional amendments including the abolition of the Interim National Assembly as provided for in the interim provisions of the 1973 constitution. The Interim National Assembly was to consist of 420 members – all former Congressmen and Senators who affirmed their option to serve and all delegates of the Constitutional Convention, provided they voted for the transitional provisions of the 1973 constitution which had already given Marcos enormous powers. This Interim National Assembly had not met. Even though this body had limited powers and could be controlled by the President, Marcos did not want to take any risk. He feared that the old politicians once assembled might show open hostility to his regime. He wanted an Interim Assembly consisting of his own nominees and appointees and fully loyal to him. The Legislative Advisory Council accordingly suggested that in place of the statutory Interim National

Assembly a new Interim National Assembly of about 200 members be created through elections and appointments. In October 1976 this constitutional amendment was put to a referendum (fourth in the series) and about 92 per cent of the voters once again said 'yes'.

In December 1977, Marcos-style politics acquired something of the atmosphere of a circus when for the fifth time the President held a referendum. Voters were asked if they wanted Marcos to continue as President (under the 1935 constitution), subsequently to become Prime Minister (under the 1973 constitution), holding both jobs after an Interim National Assembly was organised (under the 1976 constitutional amendments). In simple terms, was Marcos to continue exercising martial-law powers, whatever the guise? Once again an overwhelming majority of 21 million voters said 'yes'.

1977 turned out to be a discomforting year for the authoritarians. Democracy acquired a great boost with the launching of the human rights movement by President Carter and the collapse of Mrs Gandhi's Raj in a free election. Marcos was also subjected to domestic pressure applied by the Roman Catholic Church. At an annual conference of bishops, sixty-six of them issued a pastoral letter denouncing the martial-law regime.[36] The letter was read from every Catholic pulpit in the Philippines. Then, in August 1977, the World Law Conference of about 4000 delegates representing more than 100 countries met in Manila. A former US Attorney-General used this opportunity to condemn Marcos's regime. He said it was heartbreaking that such a conference should be held in Manila, where the martial law prevailing was the very antithesis of the rule of law to which the conference was dedicated.[37] President Marcos announced a few liberal measures at this conference: a selective amnesty for political prisoners, the lifting of a ban on international travel by Filipinos, and of the midnight curfew, and the holding by 1978 of the first local elections after five years of martial law. At this point he was, however, not willing to concede a general election. Increasing human rights pressure from the Carter administration (recurring military and economic aid from the United States was vital to the Philippines) goaded Marcos into announcing later in the year that a general election would be held in April 1978.

During the forty-five days of the election campaign, starting in February 1978, Marcos allowed democracy a walk on a short leash. Restraints on political activity were lifted during this period. Marcos did not release, however, his chief political rival, Benigno Aquino (who had been detained since Marcos imposed martial law in 1972 and sentenced to death by a military tribunal in November 1977), who decided to contest the election as the leader of the newly formed opposition party – Laban (People's Power Movement) – from his prison cell. Canvassing for him, his seven-year-old daughter brought tears to the eyes of listeners when she told a campaign rally: 'I haven't been with my father for a long time . . . please vote for my dad so he can be with me.'[38] But the Laban was too weak to match Marcos's party – the New Society Movement. It could not field more than twenty-one candidates for the election. Mrs Imelda Marcos contested a seat from Manila, and the opposition suspected that she was intending to seek the post of deputy Prime Minister (her husband will be automatically Prime Minister, as well as President, when the assembly convenes), as a stepping stone to becoming Marcos's successor. Before the election was actually held the opposition alleged that Marcos had organised large-scale rigging of the election. On the eve of the election tens of thousands of Filipinos came out in a cacophonous demonstration against Marcos, beating drums, tooting horns and banging pots and pans. The election results were a foregone conclusion. The ruling New Society Movement won the election with a large majority. The opposition seemed convinced that Marcos had not only rigged the election but resorted to 'naked terrorism' to obtain votes for his wife and twenty other candidates of his who contested twenty-one seats in Metro Manila. On 10 April, two days after election, President Marcos reimposed restrictions on political activities in the Philippines.

Marcos has not succeeded in convincing the outside world, particularly the United States, that the April election was free and fair and also a significant move towards the eventual restoration of democratic order in the Philippines. In May 1978 the US Vice-President Walter Mondale visited the Philippines and warned President Marcos that the lack of political freedom in his country might impair relations between Washington and Manila.[39] President Marcos in return warned the United States against any attempt at 'destabilising' his martial-law regime, saying this would hurt America as much as the Philippines. Marcos appears to be convinced that his martial-law regime has given political stability to the country by suppressing crime and corruption. He also believes that the country has made great economic progress under martial law. Above all, he believes that his regime has the support of the masses.

The election of the Interim National Assembly (in April 1978) in itself is by no means a significant step towards the liberalisation of the country's political affairs. So long as Marcos rules under the transitory provisions of the 1973 constitution he has powers to override the Assembly. In order to understand this point we must look at the 1973 constitution.[40] Technically the constitution is the work of the Constitutional Convention, whose 320 members were elected in November 1970, two years before martial law was declared. However, the main features of the constitution, and most certainly its transitory provisions, were drafted during the first three months of the martial-law regime, at the command of Marcos.[41] The general provisions of the constitution turn the Philippine presidential form of government (as established by the 1935 constitution) into a parliamentary one. The President becomes the nominal head of state and all the executive powers are vested in the Prime Minister, who also becomes the commander-in-chief of all armed forces. The Prime Minister is to be elected by a majority of all the members of the National Assembly from among themselves. As far as its general provisions go the 1973 constitution is like almost any other constitution of a parliamentary form of government. Its transitory provisions, however, put it in a category of its own. These provisions contemplate three stages in the transition from the old to the new government. The first stage embraces the period from the ratification of the constitution to the convening of the Interim National Assembly. This interim Assembly should have come into existence 'immediately upon the ratification of this constitution', but Marcos let nearly six years elapse before holding the election for the Assembly. The second stage begins with the convening of the Assembly and ends with its electing the interim President and Prime Minister. The third ends with the holding of the election for the regular National Assembly. During this transition period, consisting of three stages, Marcos is to exercise supreme legislative and executive powers – in the first stage as the incumbent President under the 1935 constitution, in the second and third stages as the Prime Minister under the 1973 constitution. Besides, President Marcos is the sole judge of the time when one stage should terminate and the other begin. On 12 June 1978 the Interim National Assembly was convened and Marcos became the first Prime Minister of the country, retaining the exclusive power to decide when the interim phase would be ended. However, Marcos maintains that only when the Democratic Revolution (started by him and reflected in his decrees, proclamations and orders) becomes institutionalised will he then consider terminating the martial-law regime and the 'transitory period'.[42]

Like Mrs Gandhi during her emergency rule, Marcos is not afraid of being overthrown by an army *coup*. 'Our martial law is unique', he maintains, 'in that it is based on the supremacy of the civilian authority over the military.' His orders have so far been loyally carried out by the military. And in case he is suddenly assassinated, Marcos, empowered by the 1935 constitution to choose his own successor, has already done so and kept his choice sealed, to be opened only in case of such a contingency.

INDIA

Mrs Gandhi's emergency rule in India stands apart from other authoritarian experiments in Asia, first, because it lasted for only about twenty months, from June 1975 to March 1977; second, its termination coincided with the end of the thirty-year-old Congress rule, and the coming into power of the opposition under the banner of the newly-formed Janata Party. This in turn made it possible for the emergency-rule phase to be thoroughly investigated by various commissions and committees, the foremost among them being the Shah Commission (headed by Justice J. C. Shah), which was appointed by the Janata government in May 1977 to ascertain how and why the Emergency was declared, and what excesses and misuse of powers were committed while it lasted. The Shah Commission held enquiries for a year, examined most of Mrs Gandhi's colleagues, and submitted to the Janata government by May 1978, two interim reports. Apart from the Shah Commission's proceedings, there has been a rapid growth of literature on the Emergency, contributed mostly by observers and victims. These uninhibited studies of the Emergency provide firm answers to some, though not all, of the basic questions which have been posed since June 1975: how and why Mrs Gandhi declared the Emergency; what excesses were committed during the State of Emergency; what kind of political system Mrs Gandhi tried to evolve and impose upon the people; who her close associates were and what measure of responsibility they share for some vital decisions made during this period; and what made Mrs Gandhi decide to hold elections in March 1977.

The circumstances leading to the declaration of the Emergency have been discussed in chapter 2 (see pp. 34–7). Did those circumstances merit the imposition of an internal emergency? In its first interim report submitted to the government in March 1978, the Shah Commission observed that the circumstances prevailing in June 1975 fell short of upheavals or serious disturbances, and therefore did not warrant the declaration of an emergency.[43] The Commission's observation may or may not hold water, depending on the degree of gravity one imputes to the threat which was posed by the opposition's resolve to start a nationwide mass movement solely in order to force the resignation of Mrs Gandhi. There is no denying the fact that the opposition was carried away by the judgement of the Allahabad High Court, which to all percipient observers was based on a mere technicality of law – Mrs Gandhi was found guilty of corrupt electoral practices for having used, during her 1971 election campaigns, some government facilities which normally accrued to her as the Prime Minister of India. As a result, the confrontation between the opposition and Mrs Gandhi acquired a propensity to anarchy unparalleled by any inter-élite struggle for power in the non-communist states of South and South-east Asia. The opposition's crusade against Mrs Gandhi was technically unconstitutional, for the judiciary had allowed her to remain in office until the matter was finally resolved before the Supreme Court. However, Mrs Gandhi's case does not benefit from these arguments, mainly because she had not consulted a single member of her Cabinet before declaring India to be in a State of Emergency. In April 1977, long before the Shah Commission came out with its findings, Mrs Gandhi herself conceded that she acted alone, and without consulting the Cabinet, in deciding the fateful proclamation of Emergency in June 1975.[44] An endorsement by the whole Cabinet of the gravity of the situation facing the government in those crucial weeks of June 1975, would have possibly elicited a non-biased verdict from the inquest on the justification for the declaration of Emergency. It is beyond the scope of this narrative to explain why Mrs Gandhi distrusted her Cabinet colleagues. It may, however, be observed that her style of leadership goes some way to accounting for it. Throughout the eleven years of her Prime Ministership Mrs Gandhi's style had been aggressive and uncompromising, and she had been consistent in belittling any of her Cabinet colleagues who had tried to overshadow her. As a result, at the time of the declaration of Emergency, her Cabinet consisted of a number of disaffected elements (mostly senior ministers like Jagjivan Ram, Swaran Singh, and Y. B. Chavan, who were ultimately to part company with her); and even the junior ministers, who displayed absolute obedience towards her, did so through fear rather than loyalty.

On the question of excesses committed during the Emergency, a balanced view must concede right away that no annihilation or wholesale persecution and torture of political prisoners took place at the behest of Mrs Gandhi. But Mrs Gandhi had every reason to anticipate that in such a situation, where normal channels of making protests and representations were closed and approach to the judiciary almost denied to the people, some excesses and misuse of powers were bound to be committed not only by the corrupt police force, but also by over-enthusiastic bureaucrats, ministers and chief ministers of states. Not only did she not provide any protection for the people against such behaviour, but in fact she connived at extortion and force often used by state officials in implementing such programmes as population control through vasectomy, and the improvement of the appearance of towns and cities through clearance of slum areas. Perhaps her greatest indulgence lay in allowing the chief ministers of states to use their powers and state funds to groom her young son, Sanjay Gandhi, into a national hero. The rise of Sanjay Gandhi became a humiliation to the senior colleagues of Mrs Gandhi, an enigma to the people, and a discredit to the Emergency. It cost Mrs Gandhi her credibility.

Other excesses and misuses of power manifested themselves in the demolition of some vital democratic institutions, which Mrs Gandhi carried out during the Emergency. Her Emergency began with the arrest of almost all the leaders of the opposition parties, except the Communist Party of India, which remained an ally to Mrs Gandhi's ruling Congress Party until the very end of the Emergency. Among the arrested were about sixty Members of Parliament. Twenty-six political organisations were banned. Stifling censorship was imposed on the press. Those provisions of the constitution which guaranteed fundamental rights to the citizens were made inoperative. The election due to be held in 1976 was postponed. The independence and powers of the judiciary were abridged. Most of these measures were sanctioned by Acts of Parliament. The Members of Parliament, the majority of whom belonged to the ruling Congress Party, acted throughout the Emergency as a rubber stamp for Mrs Gandhi's orders. Why did they act so passively? Did they really believe in Mrs Gandhi and her 'new order'? Or did they treat Mrs Gandhi as a Moloch against whom they dare not raise their heads? The latter explanation seems nearer to the truth, for in the post-Emergency era, when Mrs Gandhi fell out of power, many of her 'loyal' followers readily deserted her camp.

Mrs Gandhi was not as systematic and thorough in building a new political system as she was at demolishing the old one. She had no aptitude for theorising, her approach to political problems was pragmatic, though tinged with a certain amount of confusion. Unlike Ayub Khan or Ferdinand Marcos, she did not expound a thesis against liberal democracy. At the same time, she managed to bridle democracy so tightly as to make it immobile.

Of the four constitutional amendments carried during the Emergency, the last one – the 42nd Amendment to the constitution, which was enacted in December 1976 – tended to create a political system which in Mrs Gandhi's thinking was more conducive to the preservation of the unity and integrity of India. Mrs Gandhi had come to believe that India's economic progress was retarded by self-seeking politicians, who cared little about anything except how to gain economic and political power for themselves, and by the conservative judiciary which was prone to declare *ultra vires* any radical measure of the government and parliament. Indira Gandhi had further come to realise that the unity of the nation was constantly threatened by a tug-of-war between the central and state governments, and by the tendency on the part of the state governments, especially those run by non-Congress politicians, to become more autonomous. She had thus arrived at the conclusion that the only way to resolve these problems lay in the creation of a strong central executive and a fully sovereign parliament. In February 1976 a high-powered committee was set up under the chairmanship of Swaran Singh, the former Defence Minister. Its purpose was to study and suggest amendments to the constitution. The committee's negative achievement lay in its outright rejection of the idea of India opting for a presidential system of government. On the positive side it suggested several changes in the constitution, all of which were incorporated in the 42nd Amendment to the constitution. Under this Amendment, the central executive was vested with powers to override the state governments. The central government was authorised to ban 'anti-national activities and associations', and to deploy central armed forces in any state to deal with grave law-and-order situations. To ensure that the President, a mere figure-head in the constitution, was never tempted to exercise any constraint on the central executive, the 42nd Amendment further laid down that he was always to be bound by the advice of the Council of Ministers. The supremacy of parliament was also established. The judiciary was deprived of the power to enquire into any constitutional amendment passed by the parliament. Furthermore, the Amendment laid emphasis on citizens' 'duties' rather than 'rights', on 'socialism' rather than 'democracy'. A set of ten fundamental duties, including compulsory national service, was laid down, with the provision of punishment for failure to observe such duties. The preamble of the constitution was changed; the words 'sovereign Democratic Republic' were replaced by 'Sovereign Socialist Republic'.

By no means did the 42nd Amendment constitute on its own a violation of Indian democracy. None of the fifty-nine clauses of the Amendment contravened the principle of democracy. Even trimming the powers of the judiciary in order to establish the paramountcy of the parliament was in keeping with the British parliamentary tradition. Unlike the Philippine and Pakistani constitutions of 1973, the 42nd Amendment did not vest Prime Minister Gandhi with any special powers. What made the intelligentsia suspect an authoritarian design behind this constitutional amendment was the fact that it was carried out during the Emergency by a parliament which had outlived its five-year tenure. The quinquennial election, due in March 1976, had already been postponed for a year. In December 1976, when the 42nd Amendment was passed and the atmosphere had already become charged with rumours about Mrs Gandhi's villainies, most of them unfounded, hardly anybody believed that free elections would ever be held. In spite of itself, the 42nd Amendment thus came to be regarded as a device whereby Mrs Gandhi wanted to perpetuate her personal rule over India indefinitely.

On 18 January 1977, just a month after the 42nd Amendment had been enacted, Mrs Gandhi surprised everyone, her followers as well as her opponents, by announcing her intention to hold India's sixth parliamentary election in March. In this, as in other major policy decisions made during the Emergency, she acted on her own, not consulting even the senior cabinet ministers, one of whom, Y. B. Chavan, rushed back to India from Europe when he heard the news about the election. Mrs Gandhi's decision to go to the polls was mainly generated by her need to acquire legitimacy for her government, and her never-faltering belief that the masses were steadfastly with her. In order to be fully assured of her victory, she had to be careful about the timing of the election, and on this a number of factors indicated that March was by far the most appropriate month. There had been a succession of good harvests. The opposition, languishing in prison, seemed now a subdued and forgotten force, unlikely to gain any strength if brought out on a leash just a month or so before the election. Her son, Sanjay Gandhi, as it seemed in December 1976, had become a national hero, and wielded power over millions as the leader of the Youth Congress.

Soon after the announcement of the election was made, most of the opposition leaders were released and the Emergency was relaxed, though not fully lifted. On 23 January four of the non-communist opposition parties (Jan Sangh, Bhartiya Lok Dal (BLD), the Socialists and the remnants of the old Congress Party) united and launched the Janata Party under the leadership of eighty-one-year-old Morarji Desai. Mrs Gandhi's confidence was for the first time diminished when, on 2 February, Jagjivan Ram, the most senior Cabinet Minister, resigned from the Cabinet and the ruling Congress Party, formed his own Congress for Democracy Party, and joined the Janata opposition, which now became a grand coalition of five parties. The Janata fought the election pledged mainly to the restoration of democracy. Mrs Gandhi's Congress stood for 'stability' and 'integrity' and continuously warned the electorate that the victory of the Janata Party would plunge the nation into chaos.

The March 1977 election turned out to be the most significant event in the history of Indian democracy. An overwhelming majority of the poor illiterate electorate of 320 millions voted against Mrs Gandhi and the 30-year-old rule of Congress. Janata captured 300 of the 542 Lok Sabha (the lower house of the Indian parliament) seats. Mrs Gandhi and most of her close associates lost their seats.

Her Congress Party, however, retained its hold on South India, capturing most of the parliamentary seats allotted to Andhra Pradesh, Karnataka, Kerala, and Tamil Nadu. Mrs Gandhi accepted the verdict of the people gracefully, and lifted the Emergency before quitting office.

Many factors combined to bring about the defeat of Mrs Gandhi and Congress. The Emergency itself, the rise of Sanjay Gandhi, the sterilisation campaigns, the arrogant and callous behaviour of Mrs Gandhi's political associates – these had alienated the people. But perhaps the most important factor in bringing about her downfall was the rise against her of a large section of the Indian intelligentsia which during the Emergency had come to realise more the value of freedom and democracy. The educated professional class for the first time actively canvassed among the people against Mrs Gandhi and her Congress.

On 24 March 1977 the thirty-year-old Congress Raj was replaced by the Janata government, and Morarji Desai became India's fourth Prime Minister. In June 1977 Janata made further conquests when the elections for most of the North Indian state assemblies were held. It won the majority of assembly seats in Uttar Pradesh, Madhya Pradesh, Rajasthan, Haryana, Himachal Pradesh, and Orissa. It was also able to form a government in Punjab in alliance with the Sikh Akali Dal Party. In Bengal, however, a five-party leftist alliance led by the Communist Party of India (Marxist) won a clear majority, and for the first time a communist party came to rule the state in its own right. In the second round of assembly elections held in February 1978 for most of the remaining states, the Janata once again failed to gain a hold over the southern states of Andhra Pradesh and Karnataka, where Mrs Gandhi's faction of the Congress – Congress (I) – captured the majority of seats. Janata, however, managed further to strengthen its dominance over northern India by gaining the majority of seats in the Arunachal Pradesh Assembly, and a dominant position in the assemblies of Assam and Maghalaya.

Janata, however, ruled the country only for about twenty-eight months. It was indeed a short period for any democratic government to accomplish much, but more so for an 'alliance' or 'coalition' government. Although in May 1977 the five components of the Janata Party technically ceased to have their separate identities, in fact the party could not achieve any unity of purpose and consequently the Janata government, often pulled by its components in different directions, did not govern effectively. None the less it succeeded in restoring democracy to India to the fullest degree, and in devising various measures (like the 44th and 45th Constitution Amendment Acts) to ensure a safe life for the system in the country.

But most of the time and energy of the Janata leadership was consumed in resolving internal factional disputes. Within the government the struggle for power between the Home Minister, Charan Singh (the seventy-seven-year-old leader of the BKD component of the Janata Party), and Prime Minister Desai assumed tragic propensity. The fight had no ideological base. It was fuelled mainly by the personal ambition of Singh who had from the very beginning of the Janata Raj felt that he had better claim to the Prime Ministership than Desai. Though showing no sign of decay, Desai was none the less in his eighties. Had Charan Singh been in good health and also in a position to be regarded as the undisputed successor to Desai, he would possibly have waited for his chance. But he had neither of these to rely upon. Singh had already had a few heart attacks, and there was the seventy-one-year-old Jagjivan Ram, his formidable rival for the leadership of the Janata Parliamentary Party and the Prime Ministership of India. Besides, the way the Janata government had been losing its popularity, no Janata leader could be sure of the party winning the next parliamentary election. So if it was Charan Singh's life-long ambition to become the Prime Minister of India (as he himself admitted on the day be became the Prime Minister of India), his ambition had to be fulfilled during the present term of the Janata Raj. Even so, left to himself Charan Singh would have been most probably contained by Desai, for Singh was by no means given to plotting and chicanery. Singh, however, was fortunate or unfortunate in having Raj Narain as his henchman. Raj Narain continually stoked and fanned his ambition, and was most willing to bend any rule of the game in order to advance Singh's interests.

In their fight against Desai, both Singh and Narain came to defy what seemed to the Prime Minister the vital norms of parliamentary democracy. In June 1978, Desai dismissed from his cabinet both Singh and Narain for their having utterly defied the 'concept of collective responsibility that prevails in a cabinet system of government'. Charan Singh went on consolidating his support among the peasants of northern India, and at the same time agitating for his re-entry into the government. All the time and skill of the Janata leaders once again came to be spent on bringing about a reconciliation between Desai and Singh. Singh's terms of re-entry into the government were such as to make him the undisputed successor of Desai. He wanted to become the Deputy Prime Minister with the charge of the Home Ministry. The reconciliation took place in January 1979. Singh was made Deputy Prime Minister and given the charge of the Finance Ministry. At the same time the Defence Minister, Jagjivan Ram, was also elevated to the Deputy Prime

Ministership. For the first time India came to have two Deputy Prime Ministers without any clarification as to which of the two took precedence over the other. The settlement thus did not give Singh what he wanted. Besides, Raj Narain was not taken back into the government. With a frustrated Singh within and an angry Raj Narain outside the government the settlement seemed at the most to give Singh and Narain an advantageous position from whence to launch their last bid for power.

While Narain set himself the task of organising defections from the Janata Parliamentary Party, the factional fighting continued to take its toll in the Janata-governed states, where the in-fighting between the components of the Janata governments and the replacement of one Chief Minister by another became common occurrences. In due course Raj Narain formally resigned from the Janata Party, founded a Janata (Secular) Party, and by mid-July 1979 succeeded in gaining enough defectors from the Janata Parliamentary Party to reduce the Janata strength to a little over 200 in a house of 539. On 15 July 1979, Morarji Desai was thus obliged to resign and the Janata government fell from power. The following day Charan Singh resigned from Desai's caretaker government, as well as from the Janata Party and became the leader of the breakaway faction of the Janata Party.

As none of the four major national parties – Congress, Congress(I), Janata, Janata(S) – now had an absolute majority in the Parliament, any one of them which could strike an alliance with other parties was most likely to succeed in forming a government. Mrs Gandhi and her faction of Congress, having a sizeable strength in the Parliament, now came to acquire a decisive role in this politics of opportunism. Charan Singh and Raj Narain succeeded in making an alliance with Congress and, ironically enough, also gained the tacit support of their erstwhile arch enemy, Mrs Gandhi and her Congress(I). On 27 July 1979, the President was obliged to ask Charan Singh to form his government, but on condition that he 'in accordance with the highest democratic traditions and in the interest of establishing healthy conventions' sought a vote of confidence in the Lok Sabha at the earliest possible opportunity. On 28 July, Charan Singh became India's fifth Prime Minister. Y. B. Chavan, the leader of the Congress in the Lok Sabha, became the Deputy Prime Minister. For the first time India came to have a coalition government at the centre. Also for the first time the ordinary MPs and the minor national (CPI and CPM) and regional parties (AIDMK, DMK and the Akali Dal), came to count for so much in the national power game. As no political party seemed committed to any ideology, and no political leader carried any strong convictions, Indian politics came to be run more on personal than institutional grounds.

By July 1979, Mrs Indira Gandhi had already staged a come-back, partly by dint of her political skill and partly owing to the split in the Janata Party. For some time after her defeat at the 1977 parliamentary election she kept a low profile. In the meantime the Janata government went on preparing ground for her prosecution. On 3 October 1977 she was arrested on corruption charges. On the following day she was released by the Delhi metropolitan magistrate who found there was no evidence to justify her detention. This episode, on the one hand, lowered the prestige of the Janata government and, on the other, turned Mrs Gandhi almost into a martyr. At this point Mrs Gandhi realised that in order to make it difficult for the Janata government to prosecute her in future it was necessary that she become the leader of her Congress Party. The old barons of her party had come to regard her as a liability and were most reluctant to let her save her skin by becoming the president of the party. The struggle for leadership of the Congress Party led to its split, on 2 January 1978, into two factions. Mrs Indira Gandhi became president of one faction which came to be called after her – Congress(I). As most of Mrs Gandhi's erstwhile cabinet colleagues and chief ministers parted company with her by remaining allied to the opposite faction of the Congress, Mrs Gandhi used this opportunity to blame for the first time the former state chief ministers for the excesses committed during the Emergency.[45] The trial of strength between the two factions of the Congress took place at the elections to the five state assemblies which were held on 25 February 1978. Mrs Gandhi's Congress won the two southern states of Karnataka and Andhra Pradesh and established a stake in Maharashtra. Her rival congress faction suffered a crushing defeat. Soon after the elections, defections from the old congress to the new Congress(I) took place at all levels. As a result of this, Congress(I) became the leading opposition party in the parliament. Mrs Gandhi's next move was to find for herself a seat in the parliament. She contested the Chikmagalur by-election in November 1978 and defeated her Janata rival by a large majority of 77,333 votes. Her triumphant entry into the parliament, however, was short-lived. The Lok Sabha found her guilty of having committed a breach of parliamentary privilege while she was Prime Minister. On 19 December she was expelled from the Lok Sabha and imprisoned for the remaining seven days of the Lok Sabha session. The Lok Sabha might possibly have forgiven her had she apologised or expressed some regrets for having committed this technical breach of privilege, but she was throughout the Lok Sabha proceedings unrelenting as if she was determined to turn this adversity to her political advantage. On 26 December she came out of prison with her popularity further enhanced.

During the first part of 1979, Mrs Gandhi tried to unite the two Congresses. But her erstwhile colleagues, who ran the rival faction of the Congress, feared that once the two Congresses were united into a single party Mrs Gandhi would most certainly come to dominate it. They thus seized the opportunity which occurred with the split in the Janata Party. They made an alliance with Charan Singh's Janata(S) and consequently the Congress became a partner in the coalition government. But the survival of Charan Singh's coalition government solely depended on the support of Mrs Gandhi's Congress(I). Mrs Gandhi, however, would not support Charan Singh's government on 20 August – the day appointed for Singh's government to seek a vote of confidence in the parliament – unless, among other things, the two special courts erected by Desai's government in May 1979, to try the excesses committed during the Emergency, were demolished. It was a hard condition for Singh to accept for he, as a member of Desai's government, had supported the creation of these courts. Hence, no matter how desperate he was for Mrs Gandhi's support, he could not afford to lose face in public by accepting her conditions. On 20 August 1979, just before facing the parliament, Charan Singh resigned and at the same time advised the President to dissolve the Lok Sabha and hold a mid-term parliamentary election. Jagjivan Ram, now leader of the Janata Parliamentary Party, very much expected to be asked by the President to form a new government. But President Sanjiva Reddy, after consulting all the major parties and finding that almost all except the Janata Party were unanimous in demanding a fresh mandate from the electorate, dissolved the sixth Lok Sabha on 22 August and asked Charan Singh's government to continue in office as a caretaker government until a new government was formed after the election. On 26 October it was officially announced that the elections for the seventh Lok Sabha would be held on 3 and 6 January 1980.

Since the beginning of confrontation between Desai and Singh, the pre-Emergency conditions started returning to India: growing lawlessness, a rise in prices, industrial unrest and strikes, students' revolts and the frequent closure of universities, political defections and 'crossing of the floor', the revival of caste, communal and racial prejudices, and the utter lack of concern for national interests among political practitioners. Though committed to democracy, the Indian intelligentsia became increasingly disenchanted by the new, marketplace styles of their political élites. On the eve of the election the question which was generally asked was whether any of the three major political parties – Mrs Gandhi's Congress(I), Jagjivan Ram's

Janata, and Charan Singh's faction of Janata, now renamed Lok Dal and aligned with Congress – will gain absolute majority in the Lok Sabha. For, if none won an absolute majority India might plunge into an era of coalitions or Malaysia-style alliance governments, which would most probably make the Indian democratic order more unstable, more wasteful, and more ineffective than it had ever been before.

4 Problems of Disputed Lands and National Integrity

In the thirty odd years of the independence era, much of the political energy and economic resources of the countries of South and South-east Asia has been deployed in seeking and preserving their territorial identity and integrity. The problems facing most of the countries – the problems of disputed lands and boundaries, of minorities and separatism, and of communist insurgencies – arose from the legacies of their colonial past as well as from the emergence of China in 1949 as a powerful communist state. The colonial powers gave territorial unity to their respective possessions, demarcated their political frontiers, and turned them into states. The process of colonisation, however, sometimes involved adding to a particular state tracts of border lands inhabited by people who were racially, ethnically or religiously different from the majority of the people of that state. But this was by no means a feature peculiar to the European conquests in Asia. History bears witness to the same occurence in ancient and medieval times when conquerors brought different peoples under one rule. In history there is hardly an example of a state exclusively populated by peoples who belonged to the same race, spoke the same language, and practised the same religion. It would also be pointless to blame the European powers for the border skirmishes and wars which have occasionally flared up in the post-independence period. The colonial powers may seem to have acted arbitrarily and unimaginatively in drawing, and in some cases not drawing clearly, the frontiers of their imperial holdings. However, during the nineteenth and early twentieth centuries, when the political frontiers were defined, the Western powers could not even visualise their own departure from Asia, still less were they concerned for what might follow when they were gone. The primary considerations which influenced them in demarcating the frontiers of their respective dominions were physical security, administrative convenience, and compromise between their rival aspirations. During the colonial period the state was, therefore, not used as an instrument for bringing a nation into existence or, to be more precise, for moulding its diverse citizenry into an integrated nation. This task fell upon the nationalists who have, during the last three decades of the independence era, tried to perform it, in some states with a considerable degree of success.

This task, which faced every independent state in the zone, was made more complicated with the rise of China as the first communist power in Asia. The Chinese intention and capacity to reclaim lands on its hitherto vaguely defined southern frontiers (which, after the occupation of Tibet by China in 1950, extended from Pakistan in the west to Vietnam in the east) immediately gave rise to border problems between China on the one hand and Pakistan, India, Nepal and Burma on the other. At the same time, China's policy of reviving links with Chinese overseas, particularly in South-east Asia, intensified the minority problem. Further, the communist movements in South and South-east Asia were stimulated by the Chinese example, and continued to gather strength until the Sino-Soviet rupture came into the open in the early 1960s.

DISPUTED LANDS AND BOUNDARIES

In the category of disputed lands we may place, for the sake of convenience, the movements for further decolonisation which revived conflicts and confrontations between certain European and Asian states; and also disputes over territories, occasionally flaring into wars, between some of the Asian states. Disputes over boundaries and frontiers may be put into a separate category.

Only two countries – India and Indonesia – were involved in the process of further decolonisation. At the time of India's independence, France and Portugal still retained their small possessions on Indian territory. France transferred to India its five enclaves – Chandernagore, Pondicherry, Karaikal, Mahi and Yanam – peacefully, through negotiations culminating in a final treaty signed by the two countries in 1954. India agreed to let these enclaves retain their distinctive identity, which was mainly based on French culture and language. Portugal, however, was adamant about retaining its possessions – Goa, Daman and Diu – on the western coast of India. The Portuguese arguments – that it had occupied its Indian possessions for 400 years, that they formed an integral part of Portugal, and that the culture and religion of 200,000 Catholics who lived in those territories would be put in jeopardy if they went to India – seemed worthless to Nehru, who kept on reminding the Portuguese that India was a secular country and nearly five million Catholics already lived there. However, Nehru was reluctant to take military action against the Portuguese in Goa, for India's policy was to solve all problems peacefully, and any display of force on its part, he feared, would provoke the foreign powers into calling Indians hypocrites.

Nehru waited in vain for fourteen years for the Portuguese to clear out either of their own accord, or under international pressure. Then, in 1961, he came under the combined pressure of Indian and African public opinion. For the Indian public, Goa had turned into an eyesore, reminding them constantly that India was not completely free from Western dominance. The African nationalists, having been brutally treated by the Portuguese in Angola and Mozambique, had come to look up to India, and in 1961 they placed an obligation on Nehru to make the first move towards the liquidation of the Portuguese empire. Even at the last moment, Nehru hoped that the Americans would exert pressure on the unyielding Portuguese to come to a negotiated settlement, but nothing happened. Most reluctantly, Nehru had then to order the armed forces to intervene. The entire operation was over within a day with very few casualties on either side. On 18 December 1961 the Portuguese surrendered, and their territories became integrated with India, retaining fully their Portuguese cultural heritage. The forcible seizure of the Portuguese territories by India, however, aroused against the latter the ill-feeling of some Europeans, who saw in this episode nothing but a further humiliation for the West. Portugal and India cut off their diplomatic links with each other.

At about the time of Indonesian independence, the Dutch still retained their hold on Western New Guinea and the Portuguese on East Timor. Indonesia clashed first with the Netherlands over the western part of the island of New Guinea; the eastern part – Papua New Guinea – mandated to Australia by the League of Nations in 1920, eventually became independent in 1975. Even though western New Guinea was extremely mountainous and barren, providing a bare existence for its less than one million inhabitants, who were Stone-Age tribesmen, the Dutch wanted to retain their hold on it, perhaps because they thought this would enable them to remain a world power. Negotiations between the two countries began in 1949, but no progress had been made by 1956. Indonesia then began taking economic and political action against the Dutch. It repudiated its debts to the Netherlands, and in 1957, when it failed to gain the support of the United Nations Assembly for its claim, it expropriated all Dutch firms and expelled nearly all Dutch nationals. Finding the Dutch still unyielding, Indonesia then began to acquire large quantities of arms, mainly from the Soviet Union. In 1962, the Indonesian and Dutch navies clashed in the waters of Western New Guinea. Soon after the United States intervened, negotiations were resumed, and after a brief spell, during which the territory was administered by the United Nations, it was finally handed over to Indonesia in 1963. West Irian, as Western New Guinea was hitherto called, was renamed Irian Barat, and later in 1973, Irian Jaya.

More than a decade elapsed before Indonesia turned its attention to East Timor. Since the Indonesians could not firmly lay claim to it as part of their Dutch heritage, they had to wait until East Timor's internal developments reached a certain point. Portugal occupied the eastern part of Timor, over 5500 square miles of territory, in 1520, and the Dutch occupied the western part, with an area of 6120 square miles, in 1613. By treaties made in 1860 and 1914, the Portuguese and Dutch divided the island and set the boundaries for Portuguese and Dutch Timor. Western or Dutch Timor became a part of Indonesia in 1950, but the Portuguese continued to rule their part of the island. In the mid-1970s, owing to the change in the political system of Portugal and the new government's policy of decolonisation, Portuguese colonies in Africa began acquiring their independence, and the Portuguese lost their effective authority in East Timor. In August 1975, from an offshore island, the Portuguese authorities issued appeals to the warring political parties in East Timor for a conference at which the future of the country could be decided. By then, East Timor was in the grip of a civil war fought principally between the two Timorican political groups – one group was represented by the leftist Revolutionary Front for East Timor (Fretilin) which wanted to turn East Timor into an independent state; the other group was represented by such political parties as the Timorese Democratic Union (UDT) and the Apodeti, which stood for the integration of East Timor with Indonesia. President Suharto of Indonesia seized this opportunity with both hands, sent 'volunteers' (thousands of members of the Indonesian armed forces) to East Timor at the request of the 'people of Portuguese Timor', and by the end of December 1975 East Timor fell into Indonesia's lap. Thus the last colonial holding disappeared from the political map of South and South-east Asia.

Only two territories became the cause of confrontations and wars between the Asian powers. Two of the three Indo–Pakistan wars were fought over Kashimir; Borneo was the scene of a long-lasting confrontation between Malaysia and Indonesia. The Paracel and Spratly groups of islands in the South China Sea have not yet been the cause of a confrontation between China and Vietnam. China had traditionally claimed these archipelagos of the South China Sea (bounded on the west by Vietnam, on the east by the Philippines, and on the south by Borneo) as its 'sacred territories', but in the modern era until 1974 these groups of islands were considered to be under Vietnamese suzerainty. Even though the prospect of oil in and around these groups of islands had become known in the 1960s, it was only in January 1974 that China mounted a naval operation to drive off a small South Vietnamese garrison inserted into the Paracels, the most northerly island group, about 200 miles equidistant from both China and Vietnam. In November 1975, when China was firmly in occupation of the Paracels, it laid a formal claim to the Spratlys – the southernmost group, over 600 miles from China. Since 1975, with Vietnam rapidly veering away from China and falling into the Russian fold, Peking has claimed the Spratlys in increasingly bellicose tones. At present most of the Spratly Islands are controlled by Vietnam; Taiwan and the Philippines exercising control over some. The Philippines began production of oil from their part of the Spratlys early in 1979, thus supplying about 10 per cent of Manila's needs. With the Vietnamese invasion of Cambodia in December 1978, the prospect of any negotiated settlement between China and Vietnam on the disputed Spratlys, as well as on the question of Chinese refugees from Vietnam, disappeared. Though the Spratlys did not constitute the main cause for the Chinese invasion of Vietnam in February 1979, the Chinese are unlikely to forget the strategic importance of the islands. By gaining control of the Spratlys, China can command the sea route from Tokyo to Singapore, and also cut off Hanoi from almost all supplies. Unless China abandons its traditional claim to the Spratlys, which is not unlikely, the archipelago will continue to have the potential to spark off yet another war in this zone.

The state of Jammu and Kashmir was one of the three princely states which had not acceded to either India or Pakistan by the time of independence; Junagadh and Hyderabad were the other two. Junagadh's Muslim ruler wanted his predominantly Hindu state to opt for Pakistan. The Indian government intervened on the grounds that the people of the state wanted its merger with India. In November 1947 the small state of Junagadh was drawn into the Indian fold. The Muslim ruler of the predominantly Hindu Hyderabad and the Hindu ruler of Jammu and Kashmir, the population of which was 80 per cent Muslim, both ruminated on the possibility of achieving some kind of independence for their respective dominions. It was unthinkable for India's Nehru to let Hyderabad grow as a sovereign state in the very heart of India, especially when the population of that state was 85 per cent Hindu. Thus, when negotiations turned into deadlock, India intervened. In September 1948 Hyderabad became an integral part of India. Neither of these two cases, however, turned into an international crisis. But it was different in the case of Kashmir.

In October 1947, while the Maharaja of Kashmir was still evading any firm decision, his territory was invaded by Pakistani forces. The Maharaja then formally signed the state's accession to India, thereby providing India with a technical ground to intervene. Nehru was reluctant to use this ploy, but he wanted the people of the state (who were then led by his old friend and colleague, Sheikh Mohammad Abdullah) to have the chance to decide the future of the state for themselves. He also had reason to believe that, given the chance, the people might decide that the state should either accede to India or retain some kind of independence.[1] It was very unlikely, he believed, that the Kashmiris would opt for Pakistan. If the Kashmiris were to be given their chance, then India must intervene to drive out the Pakistani invaders. On 27 October India intervened. Pakistani aggression was checked, but because of the United Nations' intervention, and the consequent ceasefire agreement effected on 1 January 1949, the Pakistani forces could not be driven out of the 32,000 square miles of the western and northern regions of Kashmir which they had come to occupy. This part of the state remains today under Pakistani occupation, and the remaining part, including the Srinagar Valley and Jammu, under Indian occupation as one of India's twenty-two states, but with a special status. India's state of Jammu and Kashmir has three different territorial components – Jammu, which is predominantly Hindu, Ladakh which is Buddhist, and Kashmir which is predominantly Muslim. Pakistan's Kashmir is predominantly Muslim.

Pakistan did not reconcile itself to the division of Kashmir which the ceasefire agreement of 1949 had virtually brought about. It claimed the whole of Kashmir on the basis of the two-nation theory which implied that Hindus and Muslims constituted two separate nations, and therefore all Muslim-dominated regions of the Indian sub-continent should *ipso facto* belong to Pakistan. Thus, when it became clear that the United Nations could not rectify the situation in Kashmir, Pakistan began to strengthen itself with foreign military aid, new diplomatic ties and defence pacts, in order to launch an offensive against India. Armed hostility between the two countries broke out in April 1965 over the disputed Rann of Kutch – an unpopulated salty wasteland of about 8400 square miles, lying around India's western border with Pakistan, the Kutch-Sind border. Britain mediated, and both the parties agreed on 30 June 1965 to refer the dispute to an international tribunal. The Rann of Kutch did not give Pakistan a fuller opportunity to test its strength against India. With China on her side, and India seemingly disposed, as it appeared in 1965, towards treating the Kashmir issue as a settled fact, Pakistan invaded India's Kashmir in August 1965. This second Indo-Pakistan war saw some heavy tank engagements and fierce fighting. The Pakistanis fought with a 'now or never' kind of fervour, backed all the time by China's moral rather than military support. The United Nations intervened, and the war ended on 23 September 1965 in a draw, with no territorial gains for either party. From then onwards the Pakistani leadership became occupied in rescuing the country from the disintegration which had set in soon after the war, mainly on account of the continuing conflict between its western and eastern wings. The third Indo-Pakistan war of 1971 (see chapter 3, p. 75) was not waged on the Kashmir issue, but its outcome – the emergence of Bangladesh (East Pakistan) as an independent nation – discredited the two nations theory and decisively weakened Pakistan's claim to India's Kashmir.

Even though the Indian leaders agreed to the division of the country under pressures of various kinds, they never accepted in principle the two-nation theory, and became more aggressive in their denunciation of the theory soon after the partition, when India was left with as many Muslims, if not more, than were in the whole of what was until 1971 called West Pakistan, now Pakistan. This emphatic rejection of the two-nation theory was also motivated by the practical need to sustain secularism, to which India had committed itself for various reasons, one of them being the protection of the lives and dignity of the Muslims against the onslaught of irate Hindu communalists, who in the early years of independence seemed determined to turn India into a Hindu state and either pack off the Muslims to Pakistan or relegate them to second-class citizenship. These political considerations persuaded the Indian leaders to treat Kashmir as a prize for India's secularism. Pakistan's growing political instability also contributed to India eventually taking what seemed to the Western powers, particularly to the United States and Britain, a self-righteous stance on the Kashmir issue. The fact which was never seriously taken into account by the Western powers was that in October 1951 the Indian part of Kashmir had formed its own constituent assembly, and the assembly had formally endorsed the accession of Kashmir to India in foreign affairs, defence and communications.

The Anglo-American moral support which was initially offered to Pakistan, and the latter's inclusion in the CENTO and SEATO military–political alliances, occasionally strained India's relations with the Western powers. One of the reasons that India developed a more cordial and closer relationship with the Soviet Union was the latter's unequivocal support for India's stand on the Kashmir issue, as publically expressed by Khrushchev and Bulganin during their first visit to India in 1955. Kashmir had put India and Pakistan into the position where the enemy of the one became the friend of the other. So, when the days of the Indo-Chinese brotherhood were over, China became Pakistan's friend. The international involvement in the Kashmir affair, however, was limited to offering only moral support to one or other party. Kashmir did influence the foreign relations both of India and Pakistan, but it did not draw the big powers into the arena and turn it into a Cold War zone.

Borneo's case was different, in that it was not subjected to rival claims (see chapter 1, p. 24). Indonesia did not assert its claim over the three Borneo territories; it simply did not want those territories to enter into the proposed Malaysian federation. It was the Philippines which revived, in April 1962, its claim to one of the territories, Sabah (North Borneo), but it did not come to play a role in the confrontation between Indonesia on the one hand, and Malaysia (supported by Britain, Australia and New Zealand) on the other.

Indonesia's involvement arose mainly out of its physical proximity to the Borneo territories (Sarawak, Brunei and Sabah) on the north-western coast of the island; Indonesian Borneo (Kalimantan) comprised 208,000 square miles of the central and southern regions of this largest island of the Malay archipelago. Only the remaining 81,000 square miles of the island were occupied by the three states which had been British protectorates: Sabah since 1883, Brunei and Sarawak since 1888. The Philippine claim to Sabah arose from a deed of cession, dated in 1878, by which the Sultan of the Philippine island of Sulu, and the Sultan of Brunei, had transferred their rights in Sabah to a British company, incorporated by royal charter; the company administered the territory until 1946, when it became a British colony, although it had already become a British protectorate in 1883.[2] The Philippine contention was that the Sultan of Sulu had no right to cede Sabah, because at that time it was Spain, and not the Sultan, who was its sovereign.

Because Indonesia's policy towards the Malaysian federation was inconsistent, and the hostile posture it ultimately came to assume against Malaysia yielded no gain, and seemed pointless, it is hard to ascertain the compelling factors, if any, behind President Sukarno's move to push his country into what seemed even to the friendly Afro-Asian leaders, an awkward position. The basic facts suggest that until December 1962, when the largest political party of Brunei revolted against the state joining the Malaysian federation, and demanded that it should form an independent state of Kalimantan Utara, the Indonesian attitude towards the federation was indifferent, if not positively agreeable. It may be borne in mind that it was in May 1961 that Tunku Abdul Rahman, the Prime Minister of Malaya, had proposed the idea of a federation embracing Malaya, Singapore and the British Borneo territories. Indonesia then raised no objection, and in November 1961 Indonesia's Foreign Minister affirmed at the United Nations that Indonesia had no claim to the

Borneo territories. But on 8 January 1963, soon after the Brunei revolt, Sukarno rejected the Malaysian federation and announced his 'confrontation'. Perhaps the Brunei revolt gave Sukarno an idea that it was not all plain sailing for Malaysia, and that with some Indonesian support the Borneo territories might be enabled to remain independent, with the possibility at a later date of all or some of them merging with the Indonesian Kalimantan. Their joining the Malaysian federation, Sukarno feared, would bring Malaya next door to Indonesia. Malaya and Indonesia had not been on very good terms since 1958, when the former had sympathised with the Indonesian rebels. Further, with British support and involvement from the very beginning, the Malaysian federation, Sukarno anticipated, might be exploited by 'imperialist Britain' for tin, rubber and oil.[3] Various other arguments and consideration might have been garnered at this stage in support of Indonesia's showdown with Malaysia. Both the Indonesian armed forces, and the communists (PKI) supported the confrontation, though for different reasons – the army speculated on the prospect of increased military budgets and a reinforcement of army prestige, the communists expected the confrontation to boost their brand of radicalism. Added to these were Sukarno's penchant for histrionics and his dictum that 'a nation always needs an enemy'. Sukarno's pride was hurt at what, to his sensitive mind, seemed to be a callous indifference shown towards his protestations by the British and Malayans. While he was in the middle of negotiations, and the United Nations team was still ascertaining the opinion of the people of Sabah and Sarawak (which eventually turned out to be in favour of joining the federation), the Prime Minister of Malaya announced on 29 August 1963 that Malaysia would be formed in the following month. Thereafter Sukarno went on the warpath, and the confrontation became Indonesia's settled policy.

Beginning in September 1963, the confrontation continued until the fall of Sukarno from power on 11 August 1966. After quick and cordial negotiations with the Malaysian leaders, General Suharto formally ended it. The economic aspect of the confrontation consisted of the seizure of all British and Malaysian properties and other assets within Indonesia, and the complete severance of trade with them by Indonesia. Britain's total economic stake in Indonesia in 1963 was about £160 million. Militarily, Indonesian action was mounted in two places – Borneo and Malaya – and consisted of sabotage and small-scale guerrilla skirmishes. Britain, Australia and New Zealand, who were bound by a 1957 defence treaty to help protect the Borneo territories, had deployed by January 1965 some 12,000 Commonwealth troops and considerable naval forces in support of Malaysia. During the confrontation Indonesia became increasingly isolated. Most of the Afro-Asian nations assumed a neutral posture towards Indonesia, and quite a few avoided attending the tenth anniversary of the first Afro-Asian Conference, which was held in Djakarta in April 1965. In January 1965, Indonesia pulled itself out of the United Nations in protest against Malaysia's election to the Security Council.

In the final analysis, the confrontation turned out to be a misadventure for Indonesia. Yet it was not just an isolated example of Sukarno's indiscretion.[4] It was, perhaps, the last display of Indonesia's revolutionary fervour. It seems that a country which has won its independence on the battlefield, as Indonesia did, tends to thrive on belligerency. This phase came to an end, perhaps happily for Indonesia, with the fall of Sukarno. In comparison, Suharto's Indonesia is inward-looking, more self-confident, and less prone to simulating images of internal strength by muscle-flexing and sabre-rattling on the international stage.

Of all the boundary disputes only that between China and India flared into a war. It may first be noted that the boundaries between the states of South and South-east Asia, as demarcated by the colonial powers, were not disputed by these states in the post-independence era. It would not have been surprising in the post-colonial period to see Nepal revive its claim over certain territories on its border which it lost to India in 1816, or Burma claim the hilly tracts of Assam which came under Indian reoccupation in 1826, or Malaysia and Thailand dispute the boundary settlement made by the British in 1909, or Thailand, Laos and Cambodia each dispute the various boundary settlements made by the French and claim territories on the other side of their borders. But no such claims were revived, which meant that these states accepted the boundaries as set between them by their colonial masters. But China was not a component of the colonial order which prevailed in this region of Asia, and was therefore under no obligation to respect its boundaries, mainly with Pakistan, India, Nepal and Burma, which were vaguely demarcated during the colonial period, and without China's explicit concurrence.

The disputed territories on the Sino-Indian border were larger and strategically more important to China than the areas involved in her frontiers with Pakistan, Nepal and Burma. Thus, when the Sino-Indian border entanglement began to turn into belligerency, China hastened to make peaceful settlements of its border with Burma in October 1960, with Nepal in October 1961, and tentatively with Pakistan in May 1962, which latter agreement was eventually finalised in March 1963. China abandoned most of its old claims on the

Burmese territory, and it gained not more than fifty square miles of territory through the settlement of 1960, which demarcated the entire Sino-Burmese border from the conjunction of India, China and Burma in the west to the conjunction of Burma, China and Laos in the east.[5] In its 1961 agreement with Nepal China accepted almost the precise boundary demarcated during the period of the British Raj. Except for a few square miles just to the east of Mount Everest, which passed from Nepal to China, no other territory changed hands. In treating Nepal as a fully sovereign state, China abandoned its old claim (which had rarely been enforced in the past) to some form of suzerainty over it. The Sino-Pakistan agreement of 1963 defined the boundaries between Sinkiang province of China and the Pakistan-occupied part of Kashmir. India alleged that through this settlement Pakistan surrendered to China about 2050 square miles of the disputed Kashmir territory. Pakistan retorted that it had done no such thing, instead it had actually gained 750 square miles of territory hitherto held by China. It is difficult to ascertain what actually changed hands in that barren, mostly uninhabited, part of the Karakoram mountain range.

Sino-Indian disputes, however, took an entirely different turn. With its occupation of Tibet in 1950, China came to have 2600 miles of border with India, stretching from the conjunction of India, Afghanistan and Sinkiang in the north-west to the conjunction of India, Burma and Tibet in the north-east. Along the eastern side of the border lay three adjoining mountain kingdoms, Nepal, and the Indian protectorates of Sikkim and Bhutan. In the Sino-Indian parlance the entire border was divided into three sectors – the eastern, stretching eastward from Bhutan to Burma; the middle sector, stretching westward from Nepal to Ladakh; and the western, running along the entire Ladakh boundary with Tibet and Sinkiang. Boundaries between India and China were disputed mainly in the eastern and western sectors. The Indo-Tibetan boundary in the eastern sector had been defined by what is called the McMahon Line, drawn in 1914. But China had never explicitly accepted the McMahon Line. India had accepted the 1914 settlement, and Nehru nourished no doubts whatsoever that Indian territory extended to the south of the McMahon Line. Even though the boundary in the western sector had never been clearly defined, there was in the Indian mind the idea of a customary demarcation line, as a British heritage, which ran along the eastern edges of Ladakh, and which therefore included in the Indian domain such outlying and unoccupied regions as Aksai Chin.

Although the Chinese maps which appeared during the heyday of the Sino-Indian friendship (1954 to 1958) claimed huge chunks of

Indian territory in the eastern and western sectors, the Chinese government did not officially put forward any claim during that period; in fact, the Chinese Prime Minister, Chou En-lai evaded any discussion of the boundary whenever he was asked by Nehru to clarify China's position in the matter. As it subsequently appeared, that was not an opportune time for China to open the border question. China had been surreptitiously building its Sinkiang–Tibet highway across India's Aksai Chin, but India had no knowledge of it until after the completion of the highway in October 1957. As this highway was logistically vital to China's hold on Tibet, China would have been willing to renounce its claims in the eastern sector in return for Aksai Chin in Ladakh. In fact, Chou En-lai had some such scheme in mind from 1956 until March 1959. In November 1956, when the Sinkiang–Tibet highway was nearing completion, Chou, while visiting India, indicated to Nehru that China would be willing to recognise the McMahon Line in the eastern sector, but perhaps he was unsure of Nehru's reactions since he did not straightforwardly ask for Aksai Chin in return.[6] Perhaps this was the propitious moment for Chou to put his cards on the table. Nehru then hardly knew the location of Aksai Chin, and Indian public opinion on the issue had not yet emerged. But it was too late in January 1959 for Chou to open the Chinese case for the first time. The Indians had by then come to accuse China of deceitfulness on account of its furtive occupation of Aksai Chin.

China's willingness gently to persuade India to accept the *status quo* subsided in March 1959, when the Tibetans revolted against the Chinese rule, and the Dalai Lama found asylum in India. China became unduly apprehensive of Indian intervention in Tibet. With thousands of Tibetan refugees in India, the Indians openly condemning Chinese repression in Tibet, and the Indian government now pursuing a 'forward policy' on its borders, the Chinese were misled into believing that India was bent on undermining China's hold on Tibet. In fact India had no such designs on Tibet. It kept its border claims and grievances quite separate from its sympathy for the Tibetans. Between November 1959 and September 1962 India's belligerent movements on the frontiers were confined to reoccupying border posts lost to the Chinese, and this only with a view to strengthening its bargaining position whenever the two parties came to negotiate a settlement of their border problems. Tibet was no longer India's concern, even though the Tibetans in those crucial years looked to India for their redemption.

The Tibetan factor caused panic in the Chinese approach to the border question. Chou's letter of 8 September 1959 to Nehru was aggressive in tone and style. It accused India of taking advantage of the Tibetan disturbance in advancing its position across the

McMahon Line into Chinese territory. It also disputed India's protectorate over Sikkim and Bhutan, which aroused the ire of Nehru. The prospects for a negotiated settlement began to recede with the growth of mutual misunderstanding and distrust between China and India. In such a situation every move on the part of one party was most likely to be misinterpreted by the other. In the context also of a growing rift between China and the Soviet Union, India's purchase of the Russian MiG–21 fighters in June 1962 alarmed the Chinese leaders. India harboured no designs on Tibet then or even after, but the Chinese, given their suspicion about India, might have been led to believe that India was planning a massive attack on Tibet. A showdown with India before it was too late was the option the Chinese leadership chose. At the beginning of September 1962 the Chinese forces were ready to attack. Between 8 September and 10 October quite a few border skirmishes broke out in the eastern sector. Being unprepared for combat at that altitude, the ill-equipped Indian forces kept on retreating. On 12 October 1962 Nehru, not heeding the unpreparedness of the army, sounded a clarion call. However, this was done more in order to raise public morale than actually to push the army into an all–out action. Even at this point Nehru did not believe in the possibility of an Indo–Chinese war ever breaking out. His publicly delivered threat of 12 October, however, provided the Chinese with an excuse for military thrusts. On 20 October 1962 they attacked the Indian positions in both the eastern and the western sectors. It was, however, a rapid in-and-out action on the part of China. On 20–1 November, at the height of the victory in the mountain warfare, China unilaterally declared a ceasefire and withdrew its forces from the positions they had occupied in the eastern sector since 20 October.

China had planned in advance both its invasion as well as its retreat. Any further advance on Indian territory and any prolongation of the war might have irretrievably trapped the Chinese forces, turned China's victory into defeat and, consequently, foiled its main objective of proving, especially to the bellicose Tibetans, its superiority over India. The indirect results of this short-lived war were thus favourable to China. The war cemented China's hold on Tibet. It also enhanced China's image as a world power. The war itself was most humane; no brutalities were committed by either side, and the total loss of lives on the Indian side was not more than 1383, and was far less on the Chinese side. It was not a total war (air power was not used by either side), and not even a declared war, as both countries maintained their diplomatic relations intact. Confined as it was within a belt 50–100 miles wide on each of India's two border frontiers, it was essentially a local war.

In consequence of the war Sino-Indian border problems became frozen. It was only in February 1979 that, in pursuance of the Janata government policy of cultivating friendly and closer relations with neighbouring countries, India's Foreign Minister, Atal Bihari Vajpayee, visited China and opened negotiations with his Chinese counterparts on the border question. The Chinese leaders, while agreeing in principle to open discussions at some opportune time in the future, made some friendly gestures by expressing their willingness to stop aiding Naga and Mizo rebels in the north-east region of India. Even though the Chinese response was not very warm and enthusiastic, the Indian Foreign Minister was beginning to regard his visit as a modest success, a step towards thawing Sino-Indian relations which had remained frozen for seventeen years. But Vajpayee's mission was turned into a failure by the Chinese invasion of Vietnam. His hosts did not even tell him about the invasion; in fact, Vajpayee came to know about it from a telephone call from India. Vajpayee cut short his visit, and returned home to find Indian distrust of China revived. The Chinese failure to inform the visiting Indian Foreign Minister of the invasion was taken by the Indians as a 'deliberate, calculated and intolerable insult to India'. Indian public opinion was further enraged by a thoughtless remark reported to have been made by the Chinese Vice-Premier, Deng Xiaoping, that Vietnam was being 'punished' today exactly as India was in 1962. This statement turned the knife in the Indian wound. But there were also political reasons behind the Indian government's condemnation of the Chinese aggression. India had excellent relations with Vietnam and its ally, the Soviet Union. Also, India was appalled by China's apparent claim to be Asia's policeman and to have the right to launch a 'punitive' campaign against any country it happened to dislike. Indian support for Vietnam was displayed in many ways, including Indian willingness to let Soviet supply aircraft use Indian air space. Thus, at present, it seems very unlikely that these two giants of Asia will arrive at some mutual understanding and trust in the foreseeable future.

MINORITIES AND SEPARATISM

Though the Asian nations now seem to have nearly passed through the phase of land and boundary disputes, their national integrity still continues to be threatened by the minorities. Since the dawn of independence most of the states have been ruffled, at some time or other, by communal, regional or separatist turmoils. At the root of this problem lies the conflict of loyalties which the peoples of every incipient nation have to go through: conflict between their traditional (or primordial) attachment to tribe, region, religious sect, ethnic group or race, and their loyalty to the civil politics associated with the newly established state. This is an inevitable phase in the process of national integration. It is also potentially a dangerous phase, for whereas economic or class or intellectual disaffection threatens revolution, 'disaffection based on race, language, or culture threatens partition, irredentism, or merger, a redrawing of the very limits of the state'.[7] In the Asian context, the problem looks more severe and chronic because of the age-old traditions, the great extent to which the Asian sense of self remains bound up in the actualities of blood, race, language, locality and religion, and because of the steadily increasing importance in this century of the sovereign state as a positive instrument for 'modernisation' and the realisation of collective aims. With the rapid modernisation of social, economic and political structures, it is quite conceivable that in due course there will be no peoples left 'to play the role of submerged nationalities or underlying populations, or passive bystanders of history'.[8] Even if the cultural varieties of the sub-national types continue to exist as they do now even in such an advanced nation as Britain, they will have run out of the need for separate, autonomous or independent nations. For it is not every minority community which poses a threat to a nation; the threat comes from that community or tribe which is inspired by an overpowering desire to remove itself from the subjection to, or association with, another community or communities, and which with this end in view organises itself into a political movement for separation.

Minorities in South and South-east Asia are innumerable. We are only concerned here with significant ones, which can be broadly classified into three categories. The first category comprises the minorities which hold no live awareness of their separate identity, have accepted the national norms and ethos, and are in the process of being assimilated with the majority community, while retaining in some cases their distinct cultural symbols and religious beliefs. The Chinese in Thailand, the Buddhists in Nepal, the Jains, Buddhists, and, in a qualified sense, the Parsis, Christians, Anglo-Indians and Sikhs in India, may be put into this category. Such minorities pose hardly any threat to the process of national integration. The second category includes minorities which retain their separate identities, are unassimilated, but because of their size and geographical location, or both, do not hold the political option to agitate for separate or independent states of their own. A large number of minority communities will fall into this category: the Muslims and Untouchables in India, the Hindus in Bangladesh, the Indians and Chinese in Burma and Malaysia, and the Chinese in Vietnam and Indonesia. The problems facing such minorities are mainly communal riots and migrations. In the third category may be placed the minorities which have an intense awareness of their separate identities, are unassimilated, and hold the political option and will to separate into autonomous or independent states. Such minorities are the Tamils in Sri Lanka, the Nagas and Mizos in India, the Baluchis and Pathans in Pakistan, the Shans, Kayahs, Karens, Kachins, Chins, Arakanese and Mons in Burma, and the Muslims in the Philippines. (The small number of Thai Muslims inhabiting the four provinces on the southern tip of the country, have so far not caused any significant problem.) All these minorities have one common feature: each predominantly populates a particular region in a state. Also, the minority territories happen to be situated mostly on the fringes rather than in the heartlands of the countries concerned. The threat of separation or secession which such minorities often pose, stems solely from their advantageous geographical positions; and the fact that they inhabit the border areas of a particular country gives them the additional advantage of obtaining arms and aid from across the border.

Bengalis of the breakaway Bangladesh form a special category of their own, mainly because they did not constitute a minority in the united Pakistan (for the emergence of Bangladesh, see chapter 3, pp. 72–5). In fact they were in the majority. We will also exclude from our treatment here regional and parochial movements which were not sponsored by any minority community on any racial, ethnic, linguistic or religious grounds. The Indonesian brand of regional tensions between Javanese and non-Javanese, even though it contains some ethnic factors, will fall outside the scope of this particular enquiry.

As for the minorities in the first category, diverse factors had caused each of them to fraternise with the majority community. The case of the Chinese in Thailand explains some of the factors. In 1960 there were about twelve million Chinese residing in South-east Asia. Except for Singapore, where they formed the majority of the population, their percentage of the total population in the rest of the countries varied from 4 per cent in North Vietnam to 37 per cent in Malaya. But nowhere were they so well assimilated into the majority community as in Thailand, where they constituted about 11 per cent of the population. The specific factors which accelerated the assimilation rate of the Chinese in Thailand were intermarriage, the Thai government's non-discriminatory policy towards the immigrants, and the non-existence of Chinese schools, at least until 1910, which otherwise might have fostered a sense of separate linguistic identity among the Chinese children.[9] Intermarriage between Chinese male immigrants and Thai females took place on a large scale because until the first decade of the twentieth century Chinese women almost never emigrated to Thailand. The offspring of the mixed marriages were assimilated into society as Thais, for according to the prevailing norm anyone who used a Thai name, spoke the language, and behaved as a Thai was accepted as a Thai regardless of ancestry. Because of the government's liberal policy, there were no restrictions on ethnic Chinese making their way into the Thai ruling class; the existence of a Thai ruling class, was, of course due to Thailand being (during the colonial period) the only independent country in South-east Asia. The Thai conditions were not available to Chinese elsewhere.

Looking at the Thai-Chinese and other 'integrated' or 'integrating minorities' in this category, one is inclined to infer that the factor most conducive to their assimilation had been the unequivocal acceptance on their part of the national norms and ethos. Integration is primarily a mental process. The Sikhs, Parsis, Christians, Buddhists, Jains and Anglo-Indians in India have now come to see themselves as vital components of the Indian nation, and they talk and behave like Indians, and this is also the case with the small number of Buddhists in Nepal. Indeed, the secular and non-discriminatory policies of the Indian governments in the post-independence era have greatly softened the process of integration.

This brings us to the minorities of the second category, such as the Muslims and Untouchables[10] in India, who are still far from being fully assimilated. In their case it is really a matter of social and economic assimilation, for politically, constitutionally and legally they have equal rights with the Hindus, in fact in the matter of government employment they are more privileged than the members of the majority community. Since independence two Muslims have been President of India, the central and state cabinets have always included Muslim and Harijan ministers, and their recruitment into the Civil Service has always been weighted. Social intercourse between Harijans and Muslims, however, on the one hand and Hindus on the other, was almost non-existent until the dawn of independence, and although during the last thirty odd years some intermixing and intermarriage have taken place, these are still the exceptions rather than the common practice. Intermarriage and interdining however, are still not common among the various castes and sects of the Hindu community itself, and it is therefore quite conceivable for a non-Hindu community to become part of a Hindu India even without the basis of social intercourse. The causes, thus, for persisting communal tensions, occasionally breaking into Hindu–Muslim and Harijan–caste Hindu riots, can be traced to the attitudes towards each other of the communities concerned. The

Hindus have long discriminated against the Muslims on political, religious and historical grounds, and against their own lower-caste or casteless co-religionists – the Harijans – on cultural and economic grounds. The Muslims too have nourished and asserted their own separate identity for a long time. In the post-independence era, however, Hindu–Muslim tension has been steadily on the decline, and communal riots have become less frequent. This we may attribute partly to the Muslims gaining a greater sense of security and coming round to thinking and behaving like Indians, and partly to the Hindus gradually discarding their old prejudices and fears and accepting Muslims as their compatriots.

Harijans have constituted economically the most exploited and socially the worst discriminated against segment of Indian society. Until recently they have also been the most silent sufferers. Having become somewhat politicised through India's five general elections and many more state elections, and having also acquired the requisite initiative and courage from Mrs Gandhi's government, during the Emergency, to fight for their freedom from bonded labour and other economic servitudes, the Harijans, it appears, had by 1975 gained just enough strength to stand up for their economic and social rights, and to fight back if bullied and attacked by the higher caste Hindus.[11] This in itself constituted a monumental change in the age-old servile attitude of the Harijans. A Harijan hitting back at a caste Hindu was a much rarer event than an Indian exchanging blow for blow with a Briton during the days of the Raj. The Harijan awakening put up the backs of the land-owning and money-lending Hindus who had a vested interest in Harijan servility. From 1975 to the end of 1978 the more the Harijans stood up for their rights the more brutally they were treated by the Hindus in the rural areas of India. 1978 saw the worst crimes committed against the Harijans, particularly in the caste-ridden and most backward state of Bihar, where the state government's policy of further enhancing the Harijan quota in the public services intensified the Hindu onslaughts on the defenceless Harijans. In 1978, 412 murders and 478 rapes involving Harijans were committed in India.[12] The Indian intelligentsia, being always conscious of this shameful aspect of Indian society, writhed in agony at the sufferings of the ninety million Harijans. On 30 September 1978 Jagjivan Ram, the Harijan leader and the Defence Minister of India, called upon the members of the scheduled castes and scheduled tribes to launch a national movement for their liberation. Comparing the fate of the Indian Harijans with the 'blacks' in the United States, Ram said, 'We were patronised so long as we wanted sympathy. But they feel alarmed when we want our rights.'[13] But unlike their fellow-sufferers in the United States, Ram maintained, the Harijans were the original inhabitants of India, and physically identical with their caste-Hindu exploiters.

Jagjivan Ram, however, is not exactly the Harijan's Martin Luther King, nor are the Harijans of India exactly like the 'blacks' of the United States. Ram has exercised much more governmental power in India than any leader of a non-white minority community has so far been able to wield in the Western world. Those Harijans who by sheer force of education, industry or enterprise have forced their way out of the dungeon of poverty and cultural backwardness, have not only been readily accepted by the majority community as its own, but have also made their way easily into the core of the Indian establishment. Though exploited by the Hindus, the Harijans have never felt alienated from them. The display of assertiveness on their part promises their rapid integration with, rather than separation from Indian society.

Like the Muslims and Harijans in India, the Hindus in Bangladesh constitute an indigenous minority. They were there when that part of India became East Pakistan, and later when it emerged as the sovereign state of Bangladesh. While Bangladesh was a part of Pakistan, the tensions between the Hindus and Muslims arose whenever hostility broke out between India and Pakistan. On such occasions the Bangladesh Hindus tended to cross the border and take refuge in India. Before the last Indo-Pakistan war of 1971 they emigrated to India in large numbers and became a problem for Mrs Gandhi's government. Since the emergence of Bangladesh, the refugee problem has not been revived. There is a high degree of cultural and linguistic affinity between the Hindus and Muslims of Bangladesh, hence the minority problem there may continue to diminish unless hostility breaks out between the two countries, in which case the Bangladeshi Hindus might cross the border, for they have not yet stopped looking to India when they are fearful and insecure.

The rest of the minorities in this category are aliens, mainly Chinese and Indians in the countries of South-east Asia. They are aliens in the sense that most of them migrated to these countries during the colonial period, and continued to preserve their separate identities in the post-independence era, even after acquiring, as many did, the citizenship of the individual countries in which they lived. There were more Chinese than Indians in South-east Asia. Only in Burma and Malaysia did the Indians figure as alien minorities of any significance. But the Chinese were everywhere, as the old Chinese government (the Kuomintang) had treated the overseas Chinese as Chinese nationals, and claimed that 'where there are Chinese, there is China', the national governments of South-east

Asia were alarmed when China turned into a mighty communist power, and consequently seemed able to enforce what the previous government in China had only claimed in theory. It was also feared that communist China might use the overseas Chinese as instruments for the expansion of communism in South-east Asia. It was thus a great relief to the South-east Asian governments when China announced its policy towards the overseas Chinese at the Bandung Conference of the non-aligned countries of Asia and Africa, held in 1955. While asserting its adherence to the policy of non-intervention in the affairs of other countries, China asked the overseas Chinese (as evident by the Sino-Indonesian treaty signed in April 1955) holding double nationalities to choose within a specified period of time the nationality either of the individual countries they had been inhabiting, or of their mother country – the People's Republic of China. Those Chinese who, having chosen Chinese nationality, continued to live in the other country were asked not to take any part in the political activities of that country. The policy which China thus initiated in 1955 was to encourage Chinese nationals to adopt the nationality of their country of residence on a voluntary basis. At the same time, China was opposed to its overseas nationals being forced to change their nationality.

These principles were also incorporated in an informal agreement reached between China and Vietnam in 1955.[14] However, of the one million Chinese in Vietnam, the bulk resided in South Vietnam. According to communist China, the Ngo Dinh Diem regime of South Vietnam compelled the South Vietnamese Chinese 'to renounce their Chinese nationality, and adopt Vietnamese nationality' under decrees promulgated in August 1956.[15] Soon after the unification of Vietnam in 1975, the rift between Vietnam and China started to make itself evident, and the Chinese in Vietnam began to be treated as fifth columnists. Particularly those Vietnamese Chinese who still retained Chinese nationality were distrusted and perhaps forced to migrate to China. It is also possible that quite a number of Chinese, apprehensive of an imminent war between Vietnam and China, crossed the border of their own accord. By August 1978, China had about 160,000 Chinese refugees from Vietnam on its hands. The refugee problem, together with Vietnam's adventure in Cambodia (December 1978), intensified China's animus towards Vietnam, and caused the Sino-Vietnamese war of February 1979.

It is difficult to ascertain precisely not only the exact number of Indians and Chinese in the South-east Asian countries, but also the number of those who have acquired the citizenship of the country in which they live, and those who still retain the citizenship of their country of origin, or are stateless. This exercise becomes more difficult when applied to Vietnam, which borders China, and to Burma, which borders China, India and Bangladesh. Illegal or unregistered immigrations into Vietnam and Burma from across their respective borders have frequently occurred. In both countries the alien minorities have tended to retain the nationality of their country of origin. Burma has been mainly occupied in containing its indigenous minorities. The alien minorities have caused no serious problems, mainly because of their small size and their dispersal throughout the country.[16] In the summer of 1978, however, Burma suddenly developed a problem concerning one such alleged alien minority. From April to June of that year about 200,000 Muslims had fled into Bangladesh from the Arakan region of Burma. Denying the allegation that these Muslims were turned out of their homes at gunpoint, the Burmese government maintained that they were illegal immigrants who had entered Burma in the early 1970s when the strife between East and West Pakistan was particularly bad. The controversy over the status of these Muslims – whether they were established residents of Burma, or had entered Burma illegally in recent years – was not settled. None the less, in July 1978, the Burmese government agreed to take them back, and by March 1979 almost all the refugees had returned to Burma.

According to the 1970 census, the total population of Malaysia (Malay, Sabah and Sarawak) was nearly 10·5 million, of which the Chinese and Indians respectively constituted about 34 and 9 per cent.[17] More than 75 per cent of the Chinese and 65 per cent of the Indians were born in Malaysia or Singapore. Hence, after the country's independence, most of these Chinese and Indians became naturalised under the Malaysian constitution, which granted citizenship rights to those who were either born in Malaysia or had lived there for a certain number of years with an intention to make it their permanent home. The Chinese, Indians and Malays, however, contrast sharply in physical appearance, language, religion and mores. Since it has been the policy of the Malaysian government to preserve the Islamic character of the state, and to make Malay the official language of the country, communal riots, particularly between the Chinese and Malays, have occasionally broken out since Malaysian independence in 1957. In the 1960s the Chinese challenged the concept of the pro-Malay Malaysia in vain, and put against it the concept of a 'Malaysian Malaysia', which meant that the country belonged to all and was not to be identified with the supremacy, wellbeing and interests of any one particular community or race. There were, of course, economic factors which fuelled the tension between the Chinese and Malays. The Malaysian government's attempts to improve the lot of poor Malays involved depriving the Chinese to some extent of their virtual monopoly of the economic life of the country.

Cultural and economic grievances of the minorities, however, have been contained so far by the unique Malaysian device of the Alliance, which has hitherto enabled the Chinese and Indians to share political power (see chapter 2, pp. 57–61). As in India, so in Malaysia, it has become possible for the minorities to offer political loyalty to the state while retaining their separate cultural identities. Perhaps it is not unreasonable to expect that political integration may in due course bring about the cultural assimilation.

The minorities placed in the third category are the ones which have so far acted as the vehicles of separatism. Of all the factors responsible for activating them, perhaps the most important, and also the least mentioned, is the lust for power on the part of their individual leaders. Behind all separatist movements lies their leaders' ambition to carve out dominions for themselves. If their communities remained parts of the larger units, these leaders would hardly have the chance to wield unrestrained executive power. This is not to say that all the grievances and fears of a minority community are created by its leaders. What is suggested here is that the leaders tend to exploit the situation more for the advancement of their own personal ambition than for the good of their community. Except for the over-zealous philanthropist who sees oppression and exploitation writ large on the face of every minority community, or the romantic who believes that every linguistic community with a language and culture of its own is a nation, and as such should rightfully be a separate and independent state, or a foreign power whose interests temporarily lie in causing the disintegration of a particular state, hardly anybody else would believe, for example, that the Tamils of Sri Lanka, the Nagas of India or the Karens of Burma, would really be better off with independent states of their own. Of course there is a strong case for a minority to have its own independent state if it is being constantly persecuted, tortured, exploited and annihilated by the majority community. There is, however, no evidence to show that any minority in this part of Asia has received such treatment from the majority community, and is suffering the same fate which in the past has befallen the aborigines of America and Australia.

With the advent in 1978 of a strong presidential form of government in Sri Lanka, the Tamil separatism there appears to have subsided (for Sri Lanka Tamil separatism, see chapter 2, pp. 61–4). Having never received any clandestine support from India, the Sri Lankan Tamils were unable ever to organise themselves into a militant force. The reaction of about two million Tamil-speaking

Hindus of Sri Lanka, inhabiting the northern tip of the island around Jaffna, to the Sri Lankan government's pro-Sinhalese language and religious policies, was somewhat the same as that of the Chinese in Malaysia. They thought that they were being treated by the majority Sinhalese population as second-class citizens. They formed a separatist front in 1972, more with a view to striking political bargains and getting their grievance redressed than to putting determined efforts into the creation of a separate state for themselves. Their leaders were a little carried away by their success at the 1977 election, and put forward their demand for a separate Tamil state. President Jayewardene's emphatic 'No' to this on the one hand, and his assurance to them on the other that their grievances would be remedied, almost put an end to the incipient separatist movement.

The breakaway of Bangladesh from Pakistan in 1971 stimulated separatism among the Baluchis and Pathans, who vaguely aspired to some kind of union with their respective counterparts in Iran and Afghanistan. The Pashto-speaking Pathans of Pakistan had been receiving some encouragement from Afghanistan in their aspirations for an independent state of Pakhtunistan, which would comprise the Pathan territories of both the countries. Though Baluchi and Pathan separatism never got off the ground, much of the energies and resources of Bhutto's government, in its last days, were expended in tightening its hold on these border provinces of Pakistan.

The Indian device to contain separatism within the national fold was to create separate states for the militant linguistic or ethnic communities. India was faced with two different kinds of separatist movement: the one for the creation of separate linguistic states within the Indian union, and the other for the creation of independent sovereign states. India applied the same device to both. The movement for the linguistic reorganisation of the Indian states resulted in the creation of the Telugu-speaking state of Andhra in 1953; the division of Bombay in 1960 into two states – the Marathi-speaking Maharashtra and the Gujarati-speaking Gujarat – and the reorganisation of the old Punjab in 1966 into two separate states, the Hindi-speaking Haryana, and the Punjabi-speaking Punjab.

The movement for an independent sovereign state was led only by the tribal Nagas, numbering just over half-a-million and inhabiting the north-eastern tract of Indian territory on the Burmese border. During the days of the British Raj, the majority of Nagas had been converted to Christianity by foreign missionaries. At the time of India's independence, the most radical of the Nagas, organised as they were in the Naga National Council led by A. Z. Phizo, demanded an independent state for their tribe on the grounds that they were by race and religion different from the Hindus of India. These arguments carried no weight with the secular Nehru. India had already millions of Christians and people of Mongoloid stock in its fold. In 1955 the recalcitrant Nagas took to guerrilla warfare. India had to deploy its army. Brutalities were committed by both sides. The moderates among the Nagas, however, were instrumental in persuading their people, through the various conventions they held between 1957 and 1959, to renounce their demand for independence, and to seek a settlement of the Naga problem within the Indian Union. The result was the creation of the separate state of Nagaland within the Indian Union in 1962. Phizo had by then taken refuge in Britain, but his followers persisted in their armed hostility against India with guns and training readily made available to them by the Chinese from across the Indian border. After the Sino–Indian war of 1962, Chinese aid was made available to other restive tribes in the north–eastern region of India. India continued to contain tribal restiveness by creating separate states. By now, apart from Assam, four new states (Nagaland, Meghalaya, Manipur and Tripura) and two Union territories (Arunachal Pradesh and Mizoram) have emerged in India's north–eastern region bordering China and Burma. If China stops harbouring and training the Naga and Mizo rebels, the tribal minorities in this area may soon settle down in peace and begin strengthening their political loyalty to India.

Under the constitution of 1947 (which was replaced in 1974 by Ne Win's new constitution), Burma had contained its indigenous minorities by organising them into five separate ethnic states and special districts – the states of Shan, Kachin and Karenni (which in 1951 was renamed Kayahj), and the special districts of Chin and Karen – and giving each state representation in the country's upper legislative chamber – the Chamber of Nationalities. Unlike these states, Burma proper – incorporating almost half the territory of the Union and including more than three-quarters of the population – was governed directly by the Union government and parliament. The minorities having their own states from the very beginning (Karens acquired a state of their own in 1951), aspired to more autonomy, and some of them threatened to secede if more powers were not given to them. The tribal Kachins, Karens and Chins were opposed to the process of Burmanisation by which the language, religion, dress and customs of the dominant group were encroaching upon their way of life. Rebellions and wars occasionally broke out, but the Union government managed to keep the minorities within its fold, by employing the 'carrot and stick' policy. Within Burma proper, another form of minority problem was caused by the Arakanese and Mons, both of whom agitated for separate states. The

Burmese government, however, did not recognise them as minority groups, and their agitation gradually petered out. But a small number of dissidents, coming out of almost every ethnic group, continued their insurgent activity against the government and its supporters from their hideouts along the Burmese–Thai borders. Under Ne Win's rule the minorities have gradually come to regard themselves as integral elements in the country, even though a handful of rebel leaders, having founded the National Democratic Front in 1976, are still persisting in their fight against the government, but certainly with no clear purpose and vision.

In 1976 the Muslims formed nearly 6 per cent of the Philippines' total population of about 42 million. They inhabit the southern parts of the Philippines – Mindanao and Sulu. But of the thirteen provinces into which this region of the country is divided, the Muslims constitute a majority in only five. In the island of Mindanao itself, for example, the two million Muslims are outnumbered by four million Christians. The Muslims themselves are divided into four ethnic groups of which one – the Samals who inhabit the southern island of the Sulu archipelago – has not been deeply involved in the movement.

Muslim separatism in the Philippines has derived strength more from historical factors, and the support given to it by the Islamic countries, than from the size and location of the Muslim population in the country. The Muslims were the only Filipinos never to be totally brought under control by the Spaniards, who ruled the country for nearly 400 years. Even the Americans succeeded in extending their rule over them only after engaging in two fierce and memorable battles in 1906 and 1913. The Tausugs of Mindanao – one of the four Muslim ethnic groups – have a tradition of suicidal bravery in battle. With this kind of background, the Muslims were almost bound to become restive and rebellious at the influx of Christians from the north of the country. The superior economic advantages which the Christians enjoyed as settlers were one cause of the Muslim revolt in the first place. Foreign support in the form of firearms and ammunition came from neighbouring Sabah and distant Libya. The major Muslim backers of the revolt were Tun Datu Hadji Mustapha bin Harun, (Sabah's Minister of State until April 1976), and Colonel Qaddafi, the Libyan leader.

The Muslim resentment grew into open rebellion in 1972, and the fight between the government forces and the Muslim Moro National Liberation Front (MNLF) continued with varying intensity until December 1976, when a ceasefire agreement between the two parties was reached at Tripoli under the sponsorship of Colonel Qaddafi. The MNLF dropped its demand for an independent state, accepting as a compromise an autonomous Muslim region within the Philippines. It was tentatively agreed at Tripoli that Muslims would be allowed to set up their own legislative assembly and executive, financial, economic and educational institutions in the autonomous region.

The negotiations between the MNLF and the Philippine government, however, broke down in the summer of 1977, mainly on the question of what should be the size of the Muslim autonomous region. The MNLF wanted it to comprise all thirteen provinces. Marcos wanted this matter to be resolved by a referendum. Being aware that the non-Muslim majority of the provinces would vote against the autonomy proposal, the MNLF rejected the referendum suggestion. None the less, the referendum was held in April 1977, and the verdict of the people went against autonomy. The MNLF then renewed the fighting. Marcos, however, clearly indicated that he would like the Muslims to have some kind of political and cultural autonomy. In February 1977 he promulgated a code of personal laws for the Muslims in the Philippines, recognising their system of laws, and providing for their administration.

The eight-year-old Muslim rebellion had, by mid-1979, cost an estimated 50,000 lives. To fight the rebels the government had been steadily increasing its military spending. For example, it went up from US \$90 million in 1972 to US \$385·7 million in 1976.[18] Half the country's armed forces had been tied up in Mindanao. No negotiated settlement has yet been achieved. However, the Islamic powers appear to have stopped giving direct military aid to the MNLF, which may at some point oblige the Muslims to settle for a little less than their previous demands.

COMMUNIST INSURGENCIES

Looking at the situation in mid-1979, it appears that communist insurgencies, like minority uprisings, have ceased to be a major problem. At present there are only a small number of communist insurgents still fighting a losing battle from their hideouts on the Thai-Malaysian and the Thai-Burmese borders (see chapter 2, pp. 59–60). This, of course, does not take into account the constant fear of being invaded by a neighbouring communist state with which a non-communist state may be possessed. Here we are only concerned with internal communist revolts. However, from the present scarcity of communist uprisings, it cannot be inferred that this phenomenon has become a thing of the past and will never recur to agitate the states in this region as seriously as it did in the first two decades of their independence. For of all the factors conducive to insurgency the instability of government is the most important, and no state in this part of the world can be regarded as having passed far beyond the instability line.

At the outset of this enquiry two questions may be raised. What led to communist insurgencies in the first place. Why was the communist movement weaker in some states and stronger in others, and why did it fail to capture central power anywhere except in the Indo-Chinese states of Vietnam, Cambodia and Laos?

The answer to the first question lies partly in the change of communist strategy as symbolised by the formation of the Cominform (Communist Information Bureau) in September 1947, under the patronage of the Soviet Union. At the foundation meeting the representatives of the European communist parties accepted the thesis put forward by the Soviet delegate, Andre Zhdanov. Stressing that the world was divided into Socialist and Capitalist camps, the thesis called for an irreconcilable hostility towards the latter. The acceptance of the Zhdanov doctrine implied the rejection of the strategy which the Communist International (Comintern) had decreed in 1935 – the strategy of collaborating with Western democracies and bourgeois nationalist forces with a view to forming a united front against fascism. Zhdanov's doctrine was discussed and accepted at a communist-sponsored conference of South and Southeast Asian youth and students, held in Calcutta during February 1948. The communist leaders thus accepted the Soviet command to organise insurgencies, irrespective of the conditions prevailing in their respective countries, which in some cases involved revolting against a nationalist government and thereby acquiring unpopularity.

Soon after the clarion call was sounded at Calcutta, communist-organised insurgencies took place in those states where there was a communist party, and also, though not necessarily, a certain degree of agrarian unrest among peasants. This upsurge of militant communism involved India, Burma, Malaya, Indonesia and the Philippines. The Communist Party of India (founded in 1925) took the lead. The militant B. T. Ranadive, the prime exponent of Zhdanov's doctrine, replaced the liberal P. C. Joshi, as the party's General Secretary, and the CPI embarked upon an adventurist line of action. The peasant uprising in Telengana (Eastern Hyderadad) was propped up; strikes and sabotage were planned, and violence was openly preached. The communists, however, gained no popular support. They failed, for example, to bring the railwaymen out on strike – the single general strike they had so confidently planned for 9 March 1949. With their Russian-style revolution, they failed to make any headway against Nehru's nationalist government. By 1955 the CPI had come to abandon militancy and accept 'constitutional communism' – the view that communism could come to power in India through peaceful parliamentary means. Even in taking this stance the Indian communists were, ironically, influenced more by Russian policy towards India than by the Indian conditions. Krushchev's rise to power after the death of Stalin in 1953, and his support for Nehru's policies of non-alignment and peaceful coexistence obliged the CPI to change its views of the Nehru government.

The Burma Communist Party (founded in 1939) was divided between two factions, the Red Flags and the White Flags. The Red Flags were already in revolt in 1946. The White Flags, led by Than Tun, who had attended the Calcutta conference, went into revolt on 27 March 1948. On that day Than Tun called for insurrection at a mass meeting in Rangoon, and soon after retreated into the rural areas to rally supporters for an eventual onslaught on Rangoon. The White Flags quickly amassed a substantial guerrilla force, and after 1951 they operated in loose alliance with the Red Flags and other dissident groups – the People's Volunteer Organisation, Karen and Mon ethnic minorities. These insurgent forces dominated central and southern Burma between 1948 and 1952. Because of their disunity, mutual suspicion, and lack of objectives, they could not hold out against the government for long. By 1954 the two communist forces had been driven from their most valuable economic bases, and the BCP had become a dead political factor. By 1958 38,000 insurgents, about a quarter of whom were communists, had surrendered.

Since its formation in 1930, the Malayan Communist Party has been overwhelmingly Chinese in its membership (see chapter 2, pp. 59–60). It was revived and enthused with anti-Japanese feeling in 1937, when the war broke out between Japan and China. During the Japanese occupation of Malaya, the communist guerrillas formed the Malayan People's Anti-Japanese Army. At the time of the Japanese surrender, the MCP was in a fairly strong position, and some analysts have wondered why the Malayan communists did not take advantage of their position to block the British re-entry into Malaya and seize the governmental machinery for themselves. Instead, they co-operated with the British, surrendered their arms, and received rewards for their services. The MCP took to organising labour unions in urban areas. However, the communists soon began to realise that they would be out-manoeuvred by the Malay nationalists in the power game, and that there was no prospect of them gaining central power except by force of arms. The Calcutta conference directive thus came in handy, and the party's Secretary-General, Chen Ping, declared the 'war of national liberation'. With the

murder of three British planters in June 1948, the British government declared a state of emergency and moved to arrest the communist leaders. The Malayan communists took to the jungle, where
they became increasingly cut off from sources of supply, and their
strength and determination gradually declined. By 1955 they had
ceased to be a major threat, and became 'a stubborn but manageable
nuisance'.

In Indonesia, the beginnings of a socialist movement go back to
1914 when the Indies Social Democratic Association (ISDV) was
founded. The ISDV became a communist party in 1920, and in 1924
it acquired the name of Partai Komunis Indonesia (PKI) – the
Communist Party of Indonesia. Indonesia thus was the first country
in this region to have a communist party. In terms of membership
and following, the PKI was one of the strongest communist parties
in southern Asia. It was, however, the only communist party to have
had suffered the severest of setbacks on each of the three occasions
(1926, 1948 and 1965) that it ventured to capture power (see also
chapter 2, pp. 45–6). The first generation of Indonesian communists was destroyed by the Dutch colonial authorities following the
failure of the 1926 armed communist rebellion; 13,000 communists
were arrested, of which some were executed, some put into prison
and some deported.[19] The PKI was declared illegal, but revived
however in November 1945, and revolved round the former communist leader, Tan Malaka. There was at this time not only a crisis of
leadership in the PKI, but also a very thin boundary existed between
the nationalists and the communists.[20] Among the communists
themselves there was a division between those who followed their
own lights, and those who were faithful to the international party
line. Thus, the communist movement did not have a well-defined
objective, and the PKI could not claim to include in its membership
all who were communists or thought they were. Amir Sjarifuddin,
for example, was as much of a communist as Musso, but the former
together with Sutan Sjahrir, led the Socialist Party, which also, like
the PKI, was revived at the end of the war.

In 1945 the PKI decided to participate in the Republic's coalition
government, which was led by the leftists like Sjahrir and Sjarifuddin. The period from 1945 to 1948 was characterised by war and
negotiations carried on simultaneously between the Republican and
the Dutch forces. The coalition government fell in January 1948, and
was replaced by one led by Mohammad Hatta. Hatta did not include
in his cabinet any leftists, and tension grew between the Republican
government and the PKI. It was at this point, in August 1948, that
Musso, a leader of the Indonesian Communist Party in the 1920s,
returned from a long exile in the Soviet Union and quickly

succeeded in merging the left-wing elements into an expanded Communist Party. Musso declared that he intended to seize command of the Republic's government. Together with Sjarifuddin and other communist leaders, Musso embarked upon an intensive organisational and propaganda campaign. Suddenly, on 14 September 1948, the initiative was taken out of their hands by the local communist leaders in the city of Madiun in East Java. These local communists had become unnerved by a government order for the demobilisation of their armed forces. On that day in September they revolted. The PKI leadership was left with no alternative but to support the revolt, and the war that ensued between the PKI and Sukarno's government was brief, but bloody. Sukarno declared a state of emergency. Musso called on the people to overthrow Sukarno as a lackey of American imperialism. The government, however, had no difficulty in suppressing the revolt. By 30 September the government forces had occupied Madiun, and Musso was killed in the fighting. The rebellion was officially declared to have been finally put down on 7 December 1948. Sjarifuddin and seven other communist leaders were executed, and the PKI was thus reduced to its 'previous condition of confused anarchy'.[21] Many of the PKI branches declared their loyalty to Sukarno. The leadership of the PKI was assumed by D. N. Aidit, and in 1951 the PKI embarked on a new path of gaining power by peaceful means. This change of strategy was to place the PKI, in less than a decade, in a position of great though uncertain power. In 1959 the PKI was to claim a membership of about 1·5 million. In mid-1965, just before its demise, it claimed to have 3 million members, and its leader, Aidit, was then regarded as the political heir to the ageing Sukarno.

Launched on 7 November 1930, the Communist Party of the Philippines (CPP) was carried away by the initial response it received from the people, and also by its high-sounding objectives of overthrowing American imperialism, capitalism and feudalism, and establishing a Soviet government in the country under the dictatorship of the working class. In May 1931, when its leader, Crisanto Evengelista, openly defied the mayor's order banning the party's public meeting in Manila, the CPP was outlawed and went underground. In 1938, when the party renounced its revolutionary ambitions, it was allowed to function legally. The CPP gathered instant strength by merging with the Socialist Party (which had been founded in 1929 by Pedro Abad Santos) in the same year. It started its legal career with a membership of 55,000, of whom 50,000 had belonged to the Socialist Party.

The opportunity for the CPP to play some nationalist role, however, arose during the war, after the invasion of the Philippines by the Japanese early in 1942. The CPP launched the Barrio United Defence Corps and, in March 1942, the People's Anti-Japanese Army, better known as Hukbalahap or just Huk. The Huk was formed where the Party's peasant supporters were strongest, as in the province of Pampanga in central Luzon. Luis Taruc took command of the Huk force, which began its anti-Japanese activities in February 1942 with a guerrilla band of 300. Its strength multiplied tenfold in only seven months. Huk activities, however, were directed more towards 'eliminating the Communist Party's Filipino rivals than towards killing Japanese'.[22] Of the 25,000 people the Huks killed, only about 5000 were Japanese. At the end of the war, the CPP, toeing the Moscow line, decided to co-operate with the nationalist forces, and participated in the 1946 election held at the time of the country's independence. But the legality of the CPP-supported deputies returned to the National Congress was successfully disputed by the Liberal leaders and they were not allowed to take their seats. Luis Taruc was one of these six deputies. He left Manila for the old Huk centre, where he began to foster peasant unrest and to engage in armed activities. The Huk uprising, however, did not seem to have the direct support of the CPP. None the less, the rebellion went on gathering strength, and at the beginning of 1948 it was nearly 200,000 strong. In March 1948 the Hukbalahap was banned by the government. But the same fate did not befall the CPP, which practised constitutional politics, until the 1949 election, when its leaders realised that they would not be able to achieve either political power or agrarian reform without resorting to armed struggle. Of course by this time international communism had accepted the Zhdanov doctrine. The CPP joined hands with the Huk, which was now reorganised and given the name of the People's Liberation Army (HMB). A Provisional Revolutionary Government was formed and full-scale military operations began, plunging the country instantly into civil war.

Of all the measures the national government of the Liberal Party undertook to suppress the CPP-Huk revolt, the most effective was the appointment of Ramon Magsaysay as Secretary of Defence in September 1950. Magsaysay was perhaps the only honest, incorruptible and efficient politician in the high-ranking leadership of the Liberal and the Nationalist Parties. Like Nehru in India and Sukarno in Indonesia, Magsaysay was instrumental in paralysing and reducing insurgencies to impotence, and by 1953 the CPP-Huk armed rebellion in the Philippines was over.

'All-out force' and 'all-out friendship' were the two arms of Magsaysay's policy towards the Huk and communist rebels. Military reforms were introduced to raise the morale of the armed forces, the CPP leaders were captured and severely dealt with, and the village people were protected against acts of terrorism. At the same time, Magsaysay, believing as he did that most of the rebels were not communists at all, but people angered by governmental oppression, extended the hand of friendship to those dissidents who wanted to surrender. Land and social welfare benefits were offered to the dissidents, and a vast number of them were resettled. Magsaysay aimed at eventually removing the basic cause of discontent among the agrarian populace. It was not a mere coincidence that the Huks and communists had their stronghold in central Luzon, where there had been a steady growth in tenancy – from 38 per cent in 1903 to 54 per cent in 1939 and 60 per cent in 1948.[23] Only radical land reform could bring the 'have-nots' just above the poverty line. Magsaysay (who was elected to the presidency in 1953) died prematurely in 1957, however. But the back of the communist insurgency had been completely broken in May 1954 when Luis Taruc and his followers surrendered. By the end of 1956 the CPP controlled a Liberation Army of just 860 persons, 560 of whom were armed.

The failure of communist insurgencies in South and South-east Asia had already discredited the Zhdanov strategy before Khrushchev officially abandoned it in February 1956 at the Twentieth Congress of the Communist Party of the Soviet Union. Of the two paths open to the communists – either peaceful co-existence or the most devastating war in history – Khrushchev endorsed the former, pointing out that there were various forms of transition, even parliamentary, to socialism, and in April of the same year the Cominform was dissolved. 1956 thus marked a turning point in the communist movement. The communist parties of South and South-east Asia were virtually released from Soviet control and obliged to 'nationalise' themselves in their respective countries. With the rise of China as a communist power, communism had already acquired a nationalistic overtone. From 1956 onwards it was no longer unfashionable or unfraternal for a communist to put the interests of his country above the cause and needs of international communism. The communist movement became 'constitutional' and 'parliamentary' in most of the countries where liberal democracy functioned. However, constitutional communism achieved significant success only in India where communism has never been a mighty national force. The people of two of India's states – Kerala and Bengal – chose from time to time to vote the communists into power. But whether the communists, divided now into three identifiable parties, would be able constitutionally to capture central power in the foreseeable future, is a question which even the most optimistic of the communist leaders could not answer.

As to the second question, complex and diverse factors appear to have been responsible for the communist movement being stronger in some countries, weaker in others, and, in terms of capturing central power, a failure everywhere so far except in Vietnam, Laos and Cambodia. First, a broad distinction must be made between the 'insurgent' and the 'constitutional' communist movements. The insurgent phase began in 1947 and officially came to an end in 1956. The constitutional phase has been running since 1956. It should, however, be borne in mind that constitutional communism by no means indicates that the communists have solemnly abandoned the use of violence. Their constitutionalism is a matter of expediency. It is, none the less, possible that through their participation in democratic politics the communists might, in due course, discard altogether their revolutionary fervour and become thoroughly 'domesticated'. The change in attitude and style particularly noticeable today among India's communist leaders may support this view. After the termination of Mrs Gandhi's Emergency the communist leaders – whether Rajeshwara Rao of the CPI or Namboodiripad and Jyoti Basu of the CPI(M) – have come to align their parties with the 'democratic forces' in order to safeguard democracy in India.

The communist insurgencies collapsed mainly because they were out of tune with nationalist sentiments. Nowhere, except in Vietnam, has a communist party been either a vital component or a spearhead of the nationalist movement. In fact the communists, operating as they did in those days under the sole command of the Soviet Union, have had occasionally to act against the nationalists as in India during the Second World War, when they came out in support of the Allies, while the Indian National Congress was withholding its support on solely nationalist grounds. Until the Soviet Union joined the war the Communist Party of India was opposed to the 'imperialist war'. Inevitably the communists failed to gain mass support. Since communism was then an urban affair, run mostly by the intellectuals, it failed, in many cases, to acquire a strong rural base. Vietnam's case was different. Ho Chi Minh was the outstanding leader of the Vietnamese nationalist movement, and at the same time a brilliant and devoted communist. The Viet Minh (founded in 1941) and the Vietnam Workers' Party (founded in 1951) were throughout the principal vehicles of the nationalist movement. Nationalism was uppermost in Ho Chi Minh's mind. Occasionally he was able to make tactical sacrifices of his communist principles in order to strengthen the nationalist movement. For example, in November 1945 he dissolved the Indochinese Communist Party (which he had founded in 1930) in order to preserve unity among the nationalist forces. The National Assembly which was constituted in its place was, in fact, dominated by the Viet Minh, but the name 'communist' had to be dropped, for it would have then antagonised certain 'landlords, progressive intellectuals, and members of religious sects' whom Ho wanted to retain in the nationalist movement.

The communists played a nationalist role in Laos and a similar, though lesser part, in Cambodia. But both the Laotian Pathet Lao and the Cambodian Khmer Issarak had been supported by Ho's Viet Minh since 1950. Besides, each communist party had to encounter a popular and non-communist nationalist force as represented by Souvannaphouma in Laos and Prince Sihanouk in Cambodia. The communist victories in Laos and Cambodia would have been doubtful but for Vietnamese support and American intervention (see chapter 2, pp. 49–55). One other communist party – the Malayan – gave the impression of playing a nationalist role. But the ethnic composition of the MCP made it appear to represent Chinese rather than Malayan nationalism. The Malays were not drawn into the MCP movement. In fact they viewed it with disfavour. However, the fact that the non-communist élites in both Malaya and the Philippines were conservative gave a certain advantage to the communists in the sense that they became aware of themselves as a distinct force. The dividing line between a communist and a non-communist nationalist was clearer and sharper in Malaya and the Philippines than in Burma and Indonesia. Thus realising that they had no prospect of sharing power with the nationalists, the Philippine and Malayan communists forged their own organisation and strategy. This may partly explain why insurgent communism was stronger in Malaya and the Philippines than in Burma and Indonesia.

The Japanese occupation of South-east Asia indirectly gave the communists a unique chance to grow strong by organising resistance movements and exploiting the economic grievances of the populace. The South Asian communists did not get this chance. In South-east Asia the Malayan and Philippine communists made the most of this, and at the time of the Japanese surrender they were in positions from which they could at least make bids to capture power, as Ho Chi Minh did in Vietnam. Why did they not take advantage of their positions? Perhaps they were not prepared for the occasion; they had no plan for this eventuality which occurred rather suddenly. Also, they had no central organisation; certainly the Huks and the CPP in the Philippines constituted only a regional force and had made no efforts to expand their base. Besides, the Soviet-Western alliance was still intact, so any resistance to the re-entry of the Western powers into their colonies might have been considered by the communists as a defiance of the Moscow line. Further, the communist forces were not strong enough to face the American occupation force in the Philippines and the combined opposition of the British and Malays in Malaya.

The slow progress hitherto made by constitutional communism is due to several factors: the dearth of popular communist leaders; the inability of the communists to create a mass base; the frequent splintering of the communist parties; the deeply traditional character of the societies involved and the slow pace of their modernisation and urbanisation; and the acceptance in principle of the reformist social democratic system by most of the countries, which has cut the ground from under the feet of communism. Variations in these factors may also explain why the communist movement today is strong in India, weak in Sri Lanka, Burma, Malaysia, Thailand, Indonesia and the Philippines, and almost negligible in Nepal, Pakistan, Bangladesh and Singapore. Communism has, of course, suffered from additional disadvantages under the authoritarian rule which today prevails in all the countries except India, Sri Lanka and Malaysia. It is thus difficult to ascertain its potential in countries where the communists have had to go underground.

The communist leaders have so far emerged from the urban middle classes, and they share many traits with the nationalists with whom they are in competition. They are also highly intellectual and as such prone to factionalism. The communists of Sri Lanka, for example, are mostly the low-country Sinhalese of wealthy families, who have been educated at British universities or Inns of Court. Virtually all the top leaders of the Communist Party of Nepal are from the three most prosperous high-caste communities: the Brahmans, the Vaisya (commercial caste) and the Kshyatriya (warrior caste). The same is the case in the composition of the communist leadership in India. In fact the nationalist parties (Congress and Janata) today have more leaders from the lower strata of society than any of the three communist parties of India. Because of the predominantly urban character of leadership the communist parties have on the whole failed to create rural support. The Naxalites in India, having had strong peasant support, are an exception, but they were very much a regional force. Their influence was confined to Naxalbari – a 270 square-mile enclave in West Bengal inhabited in 1967 by about 80,000 people. The Huks of the Philippines had a similar regional and rural base. Everywhere else, except in Vietnam and Laos, the communist parties have had weak peasant support. The strength of the communist parties has lain in the urban working classes. The faster the pace of urbanisation, the stronger a communist party may thus become. The fact that India has come to acquire a fairly large urban population, owing mainly to the high pace of industrialisation, may thus account for the relatively strong position of the Indian communist parties.

The communist movement has suffered considerably from ideological or tactical controversies, often resulting in splits. By far the most divisive factor has been the Sino-Soviet breach, which occurred in the early 1960s, and accordingly split most of the communist parties into pro-Soviet and pro-Chinese factions. The Sino-Soviet schism caused clear splits in the communist parties of Sri Lanka and India; the Communist Party of Nepal (founded in 1949) avoided any open alignment with either side, though it was already divided on local issues; the majority of the communists elsewhere in Burma, Malaysia, Thailand, Indonesia and the Philippines accepted the Chinese model of revolution in the beginning, but they were a little put off by the disasters of Mao's Great Leap and the excesses of the Cultural Revolution. None the less, the communists in the non-communist countries of South-east Asia are today predominantly pro-Chinese; to what extent the present position will change on account of the 1979 Sino-Vietnamese war it is too early to say.

The Stalin–Trotsky schism of the 1920s had repercussions only in Sri Lanka, where in 1946, the communist party (Lanka Sama Samaj Party founded in 1935) split into two factions. Only in Sri Lanka have the Trotskyists become a political force. Further splits took place in 1950, 1963 and 1964, with the result that Sri Lanka came to have five communist parties. It was, however, the pro-Soviet Ceylon Communist Party which became dominant, polling 3 per cent of the total votes cast in the 1965 general election; the pro-Peking party obtained far less than 1 per cent of the vote. The Trotskyists and the pro-Moscow Communist Party put up a united front at the 1977 election, but the results turned out to be disastrous for them, and of the 130 candidates put up by the United Left Front none was elected to the parliament.

The Sino-Soviet schism caused the first split in the Communist Party of India. In July 1964 the pro-Peking faction separated from the CPI and formed the Communist Party of India (Marxist) – CPI(M). Both the CPI and the CPI(M) emerged from the 1967 general election roughly equal in strength: the CPI won 22 seats in the parliament and a total of 121 seats in the state legislatures, the CPI(M) won 19 parliamentary seats and 127 seats in the state legislatures. But from this point onward the strength of the CPI began to weaken. In the 1971 parliamentary elections the CPI secured 23 seats, while the CPI(M) won 25. In the 1977 parliamentary election the CPI won only 7 seats, whereas the CPI(M) secured 22. In the state elections held subsequently, the CPI(M) became a ruling party in West Bengal. The CPI(M) today, however, is no longer a pro-Peking party. The pro-Peking elements in the CPI(M) broke away in 1967 and formed the third party – the Communist Party of India (Marxist-Leninist). The breakaway faction consisted of what is commonly called the Naxalites. The Communist Party of China recognised the CPI(M-L) as India's only legitimate communist party. Thus in India the leadership of constitutional communism has passed from the CPI to the CPI(M). There is at present a move to form a united left front, but the CPI(M) leaders appear to be opposed to such a move. In August 1978 the CPI(M) Chief Minister of West Bengal, Jyoti Basu, condemned the CPI for having been the 'parasite' of the Congress, and the Naxalites for having always taken their orders from Peking.[24]

The deeply traditional character of the societies concerned is a factor which has militated particularly against the early, non-compromising, revolutionary brand of communism. A large majority of the population in each country is rural, consisting of peasants who are deeply religious, mostly illiterate, and poor. To preach to them the gospel of Marx and rally them round the banner of class war were Herculean tasks which the doctrinaire communist leaders could not perform. With the rise of constitutional communism, however, the communists have come to adopt increasingly the national heroes, values, norms and symbols, and to exploit local grievances. Communism has thus become nationalised and in the process lost some of its earlier characteristics. Looking at the situation that prevails particularly in India today, one gets the impression that there are communists and communist parties, but no communism.

During the first two decades of independence, almost every country in South and South-east Asia came to accept formally or informally, a socialist system of society. Since each nationalist government devised its own way to socialism, we have in view several different interpretations and varieties of the system. However, all the socialistic variations have few things in common. They have denounced the existing wide gap between the haves and have-nots, and pledged themselves to providing equal opportunities to the toiling masses.

Although no government has so far been able to redeem its pledge in full, the common man has none the less come to be the centre of all political and economic activity. As a result, the communist movement has come to lose its original claim to be the sole champion of the cause of the have-nots. The communist movement in this region of Asia has been adversely affected also by the fact that in the post-Stalin era it became possible for a non-communist country to be friendly with and receive aid from the communist powers. Nehru of India was the first to make it possible. The communist movement in India was disarmed when Nehru befriended the Soviet Union and China in the early 1950s.

5 Foreign Policy and Defence

In terms of the relations between the states of South and South-east Asia and between them and the world's super powers, the post-independence period from 1946 to 1979 may be broadly divided into two parts. The first part, stretching up to the end of 1967, was the most crucial. At the global level it was characterised by confrontation and Cold War between the two power blocs. At the regional level, the period was marked by hostilities which occasionally occurred between the individual states of southern Asia over disputed lands and boundaries, as well as over the questions of minorities and communist insurgencies. The second part of the period, from 1968 to 1979, was characterised by *détente* and cooperation at both international and regional levels. The 1979 wars between Vietnam and Cambodia and China and Vietnam were exceptions to the general trend. First put forward by India's Nehru, the principles of non-alignment and peaceful coexistence received a hostile reception in the West. But in the late 1960s they gained ground, and in the early 1970s became incorporated into the code of international conduct. The international order has thus in the last thirty odd years moved from armed confrontation to peaceful coexistence. This is not to ignore some wars and armed interventions which have taken place since 1970, and consequently defied the general trend, nor to ignore the alarmists and doom-watchers who obstinately refuse to believe in the possibility of two ideologically different political systems ever coming to coexist peacefully. What is suggested here is that peaceful coexistence has now become the dominant trend, making it difficult for any nation brazenly to interfere in the affairs of another.

CONFRONTATION AND COLD WAR, 1946–1967

Immediately after the termination of the Second World War, the world seemed to be divided into two power blocs – the Soviet and the American – each arrayed against the other in anticipation of a third world war. On 4 April 1949 the American bloc entered into the North Atlantic Treaty Organisation (NATO), which was essentially a military alliance designed to defend Western Europe against the threat of Soviet aggression. The Soviet bloc matched it by the Warsaw Pact Organisation, which was founded in 1955 as a defence pact and included the East European communist states. By then America had brought into being two more defence organisations – the South-east Asia Treaty Organisation (SEATO) and the Central Treaty Organisation (CENTO). These two were the creations mainly of John Foster Dulles, who was Eisenhower's Secretary of State from 1953 to 1959. Dulles intended to stop any further communist expansion by building defence barriers against China and North Vietnam in South-east Asia, and against the Soviet Union and its satellites in the Middle East and Europe. Linked with each other, SEATO, CENTO and NATO were to provide this barrier from the Philippines to Norway.

President Eisenhower's domino theory went into the making of SEATO, which was founded on 8 September 1954. The theory was based on the view that neighbouring states are so interrelated that, faced with the same peril, the collapse of one will lead to the progressive collapse of others. The collapse of French power in North Vietnam in 1954 occasioned the formulation and application of the theory, and SEATO came into existence to stop the progressive collapse of the remaining Indo-Chinese states. It was signed by Australia, Britain, France, New Zealand, Pakistan, the Philippines, Thailand, and the United States. It was to protect Laos, Cambodia and South Vietnam, in addition to guarding South-east Asia and the South-west Pacific. SEATO included only two Asian states – Pakistan and Thailand. Pakistan was also included in CENTO, which was originally founded under the name of the Baghdad Pact in 1955. After the withdrawal of Iraq from the pact in 1958, only four states – Turkey, Iran, Pakistan and Britain – continued to be members of CENTO; the United States did not accede to it formally, but its representatives attended the meetings of its military committee. SEATO, however, was stillborn, partly because it lacked the long-term commitment of members' forces, but mainly because it was stifled by the opposition to it of the non-aligned nations led by Nehru of India.

Nehru was alarmed at the threat to world peace posed by the two super powers, each armed against the other with nuclear weapons, military pacts and alliances; and each trying to outdo the other in recruiting allies and camp-followers. To the newly born nations of Asia and Africa, their independence seemed in jeopardy for each appeared almost obliged to join one bloc or the other. The situation seemed to Nehru suicidal and maddening. The Berlin blockade (1948) and the Korean War (1950–3) had nearly pushed the world to the brink of a third world war. The continuing bipolarisation of the world through further alignments, Nehru feared, might lead it to total destruction. The alternative he advocated was peaceful coexistence through non-alignment. Communist and non-communist states ought to forsake mutual hatred and fear and live peacefully; the super powers must adhere to the policy of non-intervention, particularly with regard to the nations of Asia and Africa; the uncommitted nations of the world must abstain from aligning themselves with one or the other bloc through political and military pacts. The larger the area of non-alignment, Nehru argued, the greater the prospect for world peace. Behind his doctrine lay Nehru's basic repugnance to the situation in which a nation like India might be reduced to the low status of a hanger-on, a camp-follower of this or that bloc, and thereby lose its identity and dignity.

Nehru's immediate concern was the preservation of peace in Southern Asia. Most of the countries in this region were faced with the problem of pursuing an independent foreign policy while at the same time seeking protection against the communist menace as posed by the emergence of communist China. To most of them China seemed an uncertain commodity, a big giant whose secret intentions and aspirations they were at a loss to fathom. For Nehru the solution of the problem lay first in insulating South and Southeast Asia against any outside intervention from America, Britain, the Soviet Union or China, and, second, in containing China in a friendly manner. The Vietnam crisis, emerging in the wake of the French defeat in May 1954 at the hands of the Viet Minh forces, gave Nehru the first opportunity to apply his solution. At a meeting of the Colombo Plan powers[1] (Indonesia, Ceylon, Burma, Pakistan and India) Nehru put forth his plan for the solution of the Indo-Chinese problem. The plan included a call for a ceasefire in Vietnam, for the complete independence of the Indo-Chinese states, and for an agreement between Russia, America, China and Britain that none of them would intervene in Indo-China. The Colombo Powers endorsed Nehru's proposals, and some lobbying was done on their behalf at the Geneva Conference of nine states (the United States, the Soviet Union, Britain, France, China, South Vietnam, North Vietnam, Laos and Cambodia) which met in May 1954 to resolve the Indo-Chinese crisis. The Geneva settlement granted independence to the Indo-China states, and India was appointed to head the three-power international control commission which was constituted to supervise the ceasefire in Vietnam, the exchange of prisoners and other related matters. Nehru was satisfied with the results of the Geneva Conference in so far as they appeared to accommodate 'united Asian opinion'. However, his plan to insulate Indo-China was not accomplished. As it turned out, all three outside powers – America, the Soviet Union and China – intervened. Perhaps the long-lasting Vietnam war would have been averted had the area been effectively sealed, particularly against American intervention in support first of Ngo Dinh Diem's and then of Nguyen Van Thieu's regimes in South Vietnam. Conditions in the 1950s, however, were not congenial to Nehru's ideas.

He did, however, succeed in dispelling from the Asian mind the fear of communist China. This he achieved first by befriending Chou En-lai, and securing in 1954 a Sino-Indian agreement on the five principles (which later came to be called Panch Sheel) of international diplomacy:

1. Mutual respect for each other's territorial integrity and sovereignty
2. Mutual non-aggression
3. Mutual non-interference in each other's internal affairs
4. Equality and mutual benefit, and
5. Peaceful coexistence.

Then Nehru introduced the friendly and reasonable face of new China to the nations of Asia and Africa at the conference of the twenty-nine Asian and African countries held in April 1955 at Bandung in Indonesia.

The Bandung Conference was the first Asian-African conference of its kind. All the countries of South and South-east Asia were represented at the conference except Singapore and Malaysia, which had not by then acquired their independence. The conference was sponsored by the five Colombo powers – Burma, Ceylon, India, Indonesia and Pakistan. Its main objects were to promote goodwill and co-operation among the nations of Asia and Africa, to consider problems of special interest to Asian and African peoples and the contribution they could make to the promotion of world peace and co-operation. It was an assembly of the aligned and the non-aligned, the communist and the non-communist countries. The participating nations had not much in common except a colonial past and a consensus against imperialism and racialism. None the less, the conference provided an opportunity to the participants, for the first time, to understand each other's problems and apprehensions. In some measure it also brought into being an Afro-Asian public opinion which the super powers were to feel obliged to take into account. But by far the most tangible achievement of the conference was the promotion of mutual understanding and trust between China and the states of South and South-east Asia. The occasion for the Chinese Premier, Chou En-lai, to offer that most relieving assurance of non-intervention arose when Cambodia and Thailand both expressed their fear of Chinese infiltration and subversion. Chou En-lai assured the participants that China had 'no intention whatsoever to subvert the governments of its neighbouring countries'.[2] He further affirmed that new China was ready to solve the problem of dual nationality of the overseas Chinese with the governments of the countries concerned 'on the basis of the strict adherence to the five principles', Chou maintained, 'we are prepared now to establish normal relations with all the Asian and African countries, with all the countries in the world, and first of all, with our neighbouring countries.'[3] These were not empty promises. During the course of the conference, Chou negotiated a treaty with Indonesia which provided for the ending of dual nationality (see chapter 4, p.132). China had already signed a treaty of friendship with Burma in June 1954, based on the five principles. It was to sign a similar treaty with Nepal in 1956. Chou thus laid the foundation for a feeling which continued to grow among the conference's delegations: that he was reasonable, conciliatory, and sincerely anxious to establish the genuineness of China's peaceful intentions.[4]

The five principles were incorporated into the final communique of the conference, and they subsequently became the dominant norms in international diplomacy. These principles went into the foundation of Indo-Soviet friendship, which began with the visit of the Soviet leaders, Khrushchev and Bulganin, to India in November and December 1955.

Nehru made it possible for the states of Southern Asia to follow an independent foreign policy by remaining non-aligned and at the same time maintaining cordial relations with and drawing economic aid from the super powers. With its genesis at the Bandung Conference, non-alignment continued to gather strength. It was formally baptised at a conference of non-aligned powers sponsored by India, Egypt, Yugoslavia and Indonesia, and held in Belgrade in September 1961, in which some thirty-five Mediterranean and Afro-Asian powers participated. At this conference non-alignment emerged as less isolationist than neutralism which it superseded, and became associated with the concept of positive neutrality, which meant collective intervention to prevent bipolarity from degenerating into open conflict.

Among the leaders of non-alignment present at this conference, Nehru was the only one to be intensely concerned about disarmament, a ban on nuclear tests, and *rapprochement* between America and the Soviet Union. The other leaders, particularly Sukarno of Indonesia, being still burdened by their old prejudices and fears, concentrated their attacks on colonialism and racialism. Indonesia's experiences of colonialism were more excruciating than those of India. Hence the Indonesians, even after a decade or so of their independence, regarded the international order as 'exploitative, and the big powers as threats to their country's independence'.[5] Sukarno was thus expressing the typical Indonesian view of the world order when he maintained at the Belgrade Conference that there were only two forces in the world: the New Emerging Forces which were the forces of freedom and justice, and the Old Established Forces, which were the old forces of domination always threatening the safety of the world.[6] For Sukarno, colonialism and imperialism were the living realities of the world, and the imperialists were exploiting their technological superiority to manipulate conditions in order that the nations of Asia and Africa could be kept eternally subservient to their selfish interests.[7]

Thus, Nehru and Sukarno held two different views of the world order, and accordingly assigned two different roles to the non-aligned force. Nehru wanted the non-aligned nations to play a positive role in the promotion of world peace by levelling down the barriers of misunderstanding and hostility which divided the world between the East and the West, or between the Soviet and American blocs. Sukarno wanted the New Emerging Force to guard and protect its own political, economic and social freedoms. The objects of non-alignment could not be defined then or in subsequent years, when it continued to grow in size as well as diversity. Nehru, however, managed to arouse the concern of the conference at the worsening of the Cold War in 1961. East–West tension had been intensified by the Cuban crisis (April 1961), and the sealing of East Berlin by a wall (August 1961). At the very time the non-aligned were meeting in Belgrade, the Russians resumed nuclear tests. Nehru guided the conference in issuing an appeal to America and Russia to stop nuclear tests and meet in a summit conference. Nehru continued exerting himself for Russo-American *rapprochement*, and he felt greatly rewarded when, in August 1963, a partial Nuclear Test Ban Treaty was signed in Moscow by Britain, America and the Soviet Union. He believed that the Treaty marked the end of the era of Cold War. Perhaps he was right. But this study takes 1968 as the terminal point, for it was in that year that the Treaty on the Non-Proliferation of Nuclear Weapons was signed by the Soviet Union and Britain. Also by then the long-standing bilateral disputes between the states of South and South-east Asia had been resolved.

During the Cold War era the non-aligned bloc also exerted its influence on global diplomacy through the United Nations and the Commonwealth. Third World countries took to the United Nations seriously and gradually came to form a majority in the General

Assembly. Within the United Nations an Asian-African bloc began to function. Though some members of this bloc were aligned, there were certain issues on which all acted together as a united force. They were collectively opposed to imperialism and racialism and all sought to mediate in the Cold War between the East and the West. They were almost united on the Suez crisis (1956) but far less so on the Korean crisis and the seating in the United Nations of the People's Republic of China. In general the bloc exerted a moderating influence, conducive to the Korean armistice of July 1953. The South and South-east Asia component of the Asian-African bloc tended to divide itself into three voting groups: the participants of SEATO – Pakistan, the Philippines and Thailand – often co-operated with the United States; India and Indonesia were less co-operative; and Burma, Cambodia, Laos, Ceylon and Nepal formed a floating group.[8] Differences of opinion on local and regional issues, which persisted among the members of the Asian-African bloc, prevented them from exercising a collective veto on a vast range of issues. By and large, the UN intervention in the bilateral disputes of Southern Asia - disputes between India and Pakistan over Kashmir, between Indonesia and Holland over West Irian, and the confrontation between Indonesia and Malaysia over the Borneo territories – were ineffective, partly because of the lack of unanimity among the five permanent members of the Security Council. For example, the Soviet Union, being committed to India's stand on the Kashmir issue, exercised its veto whenever the decision of the United Nations seemed to turn against the Indian interest.

The Commonwealth too served as a useful forum for the leaders of the non-aligned countries to express their views on general problems. The multi-racial Commonwealth continually grew in size and variety with the further dismantling of the British Empire. In 1952 there were only eight members – Britain, Australia, Canada, New Zealand, South Africa, India, Pakistan and Ceylon. In 1977 the Commonwealth included thirty-five countries, representing 1000 million people, a quarter of the world's population. It was no longer a club distinguished by the similarity of its membership. Instead it had become a place for the mingling of humanity in all its variety. In its earlier years the Commonwealth was a consolation for Britain, which felt denuded by the loss of its empire. The new members of the club likewise derived psychological satisfaction from being on equal terms with their erstwhile colonial master. The Common-wealth was, however, founded on the best and most noble of human aspirations – tolerance, brotherhood, hope, affection and mutual respect – all of them transcending the barriers of colour, class or creed.

Its main advantage was that it provided a multi-racial forum in which issues of mutual interest could be discussed without the same intensity of publicity and obligation which other international associations, like the United Nations, commanded. The Commonwealth provided an opportunity for informal contacts. Since its decisions were not registered as such, and since they were arrived at by consensus rather than by voting, the atmosphere at its meetings was relaxed. During the Cold War period, racialism and colonialism continued to be sensitive issues, particularly for the Asian and African members of the Commonwealth. South Africa was obliged to withdraw from the club in 1961 because of its apartheid policy. But whereas racialism became a disqualification, dictatorship did not. After 1958 a number of Asian and African members of the Commonwealth abandoned the British parliamentary system and opted for the authoritarian rule. But they continued to remain members of the club.

Of all the erstwhile British colonies in Southern Asia, only Burma did not join the Commonwealth. Pakistan withdrew from it after the Bangladesh war of 1971. So, of the present fourteen countries of South and South-east Asia only five (India, Bangladesh, Sri Lanka, Singapore and Malaysia) are members of the Commonwealth. During the Cold War period, tension occasionally grew between Britain on the one hand and the Asian countries on the other on such issues as the Suez crisis, Britain's proposed entry into the European Economic Community, and the British Immigration Act of 1962. On those specific occasions British interests clashed with Asian, and the fear of Britain contravening the Commonwealth ethos temporarily agitated the Asian members.

In the *détente* period, commencing in 1968, the Commonwealth focus moved from the psychological, social and political aspects to the economic. For the Asian and African members, the Commonwealth became largely a trade and investment affair. It became a forum for the have-nots to lay their claims on the haves. In the context of the North–South dialogue on the mode of bridging the gap between the rich and the poor countries of the world, the claims of the Commonwealth's have-nots perhaps implied that the average living standard of the people in the richer countries should be lowered to raise that in the poorer countries, 'much as the poor soak the rich under pressure of democracy in richer countries'.[9] The Commonwealth braced itself to meet the new challenge by floating various 'help-each-other' schemes, of which perhaps the most important was the Commonwealth Fund for Technical Co-operation founded in 1971 with resources of £400,000.

It is indeed difficult to ascertain precisely the Commonwealth's contribution to the lessening of international tension during the

Cold War era. Perhaps one has to look for it in the restraints which its two most powerful members – aligned Britain and non-aligned India – exercised on each other, and jointly at times on the two super powers. India's Nehru played some part in restraining Britain from going all the way with the United States on certain issues. Nehru was, for example, instrumental in securing the Labour government's support for the recognition of communist China. On 30 December 1949 India recognised communist China; Britain followed suit in January 1950. At the same time India used Britain to seek understanding of and exert influence upon the American bloc. Britain restrained India, particularly in the 1950s when Indo-American relations were strained, from moving too close to the Soviet bloc. At the same time, Britain leaned on India for a sympathetic understanding of the Soviet bloc. In January 1956 Nehru impressed upon Harold Macmillan the propriety of bringing the Soviet Union and the United States to a summit meeting. The credit for eventually bringing the super powers to a summit meeting thus initially belonged jointly to Britain and India.

During the Cold War period the foreign policies of the states of Southern Asia towards each other and towards the super powers were in some cases considerably influenced by the regional discord which subsisted between the individual states. In South Asia, Kashmir continued to be a bone of contention between India and Pakistan. The lingering hostility between the two great powers of Southern Asia considerably influenced their individual relations with the power blocs. As we have observed earlier, Pakistan first leaned on the Western bloc, but, finding no positive support in that quarter for its stand against India, it veered towards China when the latter became a pronounced enemy of India after the Sino–Indian war of 1962. As for India, its non-aligned policy became markedly tinged with a pro-Soviet bias mainly because of Soviet support for the Indian stand on the Kashmir issue. The other bilateral dispute of any significance in Southern Asia was between India and China over the border lands, but this was not as consequential as the dispute between India and Pakistan because it did not radically alter the foreign policy either of India or China. The United States and Britain, of course, rushed military aid to India, but their generous concern for India was non-conditional: India was not asked to modify its non-aligned policy. It continued to receive aid from both the Soviet and American blocs. The Sino–Indian war made no dent in China's international relations. Its relations with the Soviet Union continued to deteriorate independently of any Indian factor, and without any visible signs of China preparing itself for a *rapprochement* with the American bloc. In the 1960s China thus continued to remain isolated from both the blocs. None of the other bilateral discords in Southern Asia – between Pakistan and Afghanistan over the Pakhtunistan question, between India and Sri Lanka on the Tamil minority issue, and much later, during the *détente* period, between India and Bangladesh over the Ganges waters – became significant enough virtually to affect the relationship between the states concerned or their individual relations with the power blocs.

Leaving aside the continuing war between the two Vietnams, of all the remaining bilateral disputes in South-east Asia, only the ones between Indonesia and Holland over West Irian (1956–63) and Indonesia and Malaysia over the Borneo territories (1963–6) became international issues, and gave to Indonesia's foreign policy a decisively anti-Western slant. Indonesia remained technically non-aligned and grouped in this regard with India, Burma, Cambodia and Sri Lanka, but during its eight-year-old discord with Holland, it leaned heavily on the Soviet Union for military supplies. The pro-communist bias in Sukarno's policy was evident when he refused to censure communist countries on several occasions, for instance over Hungary in 1956, Tibet in 1959, the Soviet resumption of nuclear testing in 1961, and China's attacks on India in 1962. During its confrontation with Malaysia, Indonesia became further isolated not only from the Western world, but also from most of the non-aligned countries. The cordial relationship with China, which Sukarno had succeeded in establishing in 1960, collapsed in the wake of the 1965 *coup*, and was formally suspended in 1967 by Suharto. Indonesia thus stood fairly isolated at the dawn of the *détente* era, but fortunately it had a new leader who was willing to start from scratch.

While the Vietnam war and the American intervention haunted neutral Cambodia and Laos, the communist menace as posed by China and the overseas Chinese continued to agitate (in spite of Chou's assurances at Bandung) the fully aligned Thailand and the Philippines and the partially aligned Malaysia. In 1957 Malaya had entered into a defence and mutual assistance treaty with Britain. The treaty provided British assistance in case of external attack and for the training and development of Malayan armed forces. Furthermore, Britain was permitted to maintain forces in Malaya including a Commonwealth strategic reserve. Malayan policy had an anti-communist propensity, though it never became a camp-follower of the American bloc, like Thailand and the Philippines. Malaysia condemned Russian action in Hungary, opposed the occupation of Tibet by China, and quickly rallied to the support of India in 1962, when China pushed its forces deeply into northern India. Sharing thus a common bias against China and relying on the Anglo-American bloc for their security, Malaysia, Thailand and the

Philippines were so situated in relation to each other as to feel inclined to forge some kind of regional bond between themselves. Thus, together they formed in 1961 the Association of South-east Asian States (ASA) for promoting greater co-operation among themselves in a wide range of fields.

ASA, however, suffered a temporary setback when the Philippines revived its claim over Sabah during the confrontation between Indonesia and Malaysia. The confrontation also swallowed another regional association of Malaysia, Indonesia and the Philippines – Maphilindo (an acronym) – which Sukarno sponsored in July 1963 to strengthen the solidarity of the Malay race. Maphilindo was implicitly anti-Chinese.[10] However, it never passed the political blueprint stage. ASA, on the other hand, did not meet the same fate as Maphilindo. It was revived in 1966, and in August 1967 was absorbed into a new organisation, the Association of South-east Asian Nations (ASEAN), formally established in Bangkok by five founding members: Malaysia, Thailand, the Philippines, Singapore, and Indonesia. Among the seven objectives of ASEAN were the promotion of regional peace and stability and the acceleration of economic growth, social progress and cultural development.[11] The founding members also affirmed that to ensure the stability and security of the area from external interference, the continuation of foreign bases on the territories of member countries was a temporary expedient. As Indonesia's Foreign Minister, Adam Malik, later explained: 'We realize, however, that the national interest and security of each of the ASEAN countries except Indonesia necessitates the continuance, as a temporary expedient, of membership in regional alliances of a military nature, such as SEATO.'[12]

In agreeing to this proviso Indonesia made a conciliatory gesture for it was the only member of ASEAN which was non-aligned and had no foreign bases on its territory. But this was, for Suharto, a small price to pay in return for Indonesia's entry into this neighbourhood club. He wanted to pull his country out of isolation and also to repair the damage done to Indonesia's relations with its neighbours by his predecessor. Sukarno, for instance, had condemned ASA, when it was founded, as a 'neo-colonialist' and 'anti-communist' creation. Also, in the euphoric mood of the reconciliation between Malaysia and Indonesia, which followed the termination of the confrontation, it was natural for the region's statesmen to enshrine the new peace in some institutional form. In fact, ASEAN symbolised reconciliation all round: between Singapore and Malaysia, between Malaysia and the Philippines, and between Thailand and Malaysia. Singapore had not been entirely friendly towards Malaysia since it was driven out of the Malaysian federation in 1965.

Relations between Malaysia and the Philippines had been strained on account of the latter's claim to Sabah during the confrontation. The Philippines was formally to renounce its 274-year-old claim to Sabah in August 1977. Malaysia and Thailand had not been entirely happy about each other's role in the insurgency on their mutual border.

Founded almost at the beginning of the *détente* period ASEAN led a bare existence until 1976. With the rise of communists to power in all the three states of Indo-China in 1975, ASEAN became more purposeful, and acquired a second life through an elaborate treaty of amity and co-operation signed in Bali (Indonesia) on 4 February 1976 by the heads of government of the five founding countries – Suharto, Hussain Onn (Prime Minister of Malaysia), Ferdinand Marcos, Lee Kuan Yew and Kukrit Pramoj (Prime Minister of Thailand).[13] However, until 1978, the communist powers (the Soviet Union, China, Vietnam, Cambodia and Laos) continued to display their hostility towards ASEAN. They regarded it as an American stratagem devised to perpetuate American imperialism in South-east Asia.

DÉTENTE AND CO-OPERATION SINCE 1968

After 1968 *détente* progressively became the dominant trend in international relations. This trend was characterised by *rapprochement* between America and the Soviet Union, and between America and China. In South and South-east Asia the *détente* mood expressed itself in the abandonment of military pacts by the hitherto committed nations, and the pursuit by all countries of the policies of neighbourliness and peaceful coexistence.

However, international politics are never at any given time or period, entirely bent in any particular direction. The dominant trend often appears to be ruffled underneath by counter-forces. The Sino-Soviet hostility continually defied the spirit of *détente*. So did the arms race, particularly among the countries of the Third World. As a lingering legacy from the past, a sense of insecurity still continued to haunt the individual states, and occasionally cause local wars. The non-aligned bloc abandoned its peace-making role for there seemed no longer a need for it. But now it started belligerently championing the cause of the world's have-nots. Thus there began in the *détente* period an economic confrontation between the rich and the poor countries of the world. Perhaps it had to start some time or other. It is as well that it began when the world's political stage had come to be dominated by the spirit of co-operation.

The East–West *détente* was marked by the American-Soviet agreement in three different areas. By the 1968 Treaty of the Non-

Proliferation of Nuclear Weapons, the United States, the Soviet Union and Britain agreed not to transfer nuclear technology to non-nuclear countries. Some 100 other signatory states agreed not to develop nuclear weapons and technology. The treaty implied an understanding, particularly on the part of the United States, not to sell to Third World countries atomic reactors, and other necessary materials and know-how which went into the making of nuclear weapons. There were then five nuclear powers – the United States, Britain, France, the Soviet Union and China. China had carried out its first nuclear test in October 1964. India was not a signatory to the treaty, and the purpose of the treaty was somewhat defeated when, in 1974, India detonated its first nuclear device and became the sixth nuclear power in the world. However, the success of the non-proliferation treaty has so far lain in its being effective enough to prevent some forty other countries with nuclear potential from growing into nuclear powers.

Stopping the proliferation of nuclear technology was not enough, however. *Détente* required that the arms race between the two super powers must eventually stop. With this in view, the United States and the Soviet Union began the Strategic Arms Limitation Talks (SALT) in November 1969, and the first (SALT 1) agreement was reached in May 1972. The two powers signed the Treaty on the Limitation of Defensive ABM (anti-ballistic missile) Systems, and an Interim Agreement on certain measures with respect to the Limitation of Strategic Arms. The idea behind SALT was increasingly to limit the production and use of nuclear vehicles and weapons. The second SALT treaty is presently being negotiated, and when finalised it should impose further restrictions on the arms race. The success of SALT 2, like that of SALT 1, will greatly depend on the capacity of each power to verify that the other is sticking to the rules. The American capacity for verification is presently in doubt, because of the loss of its Iranian monitoring posts following the revolution which gripped Iran in 1979.

The third agreement was on the security of Europe. The tension between East and West Europe had subsisted throughout the Cold War period. The object of the Helsinki agreement – the Final Act of the Conference on Security and Co-operation in Europe signed by the heads of the thirty-five participating states, including the United States and the Soviet Union, in Helsinki in July 1975 – was to develop better and closer relations in all fields among the participating states in an effort to make *détente* a continuing process. Important for the safeguarding of peace in Europe was the commitment of the participating states to refrain from the threat or use of force and to respect the sovereignty and territorial integrity of states, and the right of self-determination of peoples. Helsinki, at last, echoed the spirit of the Bandung Conference. The norms of international relations which were set at Bandung were adopted almost *in toto* twenty years later by the Western powers.

Rapprochement between the United States and China was long overdue. Nehru had pleaded for China's entry into the United Nations on the ground that it would make China more responsible in her international relations. But the United States had always vetoed China's admission, with the result that Taiwan had continued to retain its seat in that body as representing China. America had continued to ignore communist China and no diplomatic channels existed between the two countries. The growing Sino–Soviet conflict was a conducive factor in the mellowing of the hard attitude which China and the United States had borne towards each other. President Nixon's need for leverage to offset the growing military threat of Russia and the economic threat of Japan might have induced him to draw China on to the world stage. China's continuing fear of Russian aggression on its territory had been heightened by the Russian armed invasion of Czechoslovakia in 1968. Russia had invaded Czechoslovakia, as Moscow explained, to crush heresies. The Chinese believed that China might be the next target on Moscow's list. The Vietnamese situation might have further paved the way for the Sino–American *rapprochement*. The United States was on the verge of pulling out of Vietnam. Normalisation of relations with China could thus come as a consolation to Nixon's administration.

The *rapprochement* began with the surprise visit of Dr Henry Kissinger to China in 1971. In October of the same year Taiwan was expelled from and China was admitted to the United Nations. Kissinger succeeded in paving the way for President Nixon's visit to China, which took place in February 1972. The America–China communiqué issued at the end of Nixon's visit stated the need to normalise relations between the two countries, and expressed the wish of both the countries to reduce the danger of international military conflict.[14]

Both China and the United States agreed not to seek hegemony in the Asia–Pacific region. Finally the United States undertook to reduce progressively its military commitment to Taiwan, hoping that a peaceful settlement of the Taiwan question would take place in the near future.

The process set in motion by Nixon was continued by his successors – Gerald Ford and Jimmy Carter. On 1 January 1979 the United States officially recognised China. In his message to Chairman Hua Kuo-feng, President Carter said: 'The cause of world peace will be served by this historic act of reconciliation. The estrangement of our peoples has sometimes produced misunderstanding, confrontation and enmity. That era is behind us. We can now establish normal patterns of commerce and scholarly and cultural exchange.'[15] Celebrating the occasion, one American diplomat went as far as to say that 'it was a great day in the history of mankind'.

The Sino-American *rapprochement*, however, did not seem to oblige China to observe the rules of the power game at once. The Chinese invasion of Vietnam in February 1979 utterly defied the spirit of *détente*. Of course the Chinese were opposed to *détente* from the very beginning. But why? Was it because they preferred disorder which could lead to a third world war, which in turn could bring victory to the Chinese-style revolution? One may find support for this view from the ideological utterances of Chinese leaders. While addressing the Tenth Congress of the Chinese Communist Party in August 1973, Chou En-lai described the then state of the world as being in 'great disorder', and wishfully stated that 'Such great disorder is a good thing . . . it throws the enemies into confusion and causes division among them.'[16] This view of the world was echoed by other Chinese leaders in subsequent years. Did they really believe in what they said? Or was it just the Chinese way of putting the world on its guard against the 'expansionist' Russians – the 'social imperialists', as they had come to be called in the Chinese parlance? It seems most probable that China's foreign policy in the 1970s was dominated by Russophobia; encircling and isolating the Soviet Union were its principal objectives. *Détente* between the Soviet and American blocs, in Chinese thinking, would enable the Russians to transfer their gun-power from the Western to the Chinese front and, consequently, the long-standing Sino-Soviet border dispute might flare into a war. The Chinese fears were, for instance, aroused when President Leonid Brezhnev visited Siberia, in April 1978, on an inspection tour. Was he there to inspect the preparedness of the Soviet border troops for an onslaught on China? Had the time now come when Russia was ready to 'punish' China? The Chinese did not take it as a mere coincidence that just before Brezhnev's visit to Siberia, Moscow had asked Peking to cease its long ideological battle with the Soviet Union.[17] The Chinese view of the 'expansionist Soviet Union' had already found a response from among some British Tory leaders and NATO generals. But this view was not shared by President Carter, the arch supporter of *détente*, human rights and democracy. It is believed that Carter's faith in *détente* remained unshaken in spite of the 'outrageous charges' levelled against the Soviet 'polar bear' by Chinese Vice-Premier Deng Xiao-ping during his goodwill visit to the United States in January

1979. Deng returned to China having normalised his country's relationship with the United States. China's relations with Japan had already been normalised by a peace treaty signed in August 1978.

Soon after Deng's return to China the Sino-Vietnamese war began. It is indeed puzzling that China, which had consistently displayed its fear of Soviet expansionism, should decide to 'punish' Vietnam, an ally and protégé of the Soviet Union. The Soviet Union had signed a treaty of friendship with Vietnam in November 1978. The treaty had a military clause which obliged the two countries to consult swiftly 'for the purpose of eliminating that threat', if one of them was threatened by outside aggression. Unless one attributed some kind of suicidal courage to the Chinese, it would be hard to believe that China deliberately wanted to draw the Soviet Union into a war by invading Vietnam. The most tenable explanation is that the Chinese had reason to believe (and they did not have to be extra-perceptive to do so) that the Soviet Union would do a lot of sabre-rattling but would abstain from taking direct military action. Soviet foreign policy, particularly during the *détente* era had consistently been cautious, restrained and responsible. One could say that it had been opportunist, but never adventurist. The purpose and timing of the Soviet–Vietnamese treaty were almost the same as those attending the Indo-Soviet Friendship Treaty of August 1971. The Indo-Soviet treaty was signed to deter any Chinese response to India's role in the Bangladesh affair. The Soviet-Vietnamese treaty was signed with the same purpose of deterring China from coming to Cambodia's aid. It was signed exactly one month before the formation of the Cambodian National United Front in opposition to the Pol Pot government in Phnom Penh. On 25 December 1978 Vietnam launched an offensive into Cambodia through the National United Front, and by 7 January 1979 Cambodia was 'liberated' from the 'barbarous' rule of the Khmer Rouge.

The Soviet treaties, like those with India and Vietnam, meant only Soviet backing in terms of political support, and economic and military aid. They did not imply a Soviet commitment to direct military action. They were designed essentially to work as psychological deterrents, particularly against China. The question then arises, if China was aware of this Soviet constraint, why did it not join Pakistan and Cambodia in their respective wars against India and Vietnam? Only some tentative explanations can be advanced on this question. First, like the Soviet Union, China was not adventurist. China had only one direct military involvement to its credit, which was in Korea, but that was a joint adventure with the Soviet Union. Second, the quality and quantity of China's military resources were not such as to have enabled it to rush to the aid of its ally at short notice. Both the Indo–Pakistan and the Vietnamese–Cambodian wars were sudden and short-lived. Chinese troops could not just march into Bangladesh or Cambodia, for neither of these has any border with China. The short duration of each war prevented China also from distracting India and Vietnam by creating tensions on the borders which it shared with them. Third, Chinese intervention in either case would have been construed by the non-aligned bloc as an unjustified intrusion by an outsider, for China was not closely connected with either of the local disputes. China could not afford to go down in the opinion of the non-aligned bloc and the ASEAN countries. Its cold war with Russia had obliged China to cultivate good relations, particularly with the ASEAN countries. And finally, Chinese intervention would most assuredly have given the Soviet Union a chance to show to the world that it was China, not the Soviet Union, which was pursuing expansionism.

China, however, was more interested in protecting Pol Pot's regime in Cambodia than in preventing the dismemberment of Pakistan. But the very nature of the Vietnam–Cambodia dispute and the way it suddenly developed into a fully fledged war prevented China from helping its protégé. Officially, the Vietnam–Cambodia war grew out of disputes over lands along the 750-mile-long and ill-defined Vietnam–Cambodia border. Each party claimed that the other had violated its borders and intruded into its territory. What deeper motives lay behind these border disputes and battles it is difficult to ascertain. In Cambodian thinking, Vietnam was bent on establishing its hegemony over Indo-China by absorbing Cambodia and Laos into some kind of Vietnamese federation. At one stage, in April 1978, Pol Pot, the Prime Minister of Cambodia, offered his country's cordial friendship to Vietnam in return for the latter's solemn undertaking to respect Cambodia's independence and boundaries, and to 'give up its intention to take over' the country.[18] If the subordination of Cambodia was Vietnam's intention, then it succeeded in achieving it by accelerating the border battles into a full-scale invasion of Cambodia. In this adventure Vietnam had full support of the Soviet Union. Its economic dependence on the Soviet bloc was institutionalised in June 1978, when it became a member of the East European Common Market (COMECON). China reacted by suspending all technical and economic aid to Hanoi. Beyond this, China could do nothing but watch helplessly as the Vietnamese succeeded in destroying Pol Pot's regime, and set in its place a government more compliant to Hanoi.

China's determination to punish and, to put it crudely, to knock the stuffing out of Vietnam, arose from the 'Cambodian tragedy'. In the same way that Vietnam had turned its conflict with Cambodia into a local matter, China made its aggression in Vietnam (17 February–5 March 1979) into a local, bilateral affair, warranting no interference from outsiders. China had border and refugee problems with Vietnam (see chapter 4, pp. 131–2). China claimed that, in the past six months, Vietnam had caused 700 armed provocations on the border. But the real reason for the Chinese attack on Vietnam was the latter's armed intervention to overthrow a pro-Peking regime in Cambodia.

Explaining the Chinese motive behind the aggression, Vice-Premier Deng confessed: 'We have no other aims than to explode the myth of Vietnam's claim to be the third strongest military power in the world, and we have no desire for territory.'[19] The Chinese leaders also wanted to thumb their noses at the Soviet Union, and to show that they were not afraid of the Soviet-Vietnam treaty, and they would not tolerate what Deng Xiao-ping called 'swashbuckling' in the region by the 'Asian Cuba' (Vietnam) of the Soviet Union. The Soviet Union could do nothing more than issue threats of reprisals if the Chinese penetrated more deeply into Vietnamese territory, parade its missile vessels in the South China Sea, and carry on diplomatic manoeuvres with a view to isolating China in the Third World. Premier Kosygin visited India on 2 March and urged Morarji Desai to come out with an unequivocal condemnation of the Chinese aggression in Vietnam. As India had just begun to break the ice with China, and the Janata government was vigorously pursuing a policy of neighbourliness and moderation in its international relations, Desai remained cautious and restrained in his criticism of the Chinese aggression. In the joint communiqué issued at the end of Kosygin's visit, India joined the Soviet Union in demanding 'an immediate, unconditional and total withdrawal of Chinese troops from the territory of Vietnam.'[20] It was, perhaps, a mere coincidence that the same day (15 March 1979) that the joint communiqué was issued in New Delhi, Chairman Hua Kuo-feng announced in Peking that all Chinese troops had withdrawn from Vietnam.

China's motives in waging this short-lived war against Vietnam were further clarified when peace talks between the two countries began in April 1979. The Chinese required Vietnam to withdraw its troops from Cambodia, its personnel from the Spratlys, and to receive back a large number of the ethnically Chinese refugees who had crossed into south-west China in 1978. China further required Vietnam to oppose efforts by anyone else 'to establish hegemony' in Asia – a clear reference to Hanoi's alliance with the Soviet Union. The peace talks are continuing. It is unlikely that Vietnam will ever agree to renounce its claim to the Spratlys, and it will make no real difference to Vietnam's hegemony in Indo-China if it came to accept

China's other terms. Vietnam may agree to withdraw its forces from Cambodia, mainly to please the countries of the non-aligned bloc and the ASEAN member states. But it would most certainly insist on China withdrawing its support from the Khmer Rouge insurgents in Cambodia. Such an undertaking on the part of China will automatically guarantee the security of the Vietnam-backed regime of Heng Samrin in Cambodia. By the 1977 treaty of friendship Laos had already fallen into the Vietnamese fold. Vietnam, thus, appears to have succeeded in its struggle with China for paramountcy over the Indo-Chinese region. China thus gained nothing from its aggression in Vietnam, except perhaps the small satisfaction of exploding the myth of Vietnam's invincibility.

However, China's punitive action against Vietnam did give Thailand some sense of security. Vietnam's dominance over Cambodia unnerved Thailand. Thailand mistrusted Vietnam, viewing it as an historic expansionist coveting its neighbour's rice paddies. Thailand's fear of Vietnam also arose from the role it had played in the American war against Vietnam and Laos. It had provided bases from which the air war against Laos and Vietnam was waged. Thus, during the Vietnamese aggression into Cambodia, Thailand veered towards China. In March 1978 Kriangsak Chamanand, the Thai Prime Minister, visited Peking. In November of the same year Deng Xiao-ping visited Bangkok, and assured the Thai leaders that if Thailand became a target of aggression China would not stand idly by. Thailand did not recognise the new regime in Cambodia and, as alleged by the Vietnamese, allowed Chinese supplies to pass through its territory into Cambodia to the Khmer Rouge guerrillas. Thus the Chinese military action against Vietnam was viewed by Thai leaders as China reappointing itself to its historic role as the policeman of South-east Asia, thereby supplanting the United States, which had happily relinquished the beat. But soon this feeling of security gave way to one of apprehension. If China could take action against Vietnam, it could do so against any other country in South-east Asia. It was this apprehension which goaded the ASEAN countries (Thailand, Malaysia, Singapore, Indonesia and the Philippines) into jointly issuing a statement on 20 February, appealing for an end to the fighting in Indo-China and the withdrawal of all foreign forces from the area of conflict, a criticism of both Vietnamese intervention in Cambodia and the Chinese offensive against Vietnam – though without naming either offender. Thailand now looked to the Soviet Union – which had shown in the Sino-Vietnamese war that it could keep its head when others lost theirs – as a force for moderation in Indo-China's disarray. The Thai Prime Minister visited Moscow in March 1979 to seek Soviet mediation.

Though the Sino-Soviet cold war has been running counter to the *détente* spirit, it is possible that a *rapprochement* between these two giants may take place before long. Behind the Chinese sabre-rattling and brinkmanship may lie a desire to be convinced that the Soviet Union is not really bent on the destruction of China. Much of the mud-slinging between Moscow and Peking, which is as violent as ever, is based on mutual distrust and misunderstanding, and a misconception about their respective roles in the world. The non-aligned bloc and ASEAN continue to lay pressure on the Soviet Union and China to bury the hatchet. India has begun to befriend China, and has perhaps reappointed itself to play between China and the Soviet Union the same mediatory role it played during the Cold War between the Soviet and American blocs. Some good omens are beginning to be visible. While China was 'punishing' Vietnam, the Sino-Soviet talks on border river navigation continued. The trade between the two countries has been increasing steadily despite all the acrimony. On 3 April 1979 China abrogated the twenty-nine-year-old Sino-Soviet Treaty, which was anyway an embarrassing anachronism, providing as it did for joint action against any resurgence of Japanese imperialism. At the same time the Chinese suggested that Moscow and Peking embark on new negotiations 'to settle all outstanding issues between them'.[21] It may thus be argued that if Vice-Premier Deng could dine in the White House, headquarters of the once detested imperialist arch-enemy, he could dine one day in the Kremlin.

One of the most important features of *détente* has been the gradual withdrawl of the aligned nations (Pakistan, Thailand and the Philippines) from the defence pacts. Having failed to receive any military backing from CENTO and SEATO in its wars with India in 1965 and 1971, Pakistan became indifferent towards these organisations. It formally withdrew from SEATO in 1971. In September 1975 SEATO decided to phase itself out of existence. The non-aligned bloc came to acquire a greater significance for the Asian countries, and in order to qualify for its membership it was essential that the hitherto aligned nations became fully non-aligned. CENTO thus began to look like a liability in the eyes of some of its Asian members. While visiting Pakistan in July 1976, the Turkish Foreign Minister said: 'I believe our age is not an age of confrontation but an age of co-operation and *détente*.'[22] CENTO, he advised, should therefore be re-evaluated in the context of *détente*. Turkey's growing indifference towards CENTO and the fall of the Shah's regime in Iran finally inspired Pakistan to pull out of CENTO in March 1979. By doing so Pakistan hoped that it would be admitted as a full member of the non-aligned bloc, and also that its relations with the Soviet Union would now improve.

The demise of SEATO and the withdrawal of the remaining American forces from Thailand in March 1976 turned the country into a non-aligned nation. While retaining good relations with the United States, Thailand now began improving its relations with the Soviet Union and China. The Philippines too changed its aligned status. President Marcos completely reversed his unblushingly pro-American stance under which he had sent Filipino troops to Vietnam against the wishes of Congress. His new independent foreign policy was based on his accurate reading of the world situation in which Third World power was growing, and the American role of global policeman was waning. In 1973 he normalised relations with a number of East European communist countries; in 1975 he visited China, and in May 1976 he was in Moscow. In spite of some tension lingering between China and the Philippines concerning the Sprat-lys' issue, a senior Chinese Deputy Prime Minister visited the Philippines early in 1978 to give full Chinese support to ASEAN and to dispel any fear in the Filipino mind of China's determination to support the Muslim rebellion in the southern Philippines. With the object of qualifying his country for membership of the non-aligned bloc, Marcos hosted the UNCTAD (United Nations Conference on Trade and Development) meeting in February 1976. But the Philippines failed to be recognised either as a member or an observer at the non-aligned summit meeting held in Colombo in August 1976. The Philippines was disqualified on account of the huge US military presence on its territory. With a view to modifying the terms of this US military presence, the Philippines began negotiations with the United States in November 1976.

During the *détente* era, the focus of the non-aligned bloc and ASEAN has shifted somewhat from political to economic problems, and has begun to reflect a confrontation between the haves and the have-nots of the world. Indeed, each of them continues to give some political security to its weaker members, but their main concern is the promotion of economic security and development amongst countries of the Third World. The non-aligned bloc is by far the largest. In terms of size and membership it has begun to look like a United Nations of the Third World, though it lacks structural effectiveness and cohesion. Starting with thirty-five or so in 1962, the membership of the non-aligned bloc rose to eighty-six in 1976, when it held its fifth summit meeting in Colombo. Indeed, at this meeting as at the previous summit or ministerial meetings, the bilateral disputes came out into the open and the eighty-six members lashed out at each other, but all of them were solid on two fronts: the demand for a more equitable share of the world's wealth, and the call for militant support for the Africans in South Africa. The non-aligned have-nots flexed their economic muscle for the first time to show the West that they would no longer submit to the dictates of a powerful privileged minority. Expressing the new mood and anxieties of the have-nots, Mrs Bandaranaike, Prime Minister of Sri Lanka, said that the poor could no longer depend on a favourable response from the developed nations. The poor were getting poorer and the rich richer: 'Over 100 developing countries with 50 per cent of the world's population, account for only 14 per cent of the global product. In contrast some 25 developed countries, with only 18 per cent of the world's population, account for 66 per cent'.[23]

The member states then discussed various ways and means of promoting economic co-operation between themselves, increasing their bargaining capacity with, and reducing their dependence on the developed countries. In view of the fact that the eighty-six member states run different political systems and have different inclinations, and that they cannot take a united stand on a number of political issues, it seems inevitable that they should progressively concentrate on economic problems which they share. But even in this restricted area of collective endeavour they have occasionally suffered from a crisis of identity. At the ministerial conference of the non-aligned nations held in Belgrade in July 1978, such member nations as Cuba and Afghanistan tried to force a closer link between the non-aligned bloc and the Soviet Union. India and Yugoslavia were opposed to any such move, which might eventually split the non-aligned bloc into conservative and progressive camps. Asserting that 'genuine' non-alignment was an article of faith for India, India's Foreign Minister maintained that 'all nations must resist the temptation of using the movement to further narrow national, regional or ideological interests'.[24]

At its second summit meeting held at Kuala Lumpur in August 1977, ASEAN played down the subject of future security arrangements for the region, and committed its five countries to promoting peaceful relations with Vietnam, Laos and Cambodia. The ASEAN leaders explicitly asked the states of Indo-China to drop their hostile policy against the regional grouping of the five non-communist South-east Asian nations. At this conference, ASEAN gained the economic support of Japan. Takeo Fukuda, the Japanese Prime Minister, declared that his government would extend £588 million in aid to finance the five industrial projects run by ASEAN. ASEAN thus emerged as a more cohesive unit with its focus firmly set on the economic development of the member states.

This new image of ASEAN changed the attitude of the Indo-Chinese states towards it. Both Cambodia and Vietnam had condemned ASEAN as being essentially a military front representing Western interests. By August 1978 their attitude had changed.

Vietnam was, for instance, now willing to join hands with ASEAN to make South-east Asia a zone of peace. By November 1978 the ASEAN countries had received some important visitors: the Prime Minister of Vietnam, the Deputy Prime Minister of Cambodia, the Soviet Deputy Foreign Minister, and the Chinese Vice-Premier.

However, in spite of the growing spirit of *détente* and co-operation, the nations of South and South-east Asia have continued to increase their defence expenditure every year. It is paradoxical that these countries, which have continuously championed the cause of disarmament, should themselves be so helplessly involved in the arms race. According to one estimate, although the United States and the Soviet Union dominate military spending, accounting for almost 60 per cent of the total, equivalent to the gross national product of the entire continent of Africa, the developing countries more than doubled their outlay on weapons in real terms between 1960 and 1974.[25] The massive flow of arms from the developed to the Third World countries made the latter dependent upon and more vulnerable to manipulation by the former. Fear and suspicion, national ambition, internal subversion – these have accentuated military demands for additional hardware. The worldwide urge to rearm also continues. Some nations have armed themselves to increase their power. But most nations have been arming themselves because they have felt insecure. There is thus this problem of international insecurity which has been running parallel to the dominant trend of *détente*.

6 Economic and Social Problems

The most tantalising problems facing the countries of Southern Asia are the socio-economic problems of poverty, weight of tradition and inegalitarianism. It is hard to define poverty, and harder still to identify its causes. But the tradition-mindedness of the people and the inegalitarian social structure are often seen to react against radical changes. They tend to perpetuate the *status quo*. If it is true that greater social justice follows and does not precede economic advance, then poor societies cannot be other than highly inegalitarian.

If poverty is defined as lack of command over resources relative to needs, then no society, whether developed, developing or undeveloped, is immune from this malady, for human needs multiply like germs. We have thus to go down the scale to the basic needs in order to distinguish the really poor from the rich, 'have-plentys' and 'want-mores'. The task does not become any easier unless we determine the most basic of the basic needs. The poverty line has thus come to be defined in relation to a minimum desirable level of consumption of 2400 calories per person per day in the rural areas, and 2100 calories in the urban areas.[1] According to this definition then, a large number of people in Southern Asia live below the poverty line; of the 625-odd million of India's population, 300 million people (about 46 per cent of the total population) fall into this category.[2] They live in extreme poverty, and are deprived of adequate food and other basic necessities.

Why are the Third World countries poor? Literature on this subject has grown enormously over the last three decades, and yet the experts have been unable to pinpoint the factors responsible for this continuing poverty, all we know is that 'poverty itself causes continued poverty'. We are told of the symptoms rather than the causes of poverty. In the pre-independence period the colonial powers formulated a theory to explain the poverty of the people in their colonies. The 'colonial theory' was simple and certain, but it did not hold water for long; it was discarded at the beginning of the independence era. According to this theory, the people in the backward regions were so constituted as to react differently from Europeans; that is they normally did not respond positively to opportunities for improving their incomes and living standards.[3] They were supposed to be racially inferior to the Europeans. The poverty of these people was also allied to the climatic zones of the earth they inhabited. All the under-developed countries are situated in the tropical and sub-tropical zones. The colonial theory has now completely disappeared. Race and climate are no longer considered as factors of any significance in the economic development of a region. Indeed, it would be pointless to revive 'race' as a factor, but one cannot completely ignore the hazards of the tropical climate; the extremes of heat and humidity might contribute to the deterioration of the soil and of many kinds of material goods, and they might bear some responsibility for low productivity of certain crops and animals. In some measure, the tropical climate saps human energy and initiative and possibly impairs the effectiveness and efficiency of the work-force, particularly of the agricultural workers. However, the role of climate in economic development should not be overstressed. The hazards of the tropical climate can be (and in some cases have already been) surmounted with the aid of technology.

Although the search for the 'insurmountable and unique' causes of poverty in the Third World has been given up, some analysts tend to over emphasise the role of what we may call 'transient factors', and they derive the same conclusion as the colonialists did – that non-Western societies are basically different from Western societies and, therefore, the economic development of the former must proceed on different lines. One has only to look at some Western-style changes which have taken root in the societies of Southern Asia to be able to reject firmly the hypothesis that East is East and West is West, or to put it in current economic parlance, South is South and North is North. For better or worse the countries of Southern Asia have committed themselves to Western-style economic and social development. In this age of 'interdependence' they could not do otherwise. In fact the Third World countries might make more rapid progress than the First and Second World countries were able to do in their times. This could be so because the Third World countries have the advantage of being late-starters. They have readymade models to emulate, a good deal of driving force, and the opportunity to learn from the mistakes made by the advanced countries. When Britain, for example, started its economic journey it had no model of modernity to emulate. As compared to Britain, France, Germany and Russia in the nineteenth century, the late-starters in the twentieth century have, for example, the use of more efficient modes of trade and investment, and advanced technology. Of course, the developed countries are not waiting by the wayside for the developing countries to catch up with them so that they all can run together hand-in-hand. Will the gap, therefore, between the rich and poor never be bridged?

This study is too limited to answer all the relevant questions. It proposes only to outline the main problems and the measures commonly followed by the countries concerned to resolve them.

OVERPOPULATION AND BIRTH CONTROL

Overpopulation is regarded as one of the main characteristics of poverty. The world population has passed the four billion mark. Nearly 30 per cent of the total world population lives in the fourteen countries of South and South-east Asia. India, of course, tops the list with its 625 million, but its population growth rate, which fell to 1·94 per cent in 1978, is the lowest in the region except for that of Singapore. None the less, India's population continues to increase by thirteen million (almost equal to Australia's population) every year. The relative prosperity of a country in the region, however, does not necessarily indicate a fall in its population growth rate. Leaving aside the case of Singapore (which has in operation the most severe control on births), the growth rate is high in other 'prosperous' countries – Malaysia, the Philippines, Thailand and Sri Lanka (see Table 1, p.177). Similarly, a marked decline in fertility can be achieved without any commensurate economic growth. The growth rate in developing countries fell from an all-time high of 2·4 per cent in 1970 to 2·1 per cent in 1977. In India's smallest state Kerala, which is starved of industry and has a high unemployment rate, the birth rate dropped steadily from 3.12 per cent in 1972 to 2.59 per cent in 1975.[4] This is, of course, not to deny the beneficial impact on the economy of a country of its declining birth rate. What one can infer, particularly from the case of Kerala is that factors other than economic growth can cause a decline in the birth rate, and that no society has to wait till its economy is fully developed before it can hope to tackle the runaway growth of its population. The decline in Kerala's birth rate can be attributed to the state having the highest literacy and marriage age in India. Of Kerala's women 50 per cent are literate, whereas the all-India percentage is only 19 per cent. In 1972 the average age at marriage for women in Kerala's urban areas was 18·33, as against 16·93 for urban India. The legal age for marriage in India is 18 for women and 21 for men, but the law is defied more than observed. In spite of the ban on child and early marriages, the backward and orthodox communities continue to marry their children young.

Family planning, education and employment particularly for women, will most assuredly continue to bring the fertility rate

TABLE I: POPULATION IN SOUTH AND SOUTH-EAST ASIA IN 1976

Country	Population (millions)	Birth rate (per thousand)	Death rate (per thousand)	Population growth rate (per cent)	Life expectancy
Bangladesh	76.1	47	20	2·7	43
Burma	31·2	40	16	2·4	50
Cambodia	8·3	47	19	2·8	45
India	620·7	35	15	2·0	50
Indonesia	134·7	38	17	2·1	48
Laos	3·4	45	23	2·4	40
Malaysia	12·4	39	10	2.9	59
Nepal	12·9	43	20	2·3	44
Pakistan	72·5	44	15	2·9	50
Philippines	44·0	41	11	3·0	58
Singapore	2·3	20	5	1·6	67
Sri Lanka	14.0	28	8	2·0	68
Thailand	43·3	36	11	2·5	58
Vietnam, North	24·8	32	14	1·8	48
South	21·6	42	16	2·6	40

SOURCE: *Asia Year Book (Hong Kong, 1977)*, p.52.

down. But first of all, all concerned must unanimously recognise the population explosion as a problem and a threat to mankind. But not all the countries have always considered population growth to be a problem, or believed that any correlation existed between population growth and food shortage. At the UN World Population Conference held in Bucharest in August 1974, which was the first international meeting set up between governments to deal with this problem, nearly 50 out of 120 developing nations were opposed to population control. China's delegate rejected the 'absurd theory of population explosion spread by the super powers', adding that 'it is wrong and far from the truth to say that overpopulation is the main cause of the poverty and backwardness of developing countries . . . and that a population policy is decisive in solving the problems of poverty and backwardness'.[5] That China, the world's most populous country, with about 900 million people, should be so indifferent towards the population problem, slackened the concern of many developing countries about their rising population. The radicals of Bangladesh, a country with one of the highest population growth rates and the lowest income in Asia, called the overpopulation idea a 'neo-capitalist hoax'. There grew among some developing countries the conviction that the population problem would sort itself out if only the poor countries of the world were given a fairer share in the world's resources.

This thinking on the population problem acquired additional support from some Western analysts who, in 1975, put forward their views that food shortages were not due to population pressures, and that there was no shortage of foodstuffs.[6] As for population pressures, it was pointed out that France, with a population density greater even than Indonesia's and a ratio of arable land to population not very different from India, produced enough for its domestic needs with a surplus for export. Population pressures were, therefore, not a problem in France and, given adequate fertilisers and technology, it should be economically possible for India to do likewise. The analysts further argued that there was no shortage of food, there was merely an inequality of distribution. Thus 'hunger was caused by plunder, not by scarcity'.

The denunciation of the 'population theory' had a psychological connotation. Third World countries resented being treated as the 'problem members' of the international community just because they were overpopulated and poor. Therefore, they found it consoling to believe that the haves of the world were overstressing the population theory in order to evade their obligation to share their riches equitably with the have-nots. While maintaining this posture on the international front, some countries of South and South-east Asia did, at the same time, launch population control campaigns. Even China, having internationally demonstrated its indifference towards the population question, pursued rather unobtrusively a national policy of population control, bringing its growth rate down to 1·7 per cent in the 1970s. India, however, was the first officially to encourage nationwide family planning in 1951. Taking a nationalistic view of development – the view that development was essential not just for the welfare of its citizens, but to enable the country itself to enhance its international standing – and believing that development was thwarted by excessive population growth, India put greater purpose and activism into family planning. The government legalised abortion in 1971. More vigorous birth-control campaigns were followed during the Emergency. On 16 April 1976, the new National Population Policy was announced, which provided, among other things, a monetary incentive for sterilisation. State legislatures were permitted to pass legislation for compulsory sterilisation. In 1976 one state legislature – Maharashtra – actually passed a compulsory sterilisation bill but it never acquired the presidential assent. None the less, a high number of sterilisations took place during the Emergency. The original target of 4 million for 1976-7 was reached by September 1976, and it appeared that the target was achieved not because of any legislative compulsion, but because of the involvement of all government agencies in family planning motivation.[7] Public servants were discreetly penalised for exceeding the individual family limit of three children. They were also rewarded for carrying on the sterilisation campaign among the masses, which frequently induced them to commit excesses against the common people. There is no doubt that sterilisation was a major factor in the March 1977 election which defeated Mrs Gandhi's Congress Party. The Janata government did not pursue the family planning programme with any vigour; even the word 'planning' was changed to 'welfare'. It has been estimated that under Janata rule, the number of sterilisations fell from 4 million in 1975–76 to fewer than one million in 1977–8. However, at the end of 1976 about 25 million people were using some form of contraception and about 17 million had been sterilised. Fertility in India is going down in response particularly to education, urbanisation, industrial growth, reduced infant and child mortality, improvement in employment opportunities and the status of women, and the family-planning programme. It is, of course, impossible to ascertain precisely the contribution of family planning to the decline of the birth rate in India.

In the rest of the countries of this region, family planning began in the late 1960s. By the mid-1970s all the countries had become firmly anti-natalist, except Cambodia and Laos. Singapore's crusade against population growth appears to have been most successful. There the government has devised many deterrents to population growth: government hospitals charge higher fees for each successive child that is born in government hospitals; paid maternity leave ends after the second child; income-tax relief stops after the third; and parents have lower priority in choosing primary schools after the fourth child; parents who are sterilised before the age of forty get school preference. Over 60 per cent of Singaporean married women use contraceptives. The fertility rate has steadily declined, and today Singapore has the lowest population growth rate in southern Asia. It must, however, be observed that Singapore is the most modern and urbanised country in this region, with a very small percentage of the population (2·3 per cent) engaged in agriculture. Thus the Singaporean deterrents to population growth may not be found effective in other countries of this region, in each of which the majority of the population is dependent on agriculture, and is uneducated, superstitious, and tradition-bound.

Next to Singapore are the Philippines and Thailand, where the population problem has been taken seriously. Though initially hindered by Catholic scruples, the Philippine government has devised some deterrents to population growth in urban areas. Since 1972 tax exemptions in the Philippines have only been given for a couple's first four babies; this puts the Philippines in the league of countries which have gone beyond contraception towards direct state opposition to fertility. Restrictions on abortion have been eased. Although the overall fertility has decreased by about 9 per cent since 1958, the country has still a very high population growth rate. The poor Catholic mother still carries the weight of tradition in tending to produce six to seven children. Less than 25 per cent of the women use contraceptives, and any programme to disseminate condoms widely through little grocery stores is stopped by opposition from the Catholic Women's League. In Thailand pills and contraceptives are easy to get and sterilisation is available in all government hospitals. The family planning scheme may be considered as one of the factors which brought the population growth rate down from 3·3 per cent in 1974 to 2·5 per cent in 1976. In Sri Lanka, Pakistan and Bangladesh, family planning has focused mainly on introducing contraceptives into rural areas. However, according to a 1975 estimate, only 6 per cent of those 'at risk' used contraceptives in Pakistan, and only 3 per cent in Bangladesh. In the rest of the countries of South and South-east Asia, the government commitment to family planning has not been so explicit or consistent.

The problem facing family planning in countries where the majority of the population lives in rural areas and is dependent on agriculture, is how to spread the use of contraceptives among people who are illiterate, superstitious, underemployed, and poor, and who tend to marry early in their lives and, in the absence of any welfare scheme to support them in sickness and old age, whose only form of security is their children. Even if contraceptives are made freely available to every villager, there is no guarantee that he or she will use them. The alternative of persuading or compelling them to be sterilised will arouse their indignation and suspicion, and they will use their vote to throw the government out of power, as they did in India in 1977. One may then think of shifting the focus from them to their children, hoping that through widespread education and employment opportunities their children might be brought up to behave differently from their parents. Here again one is faced with the enormous size of the younger generation. In populous countries like India and Indonesia, those under the age of 20 or 21 constitute respectively 51 and 58 per cent of the total population. In the circumstances it seems difficult for a country to achieve any rapid decline in its fertility rate without any rapid rise in its economic development and social welfare services.

FOOD SHORTAGE AND AGRARIAN REFORMS

Economists tend to disagree on the problem of food shortage. The pessimists – who believe in Malthus's theory that population, when unchecked, increases in a geometrical ratio and subsistence increases only in an arithmetical ratio – predict that there will always be a shortage of food for an increasing number of hungry people. The way things are going, they do not think that poverty will ever be overcome. The remedy they suggest, in their desperation, is based on the notion of 'triage' – the battlefield policies of a military hospital – which is to treat only those with a good chance of recovery, and to allow the rest to die. The poor thus must perish. The optimists, on the other hand, regard this problem of food shortage in the Third World countries as a transient problem. They point out that not all the world's arable land has yet been used. About half of the 7000 million acres suitable for crops is idle. Much of that is in the hungry Third World. Properly used, it is estimated that the world's potential arable land – about 2·3 times the area cultivated, say, in 1975 – could support between 10 and 13 times the present world population. The Indian subcontinent, they argue, has more arable land than the United States, with an abundant water supply and greater scope for multiple-cropping.

The situation does not look as desperate as the pessimists make out. In some countries of Southern Asia food production has out-paced population growth. In India, for example, whereas the rate of increase in population amounted to 2·08 per cent per year between 1951 and 1971, total agricultural production rose during the same period at a compound rate of 2·65 per cent per annum, and that of food grains at 2·59 per cent per year.[8] In 1977–8, India produced nearly 126 million tonnes of food grains, creating thereby a surplus reserve of 17 million tonnes. In relation to the declining fertility rate, the food situation in India looks most favourable in 1979. But this by no means indicates that India is out of the wood, once and for all. As in other developing countries, in India a rise in food production has been accompanied by a rise in consumption of food grains. Since the rise in the consumption level had been caused primarily by an increase in incomes, this 'affluence' does not necessarily suggest that the poor millions are now able to buy more food than they used to. India's surplus food grains are perhaps due only to the inadequacy of purchasing power in the bulk of the population. 1974 saw the most graphic demonstration of this uneven distribution of incomes in India when people were dying of starvation actually in sight of rice which they could not afford to buy. So even in good years of production when the *per capita* availability of food grains is not far below the minimum dietary requirements, it is owing to maldistribution of resources that so many go hungry. The inegalitarian structure of society is thus more responsible for the poverty of the masses than food shortage. Inegalitarianism inhibits economic growth by thwarting reforms which might alter the *status quo*.

All the countries of Southern Asia have, in principle, adopted improved methods of cultivation. Some have made considerable progress in replacing the old by new methods. But only a few have tried to match the technological advance with the necessary and much-needed agrarian reforms. Even where tenurial and land reforms have been devised (as in India, Sri Lanka, Thailand, and the Philippines) their successful implementation has been baulked by 'élitist conspiracy'. Being in possession of political and economic power, the élites in non-communist countries of this region have either resisted radical land reforms or so manipulated their implementation as to deprive the poor people of the benefits they were supposed to derive from such reforms. The irony of the situation is that the reforms are devised in the interests of the poor masses, but those who come ultimately to benefit from them are the rich. This point is clearly illustrated by the way certain schemes – the Green Revolution, the co-operatives, the nationalisation of domestic banks – designed primarily to enhance the productivity and creditworthiness of the poor millions have benefited mainly the richer section of the rural population.

The Green Revolution is the name given to concentrated efforts to increase productivity with greater use of improved seeds, fertilisers, pesticides and technical assistance. The dire need for some such intensive agricultural programme cannot be overemphasised, for in Southern Asia between two-thirds and three-quarters of the labour force work in agriculture, but agricultural output accounts for only about one-third of the average gross national product. The Green Revolution first began in India in 1960, and later spread to other countries of Southern Asia. Co-operatives and banks came into the picture in order to make agricultural equipment and credit available to the farmers. India nationalised its domestic banks in 1970 with a view to making government credit available to the lower strata of rural society. Such schemes did in some measure increase the productivity of the land, but because they bypassed the need for land reform they offered almost nothing to the landless labourers and the poor farmers. With an uneconomic holding and no savings whatsoever, the poor farmer could not buy the fertilisers and insecticides or use the new irrigation facilities. He thus remained a bad risk for the co-operatives and the government banks.

What are the persisting evils or drawbacks of the agrarian societies? Landless labourers, tenancy farming, landlordism, uneconomic holdings, fragmentation of land – these were the apparent agrarian disabilities from which most of the countries of Southern Asia suffered at the time of their independence. Some of the countries still continue to suffer from such exploitative agrarian conditions. The agrarian reforms which have been advocated are therefore of the kinds which would ensure redistributive growth by giving 'land to the tiller', and securing to him or her its ownership. In other words, the reforms should ensure that a farmer comes to own a consolidated economic holding and is able to use improved methods of cultivation. In the first place, not all the countries of Southern Asia are committed to introducing such agrarian reforms. And countries like India, which are so inclined, have not been able to achieve much because in these, as in the other countries of the Third World, what the governments plan and legislatures enact is not always implemented. But even if such reforms were actually implemented, they would by no means fully resolve the problem of rural unemployment.

In a country like India there may not be enough land even for tillers to have the minimum of two-and-a-half acres each. Landless labourers may not get any land at all. Therefore they have to be employed in the industrial sector. The government will thus be faced with a tremendous task, for creating jobs in the industrial sector costs much more than creating employment in the agricultural sector. None the less, this is not an impossible task to perform, especially for countries like India, Malaysia, Thailand and the Philippines, which have made steady progress over the last thirty years, and have the potential for rapid development, the 'take-off'. But whether they will succeed in creating, before long, a development-oriented egalitarian society, depends on the farsightedness of their power élites – people who in these countries hold positions of power and influence and stretch from landowners and moneylenders in the villages and the local officials in collusion with them, to industrialists, higher officials, legislators, teachers and professionals in urban areas. At present, the élites seem to be unwilling to accept or implement such reforms which have 'equalisation elements' in them, for they are reluctant to give up the advantages they enjoy. Theirs is, of course, a short-sighted view, because the productivity gains and improved opportunities that could be expected from the reforms would benefit them no less than the common people.

If the élites fail to take the initiative, pressure from below might produce the desired results. Although no non-communist country in South and South-east Asia has gone through a thorough social revolution, none the less whenever there were peasant uprisings or unrest, the élites of the countries concerned were galvanised into introducing some reforms. The spontaneous uprising of peasants against landlords in Telengana, in the late 1940s, did, on the one hand, make Nehru's government more urgent about its agrarian programme, and on the other brought into being the idealistic

Bhoodan (gift of the land) movement of Vinoba Bhava. Bhava, an ardent follower of M. K. Gandhi, began his one-man reform movement by asking the landlords voluntarily to part with a parcel of their land. The lands so collected were to be redistributed among the landless and the poorer sections of the peasantry. Bhava's movement was yet another experiment in Gandhian non-violent revolution, but it failed to produce radical results. The movement is still continuing, but its impact on agrarian conditions has been minimal. The Congress government formulated some agrarian programmes, but their implementation rested with the state governments. As a result, some of the plans took a long time to be enforced, and some have not yet been implemented. The middlemen (landlords or *Zamindars*) who during the British Raj had operated between the peasants and the government, have now disappeared from the scene, but such schemes as fixing a ceiling on land holding, and the consolidation of land, have not yet been fully implemented.

The problem which faced India during the Nehru era was how to retain democracy and at the same time make as much economic progress as communist China was supposed to be making. The Community Development Programme, which was introduced on 2 October 1952, was intended to achieve as much as China's communes. It was a programme to rejuvenate the long-dormant peasantry of India, who constituted 82 per cent of the population, and lived in India's 600,000 villages; to teach them self-help; and to mobilise their energy in changing the centuries-old face of rural India. This was to be achieved by persuasion. Village India was to be organised in blocks, each block consisting of a hundred villages. Government officers and agrarian specialists were made available at all levels within each block to guide and coach the villagers in the formulation of their needs and in pooling their efforts and resources in cooperatives. With the same object in view and using the same method of persuasion, the Janata government raised the slogan 'back to the villages', and brought into being another scheme, *Antyodaya*, which, while running parallel to various other rural development projects, aims at identifying 'the-poorest-of-the-poor' families in each area and equipping them with the means of livelihood. The *Antyodaya* was first introduced in October 1977 in the state of Rajasthan. In the following year it was introduced in a few other states of northern India. It has not yet been assimilated with an integrated rural-development plan. Even if it turns out to be a meritorious scheme, it will take long before it is implemented in all the states of India, for agrarian reforms are the charge of the state governments.

The Huk rebellion in the Philippines likewise induced the government to introduce some reforms. As the economy of that country had been operating then on capitalist lines, no attempt was ever made to eliminate landlordism. The reforms were only intended to improve the miserable conditions of the tenants by giving them some security and increasing their share in the harvest. The Agricultural Tenancy Act of 1954 reduced the landlords' share from almost 50 to 30 per cent of the net harvest on the best rice land, where the tenant provided all implements and animals, as well as labour. The Law Reform Act of 1955 aimed at the purchase and division of large estates in areas of agrarian conflict, but its scope was so limited that it failed to bring about any large-scale redistribution of land. Likewise, the Land Reform Code of 1963, which aimed at abolishing share tenancy and replacing it by a system of leaseholds, was so restricted in its operation as to affect only a small number of tenants. The Four Year Economic Development Programme (1967–70), however, was intended to convert 75 per cent of all share tenancies (which numbered some 500,000) into leasehold by 1970, and over 190,000 hectares were to be acquired for eventual redistribution to some 64,000 leaseholders.[9] The government land-colonisation scheme, in which landless Filipinos from congested parts of the country were established on new settlements created in the public domain, achieved some success, although it was heavily abused by the power élites. Large areas of public land were acquired by the rich with political influence, in the hope that unsuspecting settlers would start developing them. Only after the settlers had put in considerable labour did the 'land-grabber' appear on the scene, demanding extortionate sale prices or rents. The Philippine élite is not even formally committed to socialism. The landlord-dominated political system thrives on the belief that the equitable distribution of the agricultural product (including the distribution of land through the break-up of large holdings) would lead to a decline in output.

The progress made by Malaysia and Thailand – the two other countries in South-east Asia (besides the Philippines and Singapore) with developing economies – has not been on account of any pressure from below. Malaysia's prosperity has been dependent on prices received for rubber and tin exports. Of its four million workforce, 46 per cent is engaged in agriculture and generates nearly 40 per cent of the country's national product, which suggests that the disparity between incomes per head in agricultural and non-agricultural occupations is markedly less in Malaysia than in any other country of South-east Asia. Malaysian agriculture consists of a dominant industrial crop sector, much of which is highly capitalised, producing for its employees income levels only marginally inferior to those of workers in non-agricultural activities. The peasants in

Malaysia, therefore, are less deprived than those anywhere else in Southern Asia. Communism in this country is by no means always associated with rural discontent. Here the government and at least a substantial proportion of the population, if not a majority, feel that no major change is required from a policy of growth through capitalism and private enterprise. Government activity has thus been confined to improvements in the infrastructure, and the social and economic condition of the rural population. Thailand too faces no grave agrarian problem. It has more than adequate resources to maintain its present living standard. The country is singularly fortunate in still possessing an abundance of agricultural land in relation to its population. The average holding of a farmer, in 1950, was 10·4 acres. There was only a slight decline in this figure in 1960, even though the population had increased since 1950 at the rate of 3 per cent per year. This was so because of the steady expansion of the cultivated area at the rate of 3 per cent per year. Thus the government and the people of Thailand display a certain amount of complacency. In 1957 a government report stated:

A peculiar difficulty in the case of Thailand is that not only is there no systematic plan for economic development, but there is no very intense demand or desire for economic development. Thailand is a relatively well-to-do country. If much of its wealth consists in the opportunities provided by nature for the enjoyment of leisure and a good life, it is not out of harmony with the temperament of the people.[10]

In spite of this satisfactory state of agrarian affairs, Thailand has a substantial number of tenants. In 1970 a National Seminar on Land Problems and Policies in Thailand showed concern at the deteriorating conditions of the tenants, and the uncertainty which prevailed in the rural areas both among owners and tenants with regard to their rights and obligations.[11] It was pointed out that the situation had reduced the productivity of tenant-cultivated land, and the economic and living conditions of tenants were worsening and their indebtedness was increasing. The Seminar thus recommended that the objective of land reform should be 'land to the tiller', and the establishment of owner-operated family farms.

Both Burma and Indonesia have been under some pressure from below, as it were, to introduce necessary agrarian reforms in order to redeem the appalling conditions of their peasants. But neither has achieved any remarkable success, and the economies of both countries continue to stagnate. Both, however, are at present free from any communist threat or peasant uprising. Though bent on the wholesale nationalisation of industries and banks, Ne Win's *coup* government did not go for agricultural collectivisation. It launched a Land Reclamation Scheme which was to bring an additional million and half acres, lying fallow or under jungle cover, into production. And in 1962 the Revolutionary Council promulgated a new law – the Peasants' Rights Protection law – which protected peasant lands and farm implements from confiscation for bad debts. Some facilities for farmers to borrow money from the government were also provided.

Indonesia's problems became more complicated during Sukarno's era. It was the only country in South-east Asia to have rapidly destroyed the Western social and economic institutions implanted by colonialism. It was also perhaps the only country in the region which seemed bent on 'achieving the prosperity and power which came from industrialisation, but without the changes in social organisation and values which have been concomitants of industrialisation elsewhere'.[12] However, Indonesia was under communist pressure until 1965, and therefore it was in the Sukarno era that certain agrarian reforms were introduced. In 1960 both the Share-cropping Law and the Basic Agrarian Law were promulgated; the former fixed the level of rents for tenant farmers and provided for all tenancy agreements to be registered with the authorities. The Basic Agrarian Law fixed the minimum (two hectares) and the maximum (varying according to zones from 12·4 acres to 37 acres) on landholding, and provided for land in excess of the maximum to be confiscated and redistributed to those without land or with insufficient land. Those reforms, however, made little progress against the entrenched opposition of the larger landowners and of the custodians of customary law. Also, the government launched a transmigration scheme to remove peasants from overcrowded parts of Java to new settlements in the Outer Islands. Under Suharto's regime the belief has grown that land reform was not indispensable to improvement in agricultural productivity. The focus thus seems to have shifted from land distribution to the Green Revolution.

Communist or peasant uprisings have been very rare in Bangladesh, Nepal, Pakistan and Sri Lanka, and though the agrarian problems in these countries are as formidable as elsewhere, none has formulated any novel policy to tackle the problems. No non-communist country in this region appears to be even mildly inclined towards experimenting with collectivisation or even co-operative farming. Thus, only Vietnam, Cambodia and Laos are experimenting, though in their own different ways, with collectivisation. In the 1950s North Vietnam carried out land redistribution on a large scale – between one and two million acres of land in North Vietnam out of a total of perhaps nearly five million acres under cultivation, were redistributed. Then came the collectivisation of agriculture which the communist government regarded as the most efficient way to modernise backward peasant agricultural techniques, mechanise farming and increase productivity. The government initially encouraged the development of work-exchange teams in which peasants pool labour and farm animals, but retain ownership of their private plots of land. The Three-Year Plan (1958–60) launched an intensive drive to transform the teams into co-operatives at various levels. Eventually all land was to be owned by co-operatives which were to pay their members on the basis of work units performed.[13]

ECONOMIC NATIONALISM AND FOREIGN AID

It is difficult to define economic nationalism. Broadly, it is a system of policies and institutions created to promote national economic development.[14] Of its several features, one is the central role assigned to the regulation and control of economic relations between the country concerned and the outside world. Its other, and most important, feature is planned economic development through the mobilisation of internal resources. Analysts differ on its propriety. Some condemn it outright as 'an unmitigated evil associated with growing collectivism' which will lead the world to sacrifice the bounties of economic liberalism. Others regard economic nationalism as a necessity and believe that all countries – rich and poor – must pass through a period of economic nationalism, insulation and internal mobilisation to achieve national integration. They believe that a state can be integrated into the international economy only when it is internally integrated and egalitarian.

Indeed, economic nationalism has a touch of narrowness, insulation or chauvinism, but in certain contexts it may be regarded merely as a device for the survival of a nation. At the time of their independence, all the nations of South and South-east Asia resorted to economic nationalism, not with a chauvinistic zeal, but with a concern for their economic survival in a highly competitive world. Whether it was the right course for them to follow is a different matter. At the time they believed there was no other option. India was possibly the first country in Southern Asia to commit itself to planned growth. All the arguments in favour of planning were based on the assumption that the unplanned economic journey would take a long time (possibly as long as it had taken the Western economies to develop into their present state) to reach its destination. India could not wait for that long because its people were seized with 'high expectations'. Both 'free for all' economic liberalism and wholesale collectivisation were ruled out; the former because it represented ruthless exploitation and limitless profiteering, the latter because it was based on destruction and coercion and allowed no room for private incentive. India thus devised a mixed economy which was based on both public and private enterprise. Indian industries were divided into three categories: those which were to be exclusively owned and managed by the state, those which could be run by both state and private enterprise, and those which could be left in the hands of the private industrialists, but subjected to some official controls. The system was to be geared to a long-term planning programme. India's first Five Year Plan (1951–6) was launched in 1951. It was aimed at achieving growth both in agriculture and industry. The system which India adopted was thus neither fully capitalist nor socialist. Some economists have maintained that if India had pursued either a completely capitalist or completely social-ist strategy of economic development, a more rapid rate of growth could have been achieved. They do not realise that India's power élite was so constituted that it could not opt for either of the two extreme strategies of economic development.

The middle path of economic development, which India and the rest of the non-communist countries in South and South-east Asia followed came to be characterised by planning, nationalisation and restrictions on foreign investments, and to be sustained by foreign aid from the developed countries of the world. These countries started their economic journey on the middle path: though occasion-ally some veered to the left and some to the right, none abandoned this path for good. Planning was accepted by all, even by the Philippines, Thailand and Malaysia whose economies have re-mained based largely on private enterprise. President Macapagal, a charter member of the Free Enterprise Association of the Philip-pines, saw no contradiction between planning and private enter-prise, and introduced a 'Five Year Integrated Socio-Economic Pro-gram for the Philippines' in 1961. The plan was to achieve a 7 per cent growth rate by 1967. In the early years most of the countries focused their plans mainly on industrial growth. Rapid industrialisa-tion was the target of many plans, for it was believed that by industrialisation alone the age-old poverty could be eradicated. Later, agriculture came into focus. Malaysia's second plan (1961–5), for example, concentrated fully on the social and economic condi-tions of the rural population, leaving industrial development to private investors and entrepreneurs. However, no plan has yet attempted to raise growth by increasing the degree of distributive justice or releasing the latent productive energies of the masses by radically transforming property and production relations. By and large, all plans have so far only attempted to secure a planned growth rate over a given span of time by providing for an appropriate level of investments. As the plans have never attempted to alter the socio-economic structure of the society, they have mainly benefited the rich, created a class of 'robber barons', as in Pakistan, intensified disparities in income distribution and class distinctions and, finally, stood in the way of involving the masses in the country's development effort.[15]

To a greater or lesser degree, all countries have practised nationalisation, and set some restrictions on profit-making by foreign investors. Of all the countries, Burma has practised these devices most and, in consequence, suffered most (see chapter 3, p. 89). Next to Burma may stand Indonesia, Sri Lanka, India and Pakistan. The Philippines, Malaysia, Thailand and Singapore have practised these devices on a much smaller scale. It is indeed difficult to trace the adverse effects, if any, of nationalisation and indigenisation on the economy of a country. Even in the case of Burma, it is hard to say that excessive nationalisation alone was responsible for pulling the country's economy down. There might have been other factors responsible for the decline of its economy: the country's isolationist policy, for example, which deprived it of foreign aid. Likewise, we cannot precisely assess the adverse effect on Sri Lanka's economy of the nationalisation of the plantation industry which was carried out in 1975. In 1974 Pakistan nationalised 20 per cent of the industrial sector, including banking and shipping; and although the government claims were sharply disputed by the private sector, official estimates of increase in the production of the nationalised industries ran as high as 21 per cent.

Nationalisation or indigenisation *per se* may not be blamed for a slow growth rate. But what nationalisation does in many cases is to replace 'greedy and shortsighted' entrepreneurs with 'corrupt and slow-moving' bureaucrats. Corruption has become a way of life, and is on the increase in every country of this region except Singapore. Corruption is a major inhibition; it introduces an element of irrationality into all planning and plan fulfilment. The official exploits his position of public responsibility for private gain by threatening to obstruct and delay, and thereby impedes the processes of decision-making and execution on all levels. Corruption rampages in all the developing and underdeveloped countries, and it is a major factor in slackening the growth of their economies. Corruption, however, can be stamped out, not through education (in some cases the most educated are the most corrupt), but by stern government measures. People and the media can become more vigilant against corruption once they are assured that the corrupt cannot evade punishment. But then the government itself must be incorrupt, which is a rarity, particularly in democratic countries where the political élites use the crudest forms of corruption in their struggle for power.

Foreign aid has been the life-force of the planned economies of all the countries in this region. Aid has been given by the developed countries individually as well as collectively through the various monetary organisations of the world. The developed countries have had various considerations in advancing loans to the countries of the Third World. There was the political consideration of preventing the poorer countries coming under communist influence. In the earlier years this was the dominant consideration in the American aid programmes. There were also considerations of friendship and traditional ties which induced Britain, for example, to help Commonwealth countries like India and Pakistan. But the most important argument in favour of giving aid was that it preserved and enhanced the economic interest of the donor country. Then there were moral and humanitarian considerations; in an era of 'interdependence', it was believed, the rich ought not to ignore the poor. From the very beginning some of the aid-receiving countries believed that it was in the interest of the rich to help the poor. Nehru of India argued: 'Poverty anywhere was a danger to prosperity everywhere, just as some infectious disease somewhere might be a danger to healthy conditions elsewhere.'[16]

Just as the poor members of a joint family who have for some time lived on the alms of the rich members come to assume a militant attitude toward the whole system and to demand their shares of the total assets and resources of the family, so the aid-receiving countries too began demanding, in the late 1970s, an equitable share in the resources of the world. How could the world's resources be equitably redistributed when this involved the developed countries parting with a portion of their riches? At the summit conference of UNCTAD held in Manila in May 1979, most of the countries of Southern Asia pleaded that the developed countries must discard protectionism and buy freely and at reasonable prices manufactured goods and raw materials from the developing countries.[17] Indeed, with the beginning of the chronic oil crisis in 1973, the economies of the major industrial countries have been struck by inflation and, in order to protect individual national interest and the jobs of their electors, these countries have become relentlessly protectionist. The Willy Brandt Commission (Independent Commission on International Development Issues set up in 1977 under the chairmanship of the former German Chancellor), while urging the world leaders to recognise the importance of global co-operation in ensuring a sustainable biological environment and prosperity based on equitably shared resources, suggested yet another way of shifting resources to achieve an equitable balance between rich and poor. The suggestion was to impose some kind of international tax or levy on trade or military expenditure or deep-sea minerals, the incidence of which may fall on the rich countries.

Opinions vary on the question of whether foreign aid has been a major contributory factor in the economic growth which has, in fact, taken place in the Third World countries over the last thirty years. It must be admitted at the outset that in times of crisis caused by natural calamities – drought, floods – food aid has on many occasions salvaged the devastated countries. For example, Bangladesh, the poorest country in this region, has frequently been struck by food crises, and, lacking as it does a foreign-exchange reserve, it has had to rely on food aid from foreign countries on each occasion. Also, some countries have been able to finance with foreign aid a fair proportion of the expenditure involved in their plans. In India, for example, aid has averaged between 10 and 15 per cent of annual investment. The critics of foreign aid, however, maintain that, to start with, the total aid received by any country in a given year has been quite insignificant in relation to that country's needs; that the aid has in no case benefited the common people of the country, that it has always been misspent by the ruling élite of the country, and that consequently foreign aid has come to maintain the power of the bourgeois élite and assist 'the continuation of policies which carry forward bourgeois ambitions rather than the interests of the mass of the people'. For example, even though India has at times received as much as $1 billion in a year, taking its population into account (which is about equal to the combined populations of the whole of Africa and South America), the foreign aid in any given year may amount to not more than a few pence per head of the country's population.[18] The critics further point out that it is the ruling élite which turns up at intergovernmental meetings, negotiates aid and demands a new economic world order but without finding it opportune to stress or even mention the need for a new economic order at home.[19]

It must, however, be maintained that even if aid were completely stopped it would make hardly any difference to some countries – India, for example. The Indian economy would not crumble if deprived of aid and foreign investment, for in India landed interests and domestic capital have come to play the leading parts. Trade rather than aid is important to India. Since 1974 India has been earning the bulk of its foreign exchange by exports. But the potential market for many of India's manufactures is protected by high tariffs. What India and many other countries in South and South-east Asia need more than anything else is free and fair trade with the developed countries.

QUALITY OF THE WORKFORCE

The majority of the people in southern Asia are still afflicted by lethargy, inflexibility and illiteracy. Lack of nutrition and medical care make people easily morbid in tropical climates. Morbidity slows the pace and reduces efficiency. Tradition makes people superstitious and suspicious. It makes them resist change. People come to rely on fate rather than on their own initiative. Illiteracy, among other things, prevents people from using the facilities provided by the state. It strengthens the barrier which divides the haves and have-nots and makes communication between them almost impossible.

It has been commonly believed that almost all social evils can be eradicated through education and education alone. Thus education has figured prominently in all national schemes and every country in South and South-east Asia has, since its independence, made great quantitative progress in the educational field.[20] Over the last thirty years in every country, the number of schools, colleges and universities has increased with increases in the number of students. The progress, however, may not seem so impressive if we look at the magnitude of the problem.

In view of the steady rise in population, and of the fact that a fairly large percentage of the population in most of the countries is under twenty years of age, the provision made for mass education may in most cases seem inadequate.[21] Legislation dealing with compulsory school education has seldom been enforced. Then there is the problem of improving the quality of education at all levels. The availability of adequate schoolrooms, textbooks, writing paper and other teaching aids is usually very inadequate in primary schools. In almost every country, except, perhaps, Vietnam, the trend is more towards liberal than technical education. Everywhere there is a surplus of 'generalists' and a shortage of engineers, agricultural technicians, doctors, dentists and pharmacologists. Though many of the 'generalists' are born and brought up in villages, after their education they migrate to towns and cities in search of jobs, for rural areas hold no opportunity for their 'talents'. They swell the ranks of the 'educated unemployed'. Any programme of job-oriented rural development would require skilled labourers and middle-rank technicians, who are nowhere in abundance. Manual work is still despised, which makes secondary schools with a vocational orientation unpopular.

Education has not yet realised the hope that it would be an important factor in national integration. In Burma and Malaysia education has been intended to train the nation's youth in citizenship, responsibility and national loyalty. The poor state of the

Burmese economy has undermined the country's schemes of national education. In Malaysia the language problem has come in the way of a national school system with a Malayan-oriented curriculum. Language has been a major problem in the Philippines and India. The Philippines has a higher percentage of literates and a better developed educational system than elsewhere in South-east Asia. But here the language of instruction even in the primary grades was English until 1957. Since English was almost totally unfamiliar to many children, they had to work hard at it, finding no time to grasp other subjects. In order to reduce this waste of time and effort, in 1957 the vernacular was made the language of instruction, which meant that children in different parts of the country came to be instructed in different Philippine languages. Having struggled with this problem for a number of years India has now resigned itself to letting regional languages have priority in schools, and Hindi (officially the national language) a second place, with the option for willing students to learn English as well.

Although much has been done to educate the young, very little has been done to eradicate illiteracy, which grips the bulk of the work force in most of the countries. Except for India, perhaps, no other country has so far launched a nationwide adult education scheme to eradicate illiteracy. But then India has the highest number of illiterates in the region. In October 1978 the Janata government launched the Adult Education Programme on a massive scale. The programme aims at starting 20 to 30 adult education centres in each Community Development Block. Local school teachers, students, ex-servicemen and other retired personnel would on a voluntary basis act as instructors in these centres. The scheme excludes illiterates over 35, and focuses on those between 15 and 35, who number about 100 million. But the success of their plan as of any other, depends on voluntary co-operation, which is hard to get in India and other democratic countries. Plans, therefore, are seldom fully implemented.

★

In summing up, it may first be remarked that no country in this region has tried to evolve any new economic and social systems. All nations have followed the Western path of 'modernisation'. Indeed, certain 'modern values' have been occasionally questioned, and there have been occasional talks about reviving some traditional systems, but these have rarely deflected any country from its march towards modernity. Gandhi wanted his country not to go the Western way. But he did not work out in his own lifetime how it could be made possible. The Mahatma's greatest disciple, Nehru, spent most of his time in office fighting Gandhism. The Janata leaders have in principle revived Gandhism, but each in his or her own way. But none has rejected industrialisation, which Gandhi loathed. General Zia of Pakistan has been reviving the Islamic way of life, and at the same time trying to get all necessary aid from foreign countries in order to manufacture Pakistan's own atom bomb.

7 Some Conclusions

All the colonial systems which functioned in this part of the Asian continent exhibited two common features. First, all followed, in greater or smaller measure, the policy of cautious conservatism, which in effect revived traditionalism and set in motion certain anti-national and anti-secular forces, which not only affected the process of independence, but also the pace of integration and modernisation in South and South-east Asia. Second, all colonial powers displayed a sense of racial superiority which caused among the subject Asians an emotive reaction against a Western rule which seemed to them alien, exclusive and hypocritical. As a result of this the national movements in South and South-east Asia acquired some special features – anti-racism, pan-Asianism, and a bias towards the Soviet Union, which seemed hostile to colonialism and racism and successful in fully assimilating its Asian colonies. Beneath these similarities, however, there were differences in the styles of the colonial regimes caused partly by differences in the systems of the metropolitan countries, and partly by the variations in the historical traditions and environments that obtained among the dependencies. British and American colonial systems were liberal in introducing into their colonies the rule of law, constitutionalism and Western education. As a result, Ceylon, India and the Philippines stood well ahead of other dependencies in terms of political development. Evolution, not revolution, was throughout the *leitmotiv* of the national movement in India, Ceylon, Malaysia and the Philippines. The Dutch and French colonial systems were, on the other hand, less conducive to the growth of modern education, a professional middle class and constitutionalism, in their respective dependencies. Thus, at the time of their independence, the nations of South and South-east Asia stood somewhat differently, conditioned by the differences in their colonial legacies. Accordingly, in the post-independence era, they displayed different approaches to some common problems. The South-east Asian countries also had on their hands the legacies (mostly in the forms of political army and revolutionary nationalism) of the short-lived Japanese imperialism. It was partly due to their Japanese legacies that most of the South-east Asian countries had individually to face during the post-independence period more peasant and army revolts, and guerrilla warfare, than the countries of South Asia.

At the dawn of independence, all the countries of South and South-east Asia, except North Vietnam, adopted a Western-style democratic form of government with all its concomitants – universal suffrage, free elections, rule of law, and free press. Never during the colonial period had the Asian nationalists questioned the suitability of democratic institutions for their countries. The idea of democracy had filtered imperceptibly into their political thinking and come to dominate their aspirations for the future. For some countries, like India, democracy had become a synonym for independence itself. Besides, democracy with its concept of majority rule came in handy to the nationalists in their struggle against both imperialism and communalism. Colonial rule came to be challenged not just because it was alien, but because it was undemocratic. In Nepal and Thailand the aspiring élites based their bid for power on democratic principles because democracy alone could legitimise their claim to share power with their hereditary rulers. But nations with very little experience in constitutional politics (Indonesia, South Vietnam, Laos and Cambodia) had to make their choice at the time of their independence. They accepted democracy because it was in fashion, and because the postwar mood of the West made it almost obligatory for new nations to accept the system.

From the middle of the 1950s, however, the liberal face of South and South-east Asia began to change, and by 1975 all the countries except Sri Lanka and Malaysia had come to discard the democratic system. The Asian votaries of the democratic system had expected that it would destroy the roots of tradition, preserve the precariously balanced unity of a state, establish social and economic equality and, above all, that it would perform these functions in the minimum possible time. Democracy had been thus put to a severe test, which it had never stood before. It could not stand the test on its own, however. So in most of the countries it was sent packing. In some countries it just managed to survive, mainly because it was supported by such additional devices as the emergency. There are three specific factors which led to the collapse of democracy in Southern Asia: the undemocratic competition for power and lack of national consensus among the political élites; the political role of the military; the communist challenge and the American intervention. The first factor is the most important and complex, and is mainly responsible for the fall of democracy in the Philippines, India and Nepal. In their struggle for power the political élites tended to defy the rules of the game. They treated the tradition-mindedness, ancient fears and suspicions of the masses as political assets rather than national liabilities. The second factor emerges out of the first and explains the collapse of the system in Indonesia, Pakistan, Thailand, Burma and Bangladesh. The third is mainly applicable to South Vietnam, Laos, and Cambodia.

Of the fourteen countries in this region of Asia, ten continue to be governed dictatorially. Laos, Cambodia and Vietnam have fallen into the communist fold; authoritarian rule prevails in the remaining seven countries. Bangladesh and Thailand have not so far ventured into the problems of evolving any indigenous surrogates for Western-style democracy. India also did not try to evolve its own brand of 'democracy' while it was ruled under the Emergency for twenty months. Only five of the present ten 'unfree' countries – Pakistan, Nepal, Burma, Indonesia, the Philippines – have tried to evolve their own individual substitutes for Western democracy. Ayub Khan, King Mahendra, Ne Win, Sukarno and Ferdinand Marcos respectively, devised basic democracy, the *Panchayat* Raj, socialist democracy, guided democracy, and participatory democracy. All these surrogates had one feature in common: they attempted to turn the central government into the preserve of the ruling élite by restricting the participation of the people in the governance of their country to the local or basic levels. Pakistan's 'basic democracy' and Indonesia's 'guided democracy', collapsed with the fall from power of their respective creators.

Though each authoritarian system has its own peculiarities, yet all or most of them have broadly displayed some common features. First, all have claimed to emerge out of chaos. In physical terms, all the dictatorial regimes, except those of Nepal and Burma, came into being through the instrument either of martial law or emergency. Second, all regimes decried liberal democracy particularly for fostering the policies of opposition. Some regarded the system as out of date, some believed it was unsuited to the genius of their particular country. This led some of the regimes to evolve their individual substitutes for the Western-style democracy. Third, each regime was driven by a compulsive need to acquire 'legitimacy' in people's approval. This approval was elicited or gauged in many different ways, but never sought, except in the singular case of Mrs Gandhi of India, through a really free election based on universal franchise. This practice of seeking people's consent or acquiescence implies that non-communist authoritarianism, whether military, civilian, or monarchical, having no ideological structure of its own, tends to justify itself by the norms and standards of the very democratic system it has displaced. Fourth, all regimes, though formally claiming to be socialist, have been essentially anti-communist. None introduced any radical economic or social reforms, and none has so far shown any rapid economic growth. Last, each authoritarian ruler, though armed with supreme power, has betrayed a sense of insecurity. As none of the regimes carry any provision for a smooth transfer of power, the fear of a counter-*coup* or communist insurgency has always haunted the dictator's mind.

During the first two decades of their independence, the countries of South and South-east Asia had to deploy much of their political energy and economic resources in preserving their territorial identity and integrity, which were constantly threatened by problems of disputed lands and boundaries, of minorities and separatism, and of communist insurgencies. The era of bilateral conflicts and wars over disputed lands – starting with the Indo-Pakistan war of 1947 and running through the further decolonisation of Portuguese and Dutch possessions, and the Indo-Chinese war of 1962 – came to an end with the cessation of the confrontation between Indonesia and Malaysia in 1966. At present, only the Paracel and Spratly groups of islands in the South China Sea hold the potential to spark off yet another war between Vietnam and China. The problem of minorities has agitated almost all the countries in this region. This study has broadly classified the minorities into three categories. The first category comprises the minorities – the Chinese in Thailand, the Buddhists in Nepal, the Jains, Buddhists, and in a qualified sense, the Parsis, Christians, Anglo-Indians and Sikhs in India – who maintain no living awareness of their separate identity, have accepted the national norms and ethos, and are in the process of being assimilated into the majority community, while retaining in some cases their distinct cultural symbols and religious beliefs. Such minorities pose hardly any threat to the process of national integration. The second category includes minorities – the Muslims and Untouchables in India, the Hindus in Bangladesh, the Indians and Chinese in Burma and Malaysia, and the Chinese in Vietnam and Indonesia – who retain their separate identities, are unassimilated, but because of their size or geographical location, or both, do not hold the political option to agitate for separate or independent states of their own. The problems facing such minorities are mainly communal riots and migrations. Into the third category are placed the minorities who have an intense awareness of their separate identities, are unassimilated, and hold the political option or will to separate into autonomous or independent states. Such minorities are the Tamils in Sri Lanka, the Nagas and Mizos in India, the Baluchis and Pathans in Pakistan, the Shans, Kayahs, Karens, Kachins, Chins in Burma, and the Muslims in the Philippines. All these minorities have one common feature: they each predominantly populate a particular region in a state. Also, the minority territories happen to be situated mostly on the fringes rather than in the heartlands of the countries concerned. The threat of separatism or secession which such minorities often pose, stems solely from their advantageous geographical positions. Here again, this enquiry has ended on the optimistic note that with the subsidence of Muslim separatism in the Philippines in 1977 the minority problem has ceased to dominate the political scene. It would seem reasonable to suggest that the states of southern Asia have now passed through the crucial phase of national integration.

Two phases of the communist movement have been identified. The insurgent phase began with the establishment of the Cominform in 1947 and the publication of Andre Zhdanov's thesis. It officially came to an end in 1956. The communist insurgencies collapsed mainly because they were out of tune with nationalist sentiments. Nowhere, except in Vietnam, was the Communist Party either a vital component or a spearhead of the nationalist movement. The constitutional phase began in 1956. The slow progress hitherto made by constitutional communism is due to several factors: the dearth of popular communist leaders; the inability of the communists to create a mass base; the frequent splintering of the communist parties; the deeply traditional character of the societies involved and the slow pace of their modernisation and urbanisation; and the acceptance in principle of the reformist social democratic system by most of the countries, which has cut the ground from under the feet of communism. Variations in these factors may also explain why the communist movement today is strong in India, weak in Sri Lanka, Burma, Malaysia, Thailand, Indonesia and the Philippines, and almost negligible in Nepal, Pakistan, Bangladesh and Singapore.

As for international relations and defence, this study divides the period from 1946 to 1979 into two parts. The first part, stretching up to the end of 1967, was, at the global level, characterised by confrontation and Cold War between the two power blocs, and at the regional level, the period was marked by hostilities which occasionally occurred between the individual states of southern Asia. In bringing this phase to an end, significant roles were played by statesmen like Nehru, and international organisations like the non-aligned bloc and the Commonwealth. The period from 1968 to 1979 has been the period of *détente* and co-operation at both the global and regional levels. The period is characterised by *rapprochement* between America and the Soviet Union, and between America and China. In South and South-east Asia, the *détente* mood expressed itself in the abandonment of military pacts by the hitherto committed nations, and the pursuit by all countries of the policies of neighbourliness and peaceful co-existence. The 1979 wars between Vietnam and Cambodia, and China and Vietnam, have been taken as exceptions to the general rule. The East–West *détente* has been marked by the US–Soviet agreement in three different areas, as represented by the 1968 Treaty of the Non-Proliferation of Nuclear Weapons, SALT 1 Agreement of 1972, and the Helsinki agreement of 1975. In the *détente* era the focus of all international organisations – the non-aligned bloc, the Commonwealth, ASEAN – have moved from the psychological, social and political aspects to the economic, and they have become the forums for the have-nots of the world to lay their claims on the haves. Though the Sino-Soviet Cold War has been running counter to the *détente* spirit, it is possible that a *rapprochement* between these two giants may take place before long. Behind the Chinese sabre-rattling and brinkmanship may lie a desire to be convinced that the Soviet Union is not really bent on the destruction of China. *Détente*, however, has not yet slackened the pace of the arms race. Although the nations of South and South-east Asia are more peaceful today than at any time since the Second World War they continue to increase their defence expenditure every year, and to make beggars of themselves by acquiring more weapons of destruction from the developed world. It is, however, believed that the arms race will lose its present intensity when the spirit and mechanism of *détente* come to dominate all layers of international, regional and bilateral relations.

The most harrowing problems facing the countries of this region have been the socio-economic problems of poverty, illiteracy, weight of tradition and inegalitarianism. While the communist countries took to collectivisation, all the non-communist countries of this region, including the Philippines, Malaysia, and Singapore, took the middle path of achieving economic growth through planning and persuasion. All attempted to control population growth by family planning, to increase food production through the Green Revolution and land reforms, to support their economic nationalism with foreign aid, and to improve the quality of their work-force through mass education and medical care. In following this middle path of planned growth, some countries have occasionally veered to the left, some to the right, but none has abandoned this path for good. Inegalitarianism and widespread corruption have hampered economic growth. No country has been able to introduce radical agrarian reforms; even when reforms have been legislated the implementation has been delayed, or so manipulated as to benefit only the rich.

None the less, in the last thirty years these countries of the Third

World have achieved a rate of economic growth unprecedented in human history. In spite of a total population well in excess of 1000 million, income per head in these countries rose at an average annual rate of 3·4 per cent between 1950 and 1975. Average life expectancy has increased from forty to fifty years. The birth rate has declined in recent years; in some countries food production has outpaced population growth; there is marginally more food available today than a quarter of a century ago; and calorie consumption per head has improved in many countries. It took western Europe a century to achieve what the developing nations have done in thirty years. However, given the immense differences between the capital and technological bases of the industrialised and developing countries, it may not seem possible for the gap between them to close in the foreseeable future. But it is more important to seek to narrow the gap, not in monetary terms, but in terms of the quality of life: in nutrition, literacy, life expectancy, and the physical and social environment. These gaps can be narrowed in a reasonable period of time if the have-not countries of the South are allowed an equitable share in the world's resources, the bulk of which are presently held by the countries of the North. Most of the countries of southern Asia have nearly reached a point in their economic growth where they can do without foreign aid provided they can sell their manufactured goods and raw materials to the developed countries at reasonable prices. Some countries of the Third World are beginning to realise that it is unnecessary to think in terms of 'closing the gap' between the two worlds, for in the words of India's Morarji Desai, what they want and can achieve is 'prosperity without affluence, dignity without strife'.

Chronological Table

1945	July	C. R. Attlee forms Labour government in Britain
	August	United States drops atomic bombs on Hiroshima and Nagasaki, Japan surrenders and the Second World War ends
		Indonesian nationalists frame a constitution and proclaim the Republic of Indonesia and the struggle for independence begins
	September	Democratic Republic of Vietnam is declared by Ho Chi Minh
	October	The United Nations Organisation comes into formal existence
1946		Nepal National Congress is founded
	March	France recognises Ho Chi Minh's DRV
	July	The Philippines acquires independence
	September	The French reoccupy the whole of Indo-China
1947		United National Party is organised in Ceylon
		Foue-year-old experiment with democracy comes to an end in Thailand
	May	The Constitution of Laos curtails King's powers; the country's power élite enter the political game
	July	Aung San and six other Burmese leaders are assassinated
	August	India and Pakistan acquire independence
	September	Cominform is formed
	October	Pakistani forces invade Kashmir; the ruler of the state accedes to India; the first Indo-Pak war begins
1948	January	Burma become independent
		Mahatma Gandi is assassinated by a Hindu
	February	Ceylon becomes independent

		The Conference of South-east Asian Communists is held in Calcutta
	April	The Soviet Union begins to interfere with traffic between Berlin and West Germany
	June	Malayan communists revolt and Emergency is declared in Malaya
	September	M. A. Jinnah, founder of Pakistan, dies
		Hyderabad surrenders to Indian forces and agrees to join Indian Union
1949		The Communist Party of Nepal is founded
	January	Ceasefire agreement between India and Pakistan over Kashmir is reached
	April	NATO is founded
	October	Mao Tse-tung proclaims the foundation of the People's Republic of China
	December	Indonesia becomes independent, but Holland retains its hold on West New Guinea (West Irian)
1950		Souphanouvong of Laos founds Pathet Lao (Lao National Movement)
		China and the Soviet Union recognise Ho Chi Minh's communist government in North Vietnam
	January	Indian Constitution is inaugurated
		Colombo Conference of Commonwealth Foreign Ministers meets to prepare plans for co-operating in the economic development of Asiatic states
	February	The Soviet Union and communist China sign thirty-year treaty in Moscow
	June	North Korean forces invade South Korea; Korean War begins
	October	Communist China invades and occupies Tibet
1951		India launches its first Five Year Plan, and family planning
	February	Rana regime ends in Nepal. The King is restored to power. The kingdom begins its experiment with democratic institutions
	September	Japan Peace Treaty is signed in San Francisco. India, China and the Soviet Union oppose the terms

	October	Pakistan's Prime Minister, Liaquat Ali Khan, is assassinated
		India holds its first general election under the new constitution
		Kashmir's Constituent Assembly endorses the accession of Kashmir to India
1952		The Nepali Congress, the country's leading national party, splits into four factions
	January	American five-year loan to India
	February	Death of George VI and accession of Elizabeth II
		W. S. Churchill announces that Britain has produced her own atomic bomb
	May	Nehru forms his government; Rajendra Prasad is elected President of India
	June	United National Party under Dudley Senanayake wins Ceylon elections
	December	UN General Assembly adopts Indian proposal for Korean armistice
1953		Riots break out in Pakistan and the civilian government calls in army to restore order
	January	Dwight D. Eisenhower is inaugurated President of the United States of America
	March	J. Stalin dies
	April	Vietnamese insurgents renew offensive on Laos
		Mohammed Ali forms new ministry in Pakistan
	June	Coronation of Queen Elizabeth II; Commonwealth Prime Ministers meet in London
	July	Korean armistice is signed at Panmunjon
	September	N. Khrushchev appointed First Secretary of the USSR Communist Party
1954		Prime Ministers of India, Pakistan, Burma, Indonesia and Ceylon confer at Colombo
		Colonel Nasser becomes Prime Minister and Military Governor of Egypt
	April	Panch Sheel emerges in India's commercial and cultural agreement with China

May	North Vietnam forces under Vo Nguyen defeat French forces at Dien Bien Phu
July	Armistice for Indo-China signed in Geneva, by which France evacuates North Vietnam, the communists evacuate South Vietnam, Cambodia and Laos, and France undertakes to respect the independence of Cambodia, Laos and Vietnam
September	South East Asian Defence Treaty is signed in Manila by Britain, France, the United States, Australia, New Zealand, Pakistan, Thailand and Philippines, and SEATO comes into existence
October	Communist forces occupy Hanoi

1955   Thailand begins for the second time its experiment with democracy

Laos begins receiving American military and financial aid

India's ruling party, Congress, adopts a programme for a socialist pattern of society

Prince Sihanouk launches his scheme of a one-party democratic government

Sino-Vietnam agreement on the Chinese in Vietnam

The Nagas of India begin guerrilla warfare

Warsaw pact comes into existence

February	Democracy suspended in Nepal
April	Bandung Conference of the Asian and African nations is held; China announces its policy towards the Overseas Chinese in South-east Asia during the conference
October	Ngo Dinh Diem begins his authoritarian rule in South Vietnam as its first President
	Baghdad Pact (later to become CENTO) is made between Turkey, Iraq, Britain, Iran and Pakistan
November	The Soviet leaders – Khrushchev and Bulganin – visit India and Burma

1956   The opposition parties in Ceylon join to form Sri Lanka Freedom Party; the SLFP wins the 1956 election.

	February	At the Twentieth Congress of the Communist Party of the Soviet Union, Khrushchev endorses the policy of peaceful coexistence
		Pakistan becomes an Islamic Republic
	April	Cominform is dissolved
	July	President Nasser seizes Suez Canal
	October	Anglo-French troops bomb Egyptian airfields
	November	Soviet forces attack Budapest
		Anglo-French cease-fire in Egypt
1957	February	Second general election begins in India
	March	State of Emergency is declared in E. Indonesia and Thailand
	August	Malaya becomes independent
	October	China completes building the Sinkiang–Tibet highway across India's Aksai Chin
	November	Nehru appeals to the United States and the Soviet Union to bring about effective disarmament
1958		Burma's ruling party (AFPFL) splits
	March	N. Khrushchev succeeds N. A. Bulganin as Chairman of USSR Council of Ministers
	May	Ceylon's first Emergency is declared
	October	A successful military *coup d'état* in Thailand
		Prime Minister U Nu of Burma hands over government to the army
		Military rule begins in Pakistan under General Ayub Khan
	December	The CIA manipulates overthrow of Prince Souvanna's neutral government in Laos
		Indonesia nationalises Dutch businesses
1959		S. W. R. D. Bandaranaike, Prime Minister of Ceylon, is assassinated; Ceylon resorts to Emergency for the second time
	March	Tibetans revolt against Chinese rule, and the Dalai Lama finds asylum in India
	May	Democracy is restored in Nepal
	July	Sukarno launches Guided Democracy in Indonesia
	October	Basic Democracy is introduced in Pakistan
	November	India begins reoccupying border posts lost to the Chinese
1960	January	Election of Basic Democrats is held in

		Pakistan; Ayub Khan is elected President
	February	General election is held in Burma; Ne Win hands back the government to U Nu
	July	Mrs Sirimavo Bandaranaike becomes the Prime Minister of Ceylon – the first woman in the world to become a premier
	October	China makes border settlement with Burma
	November	John F. Kennedy is elected President of the United States
	December	King Mahendra suspends democracy in Nepal
1961		The Association of South-east Asian States (ASA) is formed
		The militants in Singapore's People's Action Party break away and constitute Barisan Sosialis
		The Kennedy administration prepares the counter-insurgency plan for Vietnam
		Ceylon is placed under Emergency for the third time
		South Africa is forced to pull out of the Commonwealth
	May	Tunku Abdul Rahman brings out his plan for a Malaysian Federation
	September	The first conference of the non-aligned powers is held in Belgrade
	October	China makes border settlement with Nepal
	December	India decolonises the Portuguese possessions of Goa, Daman and Diu
1962		India creates a separate state of Nagaland within the Indian union
		Ceylon resorts to Emergency for the fourth time
		India holds its third general election
		Prince Souvanna is restored to power at the head of a coalition government in Laos
		Nepal adopts a new constitution
	February	Elections under Nepal's Panchayat Raj begin

CHRONOLOGICAL TABLE 209

	March	The military takes over the government in Burma
	April	Ne Win launches the 'Burmese Way to Socialism'
	May	China makes border settlement with Pakistan
	June	Ayub Khan promulgates Pakistan's second constitution
	July	Burma's Revolutionary Council constitutes the Burma Socialist Programme Party
	October	China attacks India
	November	China declares ceasefire and retreats from the Indian border
	December	Brunei revolts against joining the proposed Malaysian Federation
1963		Maphilindo – the regional association of Malaysia, Indonesia and the Philippines – is formed
	April	King Mahendra of Nepal inaugurates Panchayat Raj
	May	The Dutch possession of West Irian is handed over to Indonesia by the United Nations
	August	Britain, the United States and the Soviet Union sign nuclear test ban treaty
	September	Malaya, North Borneo, Sarawak and Singapore form Federation of Malaysia. Indonesia begins its confrontation with Malaysia
	November	Military rule begins in South Vietnam President Kennedy is assassinated
1964	February	China challenges leadership of the Soviet Union
	April	India releases Sheikh Abdullah, former premier of Kashmir
	May	Jawaharlal Nehru dies. Lal Bahadur Shastri is appointed to succeed him on 2 June
	July	The Communist Party of India splits
	October	Nikita Khrushchev is replaced as First Secretary of the Soviet Communist Party by Leonid Brezhnev and as Prime Minister by Alexei Kosygin China explodes an atomic bomb

	November	L. B. Johnson is elected President of the United States
1965		F. Marcos is elected President of the Philippines
		US planes violate Cambodian territory
	January	Ayub Khan wins Pakistan's presidential election
		Indonesia withdraws from the United Nations
	February	American aircraft bomb North Vietnam
	March	Landing of 3500 American marines in South Vietnam
	April	Indian and Pakistani forces clash on Kutch–Sind border
	June	India–Pakistan ceasefire signed
	August	Singapore separates from Malaysia and becomes independent
	September	Pakistani troops cross Kashmir ceasefire line, India invades West Pakistan and bombs Lahore; the Indo-Pak war lasts for twenty-two days
	October	A communist conspiracy leads to the killing of Indonesia's six generals; massacre of the communists begins
1966		General Ne Win visits India, Europe and the United States; U Nu is released
	January	India and Pakistan make peace at Tashkent
		Lal Bahadur Shastri dies; Mrs Indira Gandhi succeeds him as India's third prime minister
	March	Sukarno falls from power; Suharto takes effective control of the government in Indonesia
	August	Malaysia and Indonesia sign a treaty to end the confrontation
1967		A third communist faction (CPI–ML) emerges in India
	February	India holds its fourth general election
	August	ASEAN is formally founded; it absorbs ASA
	December	Z. A. Bhutto forms the Pakistan People's Party
1968		Widespread unrest among university students in India

		Britain declares its intention of withdrawing its forces from Malaysia and Singapore by the end of 1971
		Treaty of the Non-Proliferation of Nuclear Weapons signed between the United States, the Soviet Union and Britain
	February	Suharto founds a new Muslim Party of Indonesia (PMI)
	March	Suharto officially takes over the presidency of Indonesia from Sukarno
	September	President Marcos signs a Bill, passed by the Congress, incorporating Sabah into the Philippines; Malaysia breaks diplomatic relations with the Philippines
1969		Ferdinand Marcos re-elected to the presidency of the Philippines for a second term of four years
		Thai and Malaysian governments agree to launch a joint offensive against communist strongholds in the border areas
	February	The Nixon administration allows the US command in Vietnam to bomb Cambodia
	March	Ayub Khan of Pakistan hands over power to General Yahya Khan
	July	India nationalises its domestic banks
	September	Ho Chi Minh, President of the Democratic Republic of Vietnam, dies
	November	The Indian National Congress splits
1970	March	Prince Sihanouk of Cambodia overthrown by a military *coup* organised by General Lon Nol
		General Yahya of Pakistan promulgates his Legal Framework Order
	June	Sukarno dies
	December	Pakistan goes to the polls for the first time since its independence; Mujibur Rahman's Awami League wins the election
1971		India holds its fifth parliamentary election
		Pakistan withdraws from SEATO
		India legalises abortions
	March	Sri Lanka is placed under a State of

		Emergency for the fifth time
		East Pakistan revolts against West Pakistan; General Yahya resorts to military action
	July	The second general election is held in Indonesia
	August	Indo–Soviet Treaty of Friendship is signed
	October	Taiwan is expelled from and China is admitted into the United Nations
	December	Ceylon adopts a new constitution and is renamed Sri Lanka
		Indo–Pak war and emergence of Bangladesh as an independent nation; Yahya Khan hands over power to Z. A. Bhutto in Pakistan
1972		Pakistan withdraws from the Commonwealth
	January	Sri Lanka's new constitution is inaugurated
		King Mahendra of Nepal dies and is succeeded by his son Birendra
	February	President Nixon visits China
	May	SALT I agreement is signed by the United States and the Soviet Union
	September	The Philippines is put under Martial Law by President Marcos
	December	Bangladesh adopts a constitution
1973		Democracy is restored in Thailand for the third time in the country's history
	January	Vietnam ceasefire agreement is signed in Paris
		Marcos calls the first plebiscite to rectify the new Philippine constitution of 1973
	March	The People's Congress of Indonesia re-elects Suharto as President
		Bangladesh holds its first election
	April	Pakistan adopts its third constitution
1974		Indian opposition parties unite against Mrs Gandhi's Congress
	January	Burma adopts a new constitution and elections are held
		China occupies Paracels
	March	The Revolutionary Council is dissolved in Burma; Ne Win becomes President

	May	India explodes atomic bomb and becomes world's sixth nuclear power
	August	The first UN World Population Conference is held in Bucharest
	October	Thailand adopts a democratic constitution
1975		Sheikh Mujib of Bangladesh discards parliamentary system, and assumes absolute presidential power
	February	An elaborate treaty of amity and co-operation is signed by the member countries of ASEAN
	April	Saigon capitulates and South Vietnam is taken over by North Vietnam
		Lon Nol's regime capitulates to communist Khmer Rouge in Cambodia
	June	Allahabad High Court finds Mrs Gandhi guilty of corrupt electoral practices
		Mrs Gandhi places India under Emergency
	July	Helsinki agreement is reached
	August	Sheikh Mujibur Rahman is assassinated and military rule begins in Bangladesh under General Ziaur Rahman
	September	SEATO decides to phase itself out of existence
	November	China lays claim to Spratlys
	December	Laos falls to the communist Lao Revolutionary Party
		Indonesia occupies East Timor
1976	February	UNCTAD meets in Manila
	March	American forces withdraw from Thailand
	April	India announces the new National Population Policy
	June	The two Vietnams are united
	August	Non-aligned summit meeting is held in Colombo
	October	Military takes over the government in Thailand and democracy is suspended
	December	The 42nd Amendment to the Indian Constitution is enacted
		The Muslims of the Philippines drop their demand for a separate state
1977		President Carter launches the human rights campaign
	January	Indian non-communist parties unite and

		launch the Janata Party
	March	General election held in Pakistan; Bhutto's party wins the election
		India's sixth parliamentary election is held; Janata Party wins the election and Morarji Desai becomes India's fourth Prime Minister
	May	Indonesia holds its third general election
		Indian government appoints Shah Commission to investigate the excesses of the Emergency
	July	Sri Lanka's fifth general election is held; the United National Party comes to power with J. R. Jayewardene as the Prime Minister
		General Zia overthrows Bhutto's government in Pakistan
	August	The second summit meeting of ASEAN is held at Kuala Lumpur
		The Philippines formally renounces its claim to Sabah
	September	Bhutto of Pakistan is arrested in connection with a political murder
	October	India introduces the *Antyodaya* scheme
1978	January	The Indian National Congress Party splits into two factions, one of which is led by Mrs Gandhi
	February	Sri Lanka adopts the presidential form of government
	March	Bhutto is found guilty by the Punjab High Court and sentenced to death
		Suharto is re-elected as President for another five years
	April	Burmese Muslims begin escaping to Bangladesh
		Election is held in the Philippines; Marcos reimposes restrictions on political activities soon after the election is over
	June	General Rahman wins the presidential election in Bangladesh
		Vietnam becomes member of COMECON
	November	Soviet Union signs treaty of friendship with Vietnam

	December	Vietnam launches an offensive into Cambodia
1979	January	The United States officially recognises China
		Chinese Vice-Premier Den Xiao-ping visits the United States
	February	General election is held in Bangladesh; President Rahman's party wins the election
		India's Foreign Minister visits China
		China invades Vietnam
	March	Sino-Vietnamese war is ended
		Pakistan pulls out of CENTO
	April	General election is held in Thailand
		Z. A. Bhutto is hanged
		Sino-Soviet Treaty of 1950 is abrogated
	May	UNCTAD meets in Manila
	15 July	Because of defections from the Janata Parliamentary Party, Morarji Desai resigns and the Janata government falls
	28 July	Charan Singh, now leader of the breakaway faction of the Janata Party, forms India's first coalition government
	20 August	Charan Singh resigns and advises the President to dissolve Lok Sabha and hold the mid-term parliamentary election
	22 August	President of India dissolves Lok Sabha and asks Charan Singh to continue as Prime Minister of caretaker government until mid-term election is held and new government formed
	September	Local elections held in Pakistan
	8 October	Jaya Prakash Narayan, founder of India's Janata Party, dies
	16 October	General Zia cancels election to be held in Pakistan on 17 November, bans all political parties, imposes strict censorship on press and tightens martial-law control
	28 October	India's seventh parliamentary election (to be held in 1980) is officially announced in New Delhi

Select Bibliography

This is not a comprehensive bibliography; many of the books which have been consulted and found useful are not listed here. Only those which are either relevant to the topics discussed in this work or which are mentioned in the references are listed. As there are not many books on the developments which have taken place in the present decade, this work had to rely heavily on newspapers and periodicals, particularly for the period from 1972 to 1979. In addition to the general list given there is a section for each country discussed in the text. These sections appear according to the order in which the countries are found geographically from west to east.

GENERAL

J. S. BASTIN, and H. J. BENDA, *A History of Modern South-east Asia* (Englewood Cliffs, N.J., 1968).
C. E. BLACK and T. P. THORNTON (eds), *Communism and Revolution* (Princeton, N.J., 1964).
MICHAEL BRECHER, *The New States of Asia: A Political Analysis* (London, 1963).
J. H. BRIMMELE, *Communism in South-east Asia* (London, 1959).
HANS-DIETER EVERS (ed.), *Modernization in South-east Asia* (London, 1973).
GEOFFREY FAIRBAIRN, *Revolutionary Warfare and Communist Strategy* (London, 1968).
D. FIELDHOUSE, *The Colonial Empire* (London, 1966).
RUSSELL H. FIFIELD, *The Diplomacy of South-east Asia 1945–1958* (New York, 1958).
DONALD W. FRYER, *Emerging South-east Asia: A Study in Growth and Stagnation* (London, 1970).
J. S. FURNIVALL, *Colonial Policy and Practice* (New York, 1956).
FRANK H. GOLAY and OTHERS (eds), *Underdevelopment and Economic Nationalism in South-east Asia* (Cornell, 1969).
D. G. E. HALL, *A History of South-east Asia* (London, 1968).
History of the Twentieth Century (London, 1976).
GUY HUNTER *South-east Asia: Race, Culture and Nation* (London, 1966).

JOHN J. JOHNSON (ed.), *The Role of the Military in Underdeveloped Countries* (Princeton, N.J., 1967).

G. M. KAHIN, *The Asian-African Conference: Bandung, Indonesia, April 1955* (Cornell, 1956).

G. M. KAHIN (ed.), *Government and Politics of South-east Asia* (Cornell, 1964).

ALASTAIR LAMB, *Asian Frontiers* (London, 1968).

PETER LYON, *War and Peace in South-east Asia* (London, 1969).

JOHN T. MCALISTER (ed.), *South-east Asia: The Politics of National Integration* (New York, 1973).

H. J. VAN MOOK, *The Stakes of Democracy in South-east Asia* (London, 1950).

MILTON OSBORNE, *Region of Revolt: Focus on South-east Asia* (Canberra, 1970).

V. PURCELL, *The Chinese in South-east Asia*, (London, 1965).

Report to the Combined Chiefs of Staff by the Supreme Allied Commander South-east Asia, 1943–1945, Vice-Admiral the Earl Mountbatten of Burma (London, 1951).

SAUL ROSE (ed.), *Politics in Southern Asia* (London, 1963).

ROBERT A. SCALAPINO (ed.), *The Communist Revolution in Asia* (Englewood Cliffs, N. J., 1965).

ARTHUR M. SCHLESINGER, *A Thousand Days* (London, 1967).

GUY WINT (ed.), *Asia Handbook* (London, 1969).

PAKISTAN

Z. A. BHUTTO, *The Myth of Independence* (London, 1968).

G. W. CHOUDHURY, *Constitutional Development in Pakistan* (London, 1969).

HERBERT FELDMAN, *The End and the Beginning: Pakistan 1969–1971* (New Delhi, 1975).

ROUNAQ JAHAN, *Pakistan: Failure in National Integration* (New York, 1972).

AYUB KHAN, *Friends not Masters* (London, 1967).

D. P. SINGHAL, *Pakistan* (Englewood Cliffs, N.J., 1972).

LAURENCE ZIRING, *The Ayub Khan Era* (New York, 1971).

INDIA

KRISHNAN BHATIA, *Indira* (London, 1974).

PAUL BRASS, *Factional Politics in an Indian State* (Berkeley, Cal., 1965).

R. H. CASSEN, *India: Population, Economy, Society* (London, 1978).

218   SOUTH AND SOUTH-EAST ASIA, 1945–1979

T. DRIEBERG and SARLA JAGMOHAN, *Emergency in India* (New Delhi, 1975).
A. H. HANSON and JANET DOUGLAS, *India's Democracy* (London, 1972).
R. HARDGRAVE, *India* (New York, 1970).
W. H. MORRIS-JONES, *The Government and Politics of India* (London, 1971).
KULDIP NAYAR, *India: the Critical Years* (New Delhi, 1971).
Jawaharlal Nehru's Speeches, 1946–1964, 5 vols (New Delhi, 1949–69).
B. N. PANDEY, *Nehru* (London, 1976).
MOHAN RAM, *Maoism in India* (New Delhi, 1971).
DAVID SELBOURNE, *An Eye to India* (London, 1977).
D. E. SMITH, *India as a Secular State* (Princeton, N.J., 1963).
MYRON WEINER, *Party Building in a New Nation: the Indian National Congress* (Chicago, 1967).

BANGLADESH, SRI LANKA AND NEPAL

L. S. BARAL, 'The First Panchayat Election in Nepal, 1962–1963', *International Studies* (July–Sept 1973).
B. H. FARMER, *Ceylon: A Divided Nation* (London, 1963).
A. GUPTA, *Politics in Nepal* (Bombay, 1964).
R. KEARNEY, *Cummunalism and Language in the Politics of Ceylon* (Durham, N. Carolina, 1967).
ANTHONY MASCARENHAS, *The Rape of Bangladesh* (New Delhi, 1971).
L. E. ROSE and M. FISHER, *The Politics of Nepal* (London, 1970).
R. SHAHA, *Nepali Politics* (New Delhi, 1975).
W. H. WRIGGINS, *Ceylon: Dilemmas of a New Nation* (Princeton, N.J., 1960).

BURMA

RICHARD BUTWELL, 'Ne Win's Burma: At the End of the First Decade', *Asian Survey* (October 1972).
N. R. CHAKRAVARTI, *The Indian Minorities in Burma* (London, 1971).
W. C. JOHNSTONE, *Burma's Foreign Policy* (Harvard, 1963).
MYA MAUNG, *Burma and Pakistan: A Comparative Study in Development* (New York, 1971).
HUGH TINKER, *The Union of Burma* (London, 1957).
FRANK N. TRAGER, *Burma: From Kingdom to Republic* (New York, 1966).

LOUIS J. WALINSKY, *Economic Development in Burma, 1951–1960* (New York, 1962).

SINGAPORE AND MALAYSIA

I. BUCHANAN, *Singapore in South-east Asia: An Economic and Political Appraisal* (London, 1972).
T. J. S. GEORGE, *Lee Kuan Yew's Singapore* (London, 1973).
J. M. GULLICK, *Malaysia* (London, 1969).
J. M. GULLICK, *Malaysia and its Neighbours* (London, 1967).
D. LIM, *Economic Growth and Development in W. Malaysia 1947–70* (Kuala Lumpur, 1973).
GORDON P. MEANS, *Malaysian Politics* (London, 1970).
R. S. MILNE, *Government and Politics in Malaysia* (Boston, Mass., 1967).
Population and Housing Census of Malaysia 1970 (Kuala Lumpur, 1972).
JAMES C. SCOTT, *Political Ideology in Malaysia* (Yale, 1968).

THAILAND

N. JACOBS, *Modernisation without Development: Thailand as an Asian Case Study* (New York, 1971).
G. A. MARZOUK, *Economic Development and Policies: Case Study of Thailand* (Rotterdam, 1972).
DONALD NEUCHTERLEIN, *Thailand and the Struggle for Power in South-east Asia* (Ithaca, N.Y., 1967).
G. W. SKINNER and T. KIRSCH, *Change and Persistence in Thai Society* (Cornell, 1975).
DAVID A. WILSON, *Politics in Thailand* (Cornell, 1962).

CAMBODIA, LAOS AND VIETNAM

A. J. DOMMEN, *Conflict in Laos: the Politics of Neutrality* (London, 1971).
G. M. KAHIN and JOHN LEWIS, *The United States in Vietnam* (New York, 1967).
JEAN LACOUTURE, *Ho Chi-minh* (London, 1969).
M. LEIFER, *Cambodia: The Search for Security* (London, 1967).
JOHN MCALISTER, *Vietnam: The Origins of Revolution* (New York, 1969).
On Viet Nam's Expulsion of Chinese Residents (Peking, 1978).

M. E. OSBORNE, *Politics and Power in Cambodia: The Sihanouk Years* (Melbourne, 1973).

DOUGLAS PIKE, *Viet Cong* (Cambridge, Mass., 1966).

NORODOM SIHANOUK, *My War with the CIA* (London, 1973).

RALPH SMITH, *Viet-nam and the West* (London, 1968).

R. M. SMITH, *Cambodia's Foreign Policy* (Cornell, 1965).

DONALD ZAGORIA, *The Vietnam Triangle: Moscow, Peking, Hanoi* (New York, 1967).

J. ZASLOFF, *The Pathet Lao* (Lexington, Mass., 1973).

J. ZASLOFF (ed.), *Communism in Indochina* (Lexington, Mass., 1975).

INDONESIA

H. J. BENDA, *The Crescent and the Rising Sun: Indonesian Islam under the Japanese Occupation* (The Hague, 1958).

D. K. EMMERSON, *Indonesia's Élite* (Cornell, 1976).

HERBERT FEITH, *The Decline of Constitutional Democracy in Indonesia,* (Cornell, 1968).

J. M. VAN DER KROEF, *Indonesia since Sukarno* (Singapore, 1971).

J. D. LEGGE, *Sukarno* (London, 1972).

D. S. LEV, *Transition to Guided Democracy* (Cornell, 1966).

J. A. C. MACKIE, *Konfrontasi: The Indonesia–Malaysia Dispute 1963–1966* (London, 1974).

RUTH MCVEY (ed.), *Indonesia* (Yale, 1967).

PETER POLOMKA, *Indonesia since Sukarno* (London, 1971).

FRANKLIN B. WEINSTEIN, *Indonesian Foreign Policy and the Dilemma of Dependence: From Sukarno to Soeharto* (Cornell, 1976).

THE PHILIPPINES

R. E. AGPALO, *The Political Élite and the People: A Study of Politics in Occidental Mindoro* (Manila, 1972).

BETH DAY, *The Philippines* (New York, 1974).

FRANK H. GOLAY, *The Philippines: Public Policy and Economic Development* (Ithaca, N.Y., 1961).

EDUARDO LACHICA, *The Huks: Philippine Agrarian Society in Revolt* (New York, 1971).

C. H. LANDE, *Leaders, Factions and Parties: The Structure of Philippine Politics* (New Haven, 1965).

DAPAN LIANG, *Philippine Parties and Politics* (San Francisco, 1971).

FERDINAND E. MARCOS, *The Democratic Revolution in the Philippines* (Englewood Cliffs, N.J., 1974).

G. P. SICAT, *Economic Policy and Philippine Development* (Quezon City, 1972).

NEWSPAPERS AND PERIODICALS

Asia Year Book (Far Eastern Economic Review, Hong Kong).
Asian Recorder (New Delhi).
The *Guardian* (London).
The *Hindustan Times* (New Delhi).
Keesing's Contemporary Archives (Bristol).
The *Observer* (London).
The *Statesman* (New Delhi).
The *Statesman Weekly* (Calcutta).
The *Sunday Times* (London).
Third World Quarterly (London).
The Times (London).
The Times of India (New Delhi).

Notes and References

1. DECOLONISATION AND THE EMERGENCE OF SOUTH AND SOUTH-EAST ASIA

1. D. Fieldhouse, *The Colonial Empire* (London, 1966) p. 377.
2. Ralph Smith, *Vietnam and the West* (London, 1968) p. 97.
3. H. J. van Mook, *The Stakes of Democracy in South-east Asia* (London, 1950) p. 107.
4. Fieldhouse, *Colonial Empire*, p. 402. See also D. J. Steinberg (ed.), *In Search of South-east Asia* (London, 1971) p. 337.
5. G. M. Kahin (ed.), *Government and Politics of South-east Asia* (Cornell, 1964) p. 679.
6. Report from Manila in the *Sunday Times* (2 May 1976).
7. Quoted in S. Sjahrir's *Out of Exile* (New York, 1949) p. 112, and cited in Kahin (ed.), *Government and Politics*, p. 195.
8. H. J. Benda, *The Crescent and the Rising Sun* (The Hague, 1958) p. 195.
9. J. S. Bastin and H. J. Benda, *A History of Modern South-east Asia* (Englewood Cliffs, N.J., 1968) p. 190.
10. *Report to the Combined Chiefs of Staff by the Supreme Allied Commander, South-east Asia, 1943–1945*, Vice-Admiral the Earl Mountbatten of Burma (London, 1951).

2. THE CRISIS OF DEMOCRACY

1. Francis Carnell, 'Political Ideas and Ideologies in South and South-east Asia', in Saul Rose (ed.), *Politics in Southern Asia* (London, 1963) p. 266.
2. Cited in B. N. Pandey, *Nehru* (London, 1976) p. 197.
3. Herbert Feith, *The Decline of Constitutional Democracy in Indonesia* (Cornell, 1968) p. 39.
4. Ibid.
5. For North Vietnam's constitution, see G. M. Kahin (ed.), *Government and Politics of South-east Asia* (Cornell, 1964) pp. 475–9.
6. Ibid., p. 488.
7. Pandey, *Nehru*, p. 337.
8. Myron Weiner, *Party Building in a New Nation* (Chicago, 1967) p. 15.
9. Paul Brass, *Factional Politics in an Indian State* (Berkeley, 1965) p. 2.
10. Cited in Rose (ed.), *Politics in Southern Asia*, p. 281.
11. Entries in Nigalingappa's Diary, as quoted by Kuldip Nayar, *India: the Critical Years* (New Delhi, 1971) pp. 25–6.
12. Max Beloff, 'The Decline of Liberalism', in *History of the 20th Century* (London, 1976) p. 491.
13. *Asia Year Book* (Hong Kong) p. 169.
14. 'The Prime Minister's Broadcast on June 26', in T. Drieberg and Sarla Jagmohan, *Emergency in India* (New Delhi, 1975) Appendix 1, pp. 106–7.

15. Ferdinand E. Marcos, *The Democratic Revolution in the Philippines* (Englewood Cliffs, N.J., 1974) pp. 109–29.

16. Peter Hazelhurst, 'President Marcos: Tolerant and Ruthless Man of Law', in *The Times* (22 September 1976).

17. Cited in Dapan Liang, *Philippine Parties and Politics* (San Francisco, 1971) p. 394.

18. *Asia Year Book* (Hong Kong, 1972) p. 269.

19. Kahin (ed.), *Government and Politics*, p. 716.

20. Beth Day, *The Philippines* (New York, 1974) p. 32.

21. Cited in A. Gupta, *Politics in Nepal* (Bombay, 1964) p. 162.

22. David A. Wilson, 'The Military in Thai Politics', in John J. Johnson (ed.), *The Role of the Military in Under-developed Countries* (Princeton, 1967) p. 255.

23. Quoted in *The Times* (7 October 1976).

24. Guy J. Pauker, 'The Role of the Military in Indonesia', in Johnson (ed.), *Role of the Military*, p. 214.

25. J. D. Legge, *Sukarno* (London, 1972) p. 378.

26. See Anthony Mascarenhas in the *Sunday Times* (17 August 1975).

27. Lucian W. Pye, 'The Army in Burmese Politics', in Johnson (ed.), *Role of the Military*, p. 234.

28. Ibid., p. 249.

29. Hugh Tinker, 'Burma', in *Asia Handbook* (London, Penguin, 1969) p. 293.

30. D. P. Singhal, *Pakistan* (Englewood Cliffs, N.J., 1972) pp. 78–89.

31. Arthur M. Schlesinger, *A Thousand Days* (London, 1967) p. 428.

32. Ibid.

33. Ibid., p. 274.

34. Norodom Sihanouk, *My War with the CIA* (London, 1973) p. 46.

35. William Shawcross, 'Cambodia: The Blame', in the *Sunday Times* (12 December 1976).

36. Ibid.

37. Sihanouk, *My War*, p. 38.

38. Ibid., p. 26.

39. Cited in T. J. S. George, *Lee Kuan Yew's Singapore* (London, 1973) p. 130.

40. Gordon P. Means, *Malaysian Politics* (London, 1970) p. 414.

41. *The Times* (21 June 1977).

42. Ibid. (10 February 1976).

43. B. H. Farmer, 'Politics in Ceylon', in Rose (ed.), *Politics in Southern Asia*, pp. 57–8.

3. THE AUTHORITARIAN ALTERNATIVE

1. Freedom House (New York) Survey of 1976, *The Times* (22 December 1976).

2. *The Times* (23 October 1977).

3. Under this constitution the Prime Minister (General Kriangsak) nominates the 225 members of the Upper House (the Senate), who together with the 301 elected members of the Lower House elect the Prime Minister. The constitution allows for a non-elected Prime Minister.

4. Ayub Khan, *Friends not Masters* (London, 1967) p. 206.

5. Ibid., p. 187.

6. Ibid., p. 226.

7. Ibid., p. 240.

8. Bhutto might have felt further aggrieved because Ayub did not even mention him in his autobiography, *Friends not Masters*, two chapters of which are devoted to

Pakistan's foreign policy during the period when Bhutto was his Foreign Minister. This must have prompted Bhutto to prepare his own rejoinder – *The Myth of Independence* – in November of the same year.

9. Rounaq Jahan, *Pakistan: Failure in National Integration* (New Yoek, 1972) p. 186.

10. *Asian Recorder* (1973) p. 11621.

11. *The Times* (6 September 1976).

12. Bhutto's speech at the opening of his election campaign on 23 January 1977, as reported in *The Times* (24 January 1977).

13. Ibid.

14. S. Nihal Singh in the *Statesman Weekly* (30 July 1977).

15. As reported in *The Times* (11 November 1977).

16. Nehru's speech in the Indian parliament, 20 December 1960, *Jawaharlal Nehru's Speeches*, vol. IV (New Delhi, 1964) pp. 272–4.

17. As reported in *The Times* (15 December 1975).

18. Freedom House observations, *The Times* (20 January 1978).

19. Richard Butwell, 'Ne Win's Burma: At the End of the First Decade', in *Asian Survey*, XII, no. 10 (October 1972).

20. *The Times* (17 March 1977).

21. *Asia Year Book* (1977) pp. 130–1.

22. J. D. Legge, *Sukarno* (London, 1972) p. 284.

23. Herbert Feith, 'Dynamics of Guided Democracy', in Ruth McVey (ed.), *Indonesia* (Yale, 1967) p. 373.

24. Ibid., p. 367.

25. Ibid.

26. Peter Polomka, *Indonesia since Sukarno* (London, 1971) p. 96.

27. Ibid., p. 153.

28. *Keesing's Contemporary Archives* (1971) p. 24908.

29. The *Sunday Times* (22 January 1978).

30. *The Times* (6 February 1978).

31. Report by Brian Moynahan in The *Sunday Times Magazine* (12 March 1978).

32. The *Guardian* (1 April 1978).

33. F. Marcos, *The Democratic Revolution in the Philippines* (Englewood Cliffs, N.J., 1974) pp. 97–8.

34. Ibid., pp. 155–6.

35. Ibid., p. 97.

36. *The Times* (28 June 1977).

37. Ibid., editorial (23 August 1977).

38. The *Sunday Times* (26 February 1978).

39. *The Times* (4 May 1978).

40. Constitution of the Republic of the Philippines (1973), Appendix A in Marcos, *The Democratic Revolution.*

41. Marcos, *The Democratic Revolution*, p. 209.

42. Ibid., p. 212.

43. As reported in The *Statesman Weekly* (18 March 1978), also in *The Times* (15 March 1978).

44. Mrs Gandhi's interview with the *Statesman* of Calcutta, as reported in the *Times* (7 April 1977).

45. The *Statesman Weekly* (18 February 1978).

4. PROBLEMS OF DISPUTED LANDS AND NATIONAL INTEGRITY

1. B. N. Pandey, *Nehru* (London, 1976) p. 311.

2. *The Times* guide to Philippine claims to North Borneo, published in *The Times*

(2 May 1962), and reproduced in J. M. Gullick's *Malaysia and its Neighbours* (London, 1967) pp. 148–51.

3. J. D. Legge, *Sukarno* (London, 1972) p. 364.

4. Some tenable explanations of the reasons for Sukarno launching the confrontation are offered by J. A. C. Mackie in his authoritative study of the event, *Konfrontasi: The Indonesia–Malaysia Dispute 1963–1966* (London, 1974) pp. 325–35.

5. Alastair Lamb, *Asian Frontiers* (London, 1968) p. 156.

6. Pandey, *Nehru*, p. 369.

7. Clifford Geertz, 'Primordial Sentiments and Civil Politics in the New States', in John T. McAlister (ed.), *South-east Asia: The Politics of National Integration* (New York, 1973) p. 45.

8. Karl W. Deutsch, 'The Growth of Nations', in McAlister, *South-east Asia*, p. 36.

9. G. William Skinner, 'Chinese Assimilation and Thai Politics', in McAlister, *South-east Asia*, pp. 384–8.

10. Constituting the lowest stratum of the Hindu community, they have been styled differently in the different languages of India. They were first called 'Untouchables' by their own leader, Dr B. R. Ambed Kar, who himself belonged to this caste. Gandhi coined the word 'Harijans' (People of God) for them during his 1933–4 campaign against untouchability. The early governmental term for them was 'Depressed Classes', which was replaced by 'Scheduled Castes' in 1935, when these castes were placed on schedule as qualifying for special rights.

11. Harijan representation in the Indian legislatures today (1979) amounts to 78 in the Parliament, and to a total of 538 in the state legislatures.

12. Government of India statement of 21 February 1979 as reported in the *Statesman Weekly* (24 February 1979).

13. *Sunday Standard* (1 October 1978).

14. People's Republic of China, *On Viet Nam's Expulsion of Chinese Residents* (Peking, 1978) p. 32.

15. Ibid., p. 34.

16. At the time of its independence, Burma had not more than a million people of Indian origin. In the 1960s a large number of them left for India, bringing the Indian strength down to, possibly, a quarter of a million. In 1960 there were about 350,000 Chinese in Burma.

17. *Population and Housing Census of Malaysia 1970: Community Groups* (Kuala Lumpur, 1972) pp. 45–6.

18. Dennis M. O'Leary's report on the Muslim rebellion in the Philippines, *The Times* (22 September 1976).

19. Guy J. Pauker, 'The Rise and Fall of the Communist Party of Indonesia', in Robert A. Scalapino (ed.), *The Communist Revolution in Asia* (Englewood Cliffs, N.J., 1965) pp. 275–6.

20. Ruth T. McVey, 'The South-east Asian Insurrectionary Movements', in C. E. Black and T. P. Thornton (eds), *Communism and Revolution* (Princeton, N.J., 1964), p. 160.

21. J. H. Brimmele, *Communism in South-east Asia* (London, 1959) p. 236.

22. Ibid., p. 213.

23. Eduardo Lachica, *The Huks: Philippine Agrarian Society in Revolt* (New York, 1971) p. 41.

24. Jyoti Basu's Speech of 6 August as reported in the *Times of India* (7 August 1978).

5. FOREIGN POLICY AND DEFENCE

1. The Colombo Plan was a project started in 1950 for co-operative economic development in South and South-east Asia. The project was devised in 1949 at a

226 SOUTH AND SOUTH-EAST ASIA, 1945–1979

conference in Ceylon by the British Commonwealth Foreign Ministers.

2. Chou En-lai's speech of 19 April 1955 in G. M. Kahin, *The Asian-African Conference: Bandung, Indonesia, April 1955* (Cornell, 1956) p. 55.

3. Ibid.

4. Ibid., p. 15.

5. Franklin B. Weinstein, *Indonesian Foreign Policy and the Dilemma of Dependence: From Sukarno to Soeharto* (Cornell, 1976) p. 354.

6. J. D. Legge, *Sukarno* (London, 1972) p. 344.

7. Ibid.

8. Russell H. Fifield, *The Diplomacy of South-east Asia 1945–1958* (New York, 1958) p. 474.

9. Roy Lewis, 'Now is the Time to Break Silence', in *The Times*, Commonwealth Supplement (8 June 1977).

10. Peter Lyon, *War and Peace in South-east Asia* (London, 1969) p. 157.

11. The ASEAN declaration: Bangkok, 8 August 1967, as reproduced in *The Times* supplement, ASEAN (8 August 1972).

12. Adam Malik's statement, August 1972, ibid.

13. 'Treaty of Amity and Co-operation in South-east Asia', as reproduced in the *Asia Year Book* (Hong Kong, 1977) pp. 58–9.

14. The America–China communiqué as reproduced in *Asia Year Book* (Hong Kong, 1973) pp. 64–6.

15. *Times of India* (2 January 1979).

16. *Asia Year Book* (Hong Kong, 1974) p. 125.

17. *The Times* (3 April 1978).

18. Ibid. (14 April 1978).

19. The *Guardian* (28 February 1979).

20. Ibid. (16 March 1979).

21. Denis Bloodworth's report in the *Observer* (22 April 1979).

22. *The Times* (15 July 1978).

23. Ibid. (21 August 1976).

24. The *Hindustan Times* (1 August 1978).

25. *Asia Year Book* (Hong Kong, 1977) p. 47.

6. ECONOMIC AND SOCIAL PROBLEMS

1. The Indian Planning Commission's definition as reported in *The Statesman* (27 November 1978).

2. World Bank Report, as reported in the *Times of India* (14 September 1978).

3. Gunnar Myrdal, 'Underdevelopment and the Evolutionary Imperative', in the *Third World Quarterly* (April 1979) p. 24.

4. Darryl D'Monte, 'Declining Birth Rates', in the *Times of India* (16 September 1978).

5. *Asia Year Book* (Hong Kong, 1975) p. 59.

6. Ibid. (1976) p. 57.

7. R. H. Cassen, *India: Population, Economy, Society* (London, 1978) p. 183.

8. Surinder Sud, 'Real Truth about Food Surpluses', in the *Times of India* (15 November 1978).

9. Donald W. Fryer, *Emerging South-east Asia: A Study in Growth and Stagnation* (London, 1970) pp. 196–7.

10. As quoted in G. M. Kahin (ed.), *Government and Politics of South-east Asia* (Cornell, 1964) p. 61.

11. G. A. Marzouk, *Economic Development and Policies: Case Study of Thailand* (Rotterdam, 1972) pp. 187–8.

12. Kahin (ed.), *Government and Politics*, p. 258.

13. Ibid., p. 502.

14. Frank H. Golay and others (eds), *Underdevelopment and Economic Nationalism in South-east Asia* (Cornell, 1969) p. 2.

15. B. M. Bhatia, 'Pakistan's Economy', in the *Statesman* (17 November 1978).

16. Quoted in B. N. Pandey, *Nehru* (London, 1976) p. 320.

17. Proceedings of UNCTAD as reported in the *Statesman Weekly* (12 May 1979).

18. Cassen, *India*, p. 332.

19. Myrdal, 'Underdevelopment . . .', p. 40.

20. In India, between 1950–1 and 1972–3, the number of primary schools increased from 209,671 to 414,406; of middle schools from 13,596 to 94,199; of high schools from 7288 to 38,488; and of colleges and universities from 632 to 4105. In Thailand, the enrolment in primary schools increased from 1,828,240 in 1944, to 2,937,534 in 1954; in universities from 3266 in 1948 to 5286 in 1953. In Burma, the enrolment in primary schools rose from 737,000 in 1954 to 1·48 million in 1959. In Western Malaysia at the end of 1961, there were 1·2 million children (or approximately 17 per cent of Malaysia's population) attending primary schools; and at the same time 21 per cent of Singapore's population was enrolled in primary and secondary schools. In South Vietnam the increase in enrolment in primary schools was 100 per cent from 1955 to 1960. During Indonesia's first Five Year Plan, which ended in 1974, the number of children in elementary schools increased from 12·3 million to 13·6 million. And so on.

21. In 1977 in India 51 per cent of the population was under 20; in Bangladesh 55 per cent was under 21; in Burma 40 per cent under 15; in Laos 42 per cent under 15; in Malaysia 58 per cent under 21; in Pakistan 52 per cent under 21; in the Philippines 49 per cent under 19; in Sri Lanka 39 per cent under 15; and in Thailand 56 per cent of the population was under 21.

Index